As the Wind Blows IT LISTETH

If we want to be honest, there is no life that is more valuable than another

Each person that we see during our daily lives is the "harvest." This is what Jesus meant when He said I will make you fishers of men. He wants to reach them with the Gospel. The question is, will we join Him in His Harvest?

Contents

As the Wind Blows

IT LISTETH

Chapter 1
Every person has a childhood

If we want to be honest, there is no life that is more valuable than another, but we all think about ourselves first. Now granted, some people are more giving and caring than others, this is good, and we may hold them in great respect, but most of us live in our own personal universe, thinking of ourselves most of the time. Here is a peek into my universe.

My mother and father grew up within a few blocks of each other. They became childhood sweethearts and were married very young. After their first child was born, a girl, my father joined the Navy. He served in the Mediterranean during World War II. He was home for a short time, and the Navy called him back to serve in the Korean

War. While on the ship, he found out that my mother was pregnant with their second child (Me). It was many months until my mother introduced me to my father. I was born prematurely at seven months, and my father told me they could fit me in a shoebox.

We lived in a small home in Washington, DC. My mother was a very loving homemaker, and my father was a plumber. Finances did not come easy, but they made it work. By the time I was four, they had saved enough money to buy a house in Maryland. Considering that my father was a second-generation Italian, that was very impressive. Taking into consideration that my grandfather came to America on a ship from Naples, Italy. He landed on Ellis Island and, in a short time, was able to establish himself as a tailor. He then sent for my Sicilian grandmother. They moved to Washington, DC, and raised my father and his four sisters.

We had a happy home; in fact, I cannot remember my parents eve r arguing. I do remember them playing a lot of tricks on us, though . One time during Halloween, they put a sheet over their heads, bu rnt two holes in it with cigarettes, then tapped on the living room wi ndow after dark. When we looked out the window, we about wet o ur pants. We had picnics at the beach and played games together. They would do all they could to bring joy into our lives.

We were shocked when mom and Dad split up and were divorced very soon afterward. I did not find out why, until I was an adult. Neither one of them ever got over the divorce. Both told us before their deaths that they wished they would have worked out the incident rather than divorce.

My father remarried within a year. The woman he married had two children of her own, making the members of our family living in the house six. My mother took the youngest daughter and moved to Ohio. She had two other children while living there. For me, the joy in our home disappeared. It totally changed within a few months.

I became very rebellious. I was accustomed to a loving mother who showed her affection daily, with her saying; I love you and giving me constant kisses and hugs. The new woman in my father's life was hugely different. She had not grown to understand that children need affection. The combination of losing my mother and having another woman come in her place was hard enough, but a woman who did not know how children need love and affection was too much for me to take.

As my preteens went by, I received so many spankings I cannot remember the number. From the time I was seven to my seventeenth birthday, I spent about two years in my room for punishment. Looking back, I believe they just did not know how to deal with me. They were struggling financially, and my constant rebellious actions made things harder, so they would send me to my room.

I was a hard worker. I served newspapers, shoveled snow in the winter, and cut grass in the summer. I kept money in my pocket so that I could go to the teen club. I loved music and dancing. My money caused me trouble too. My friends and I would convince homeless drunks to buy whiskey and other drinks for us, and we would drink before going to dances. I did use the money earned to do wholesome things, too, like going bowling, skating, and going to movies.

I do appreciate some of the things I was able to do with my Dad during my teen years. He would take Ron, my brother, and me on jobs. At the time, I had a love/hate feeling about it. I loved going out with my Dad, but I hated plumbing.

Some jobs were just disgusting. On some of them, we had to clear out the main sewer lines in Washington, DC. The apartment buildings he had contracted with were multi-unit buildings with one hundred or so people living in them. I do not want to go into details;

suffice to say while trying to clear the main drains, some people on the upper floors would flush their toilets. I am sure you get the picture.

(Please note: names in this book are changed to protect the privacy of those in my life.)

Some things happen in my life that woke me up to the existence of God. When I was fifteen, my best friend Mark and I passed by a tent revival meeting, seeing the people on stage sharing how God had healed them. I thought I would trick everyone, so I started screaming, my foot my foot. I received a lot of attention, and then we ran away. A few months later, I wanted to get some money to go dancing at the teen club. It was late in the afternoon, and I needed to finish fast. I knew one of my clients wanted their lawn cut, so I ran over to their house and got the job. While I was cutting the grass on the back of the property, I had to push the mower down the hill while standing on top, and the drop off was about three feet. On one of the sections, my foot slipped and went under the running lawnmower. Lawnmowers at this time did not have the safety stop, so two toes on my left foot were cut like a butcher fillets a sirloin steak.

When my Dad heard what had happened, he ran to my aid. He drove way too fast. While cutting through traffic, I could hear the horns from other cars blowing at him. After getting to the hospital, the surgeon could sew them back together, but the toe next to the big toe is smaller and twisted about thirty degrees. Both toes had metal splints in them, and it took about six months to heal. My cast had been signed by many of my friends as it was five months before I got the form off. But not to worry, I still love to dance even till today.

I went to Bladensburg Vocational High School. I enjoyed working with my hands, so I took different trades to see which one I wanted to pursue as a profession. First, I tried mason work for a year,

4

learning how to lay brick and block. It was fun, but it did not fulfill the need. I tried HVAC next. Again, I was not too fond of it, so I changed to auto mechanics. It was great to learn these trades, as I used them throughout my life, in the USA, and while serving as a Missionary for 17 years in South America and Spain.

One of my best memories as a teenager is when my Dad called me and ask me to come down from my room to help him shingle the roof. I had just graduated from high school and was doing some celebrating the night before. I had no idea dad knew I was drunk the night before. He was making me carry the bundles of shingles up the ladder while he installed them. After about an hour or so, I was getting tired. Dad signaled me to say something. He leaned over towards me and said, "I know you were drunk last night. I will not tell your stepmother, but do not do it again." This touched my heart more than all the whippings and punishments that I ever received because I felt he was on my side.

Contents

Chapter 2
Military service and experience

I graduated from High School at seventeen, and my father gave me a choice. He said, "I know the Military Service will make a man out of you, so you can join the Navy, or I will call the army and get them to enlist you." This was a tough choice for me. By this time, America had been fighting the Vietnam War for twelve years. There were about 3.5 million war-related deaths, 58,000 were Americans, with  nothing to speak of as a result. I believed we needed to withdraw. Knowing my father was a man of his Word (One thing I still admire him for), I knew I had to go into the Navy.

I went through boot camp at "The Keel" in the Great Lakes. I will never forget walking in line to get my Military vaccines. These vaccines were given with air-jet guns and in both arms at the same time. The next morning, I could barely lift my arms. During my time at boot camp, I caught double pneumonia. It was below freezing  most of the time. The clothes would freeze on the clotheslines. The pants and shirts would be as hard as a board. I can remember times when the commander ordered to put them on frozen.

After Boot Camp, I the Navy stationed in San Diego, California, on the USS *Samuel Gompers* (AD-37). She was a destroyer tender, the first of her class. They designed it to be a floating U.S. Navy repair shop for Battleships, either in port or at sea. The vessel got the name from Mr. Samuel Gompers because he was a distinguished American labor leader during the late nineteenth century.

Although I was still not sold on America being in the Vietnam War when onshore, I thought I was in heaven. San Diego's climate was delightful. People were friendly, and I was free to go ashore most weekends.

The military tours of the Samuel Gompers were Guam, Hawaii, Philippines, Hong Kong, Japan, and off the coast of Vietnam. It was great seeing all these Countries. I began to understand that people

 are the same all over the world. People of all Nations had families they loved. They all were doing what they could to survive and live a full life. I came to understand how God loves all the peoples of the

world.

I will never forget what happened in Japan on the ship. Jim, a buddy on the Gompers and I wanted to go to the 1970 World Expo. It was held in Osaka, Japan, and was called the Progress and Harmony for Mankind. I remember we arrived way before the gates open. It was still dark, and we could not get in. There was no one around, so we laid down on the benches that were outside the gates. We both fell asleep, and when I woke up, I had Japanese people sitting on the bench all around my body: one by my head, another where my knees bent, and another where my feet left space. I could not see Jim as there were so many Japanese people on the sidewalk. It amazed me how quiet and respectful they were.

In the World Expo, Jim being six foot three, could easily see over everyone's heads, but I could see over their heads. This was something out of the normal for me as I was only five feet five inches tall. There were so many people we could barely walk, so we made a plan of how to change things up. Please remember we were eighteen years old and crazy. We planned to count three and yell. When we did, everyone moved, some to the left and some to the right. We were amazed. We ended up walking right through the middle, and no one said anything, and no one got mad. I guess they realized that we were ignorant young men. Being sixty-eight years old now, I understand that they had the gift of humility, something of which we knew nothing.

Like other military personnel, I was introduced to drugs while overseas. This addiction went on for about three years after being discharged out of the Navy. I continued into heavier drugs, doing everything from Marijuana, Mescaline, Acid, and more. I thank God that I did not do heroin or ever use a needle. God had mercy on me.

While on tour, the ship's medic assigned me to the Hospital in Manila, Philippines. I needed to have research on my foot injury. While there, I met many young men who had returned from the battle. Many had different parts of their bodies amputated. It was hard to see. Many were crying out in pain. Hearing the stories of what had happened to them made me sad and mad. It horrified me to see what one young soldier in his twenties showed me. He had pictures of what he did to a young woman. He made a marijuana bag out of her breast. I will never get these pictures out of my mind. Horrible things happen in the minds of the men that fight hand-to-hand combat. I was devastated, and my life changed after this.

The Hospital in Manila could not help me, so the medics flew me back to the Bethesda Naval Hospital to do a more extensive study on my foot. As I said earlier, I slipped under a lawnmower and cut two toes nearly off when I was fourteen. A box fell on the injured foot in San Diego when I was working in a Navy warehouse. I believe I was having a mental breakdown as I could not stop thinking about a way to get out of the war after seeing the horrors of what the war had done while in the hospital in the Philippines.

Contents

Chapter 3
Why do we go through HARDSHIPS?

When on liberty from the Bethesda Hospital, I was walking down the streets of Georgetown in Washington, DC. It was about three in the morning, and I met a woman in a tattered white dress. She started telling me how God loved me and wanted to have a relationship with me. After listening to her for about thirty minutes, I told her, "I have to leave." In less than a minute, I changed my mind. I looked everywhere for her. I ran up and down the streets looking for her. She was gone; it seemed as though she disappeared. To this day, I believe she could have been an Angel.

A few weeks later, I went out with some old friends. They introduced me to Bill. He owned a fifty-seven Chevy, a great car to drive around looking for girls, so we drove around. We met some girls by a restaurant called Jerry's Hotdog Stand. As we talked to the girls, a huge man, about six feet five inches tall and weighing nearly three hundred pounds, came walking over to us and started beating up Bill. We were all surprised at this, and we knew we had to stop the fight. All of us together started to do whatever we could to stop him. We were able to stop him, and he left. Later, Bill told us that the attacker was one of the leaders of the motorcycle group called the Pagans.

About twenty minutes later, I saw the Pagan leader coming back. I also noticed he had a knife, so I yelled, "HEY" to get everyone's attention. When I did, he leaped at me and swung the blade. He might have picked me because I was in my gaberdine Navy uniform. "This was my favorite uniform because I had it made in Hong Kong." All I could do was lift my hands to block the knife as it came down towards my neck. It cut off my left-hand ring finger at the distal phalanx, the middle finger halfway through, about a third the way through my index finger, and cut the bottom of my thumb on the right hand. When I saw what had happened to my hand, I ran for my life. He was right behind me until I lost him. I thank the Lord I got away.

I was not ready to die. After looking back, I know God saved me for His purpose. I returned to the car after I learned the Pagan had left. I went into the restaurant and told the server behind the counter that I needed a rag. He told us to get out of his restaurant. I told him in some very descriptive words if you do not give me a clean rag, I am going to come back there and cut your XXXX fingers off. He gave me a rag and called the police. The police called an ambulance, and then the policeman told me, if you find your finger, the surgeon should be able to put it back on.

Being in shock, I did not feel pain yet, so I yelled, "Finger Hunt." When my best friend Mark found it, I asked him to bring it to me. He said no way, so I walked over and picked up the piece of my finger off the ground. I put it back in place and replied, "it still fits." The policeman told me to place the cut off part of the finger in a rag. This was not a good thing to do as the cloth pulled all the blood out of it. The tissues were dead by the time we arrived at the hospital. My hand swelled up to be as big as a softball. The pain was constant and difficult to bear.

When in the hospital, my father told me that the Pagan motorcycle group tried to get to me in the hospital then threatened to burn down my father's restaurant if the charges were not dropped. I did not want to take this chance, so I dropped the charges. This attacker was put in jail for another offense later.

After my hand had healed up, I returned to San Diego to find my ship. The Samuel Gompers had already shipped out, so the Navy assigned me to a small destroyer. It was so different while underway. Being a much smaller ship, it did not take the open seas as well as the Gompers. I was amazed it did not sink. The quarters were tiny, and it was hard to sleep. When the ship landed in the Philippines, they transferred me back to the Gompers. Before leaving for the hospital, I worked in the boiler room. I was delighted to go into the ship fitter's unit instead of the boiler room. Then I was incredibly grateful to be assigned to the library. It would be my third and last tour overseas.

After my discharge from the service, I stayed in San Diego for about five months. Then I moved to Akron, Ohio, to be close to my mother, grandmother, sister, half-brother, and half-sister. After getting there, I found out that my mother was going through a tough time. She was drinking a lot, and the man she was with was abusive to her and my siblings. I chose to stay at her house instead of finding a place. I wanted to do what I could to stop this person from hurting my family.

One evening they got into an argument, and it got physical. The boyfriend was six foot three and weighed about three hundred pounds. My mother weighed about one hundred and twenty pounds, and I weighed about one hundred and thirty-five pounds. I knew I could not allow him to hurt my mother, so when I confronted him, I said I am sure I will not be able to beat you, but one thing is for sure I will hurt you before you get past me. I was so thankful that he backed down and left the house.

A month or so passed, and my mother was doing better, so I got an apartment. I started welding school with the vision to get rich by working on the Alaskan pipeline. They were paying a lot of money per day, and I thought after two years, and over time I would be set.

After passing the welding certification test for flat and vertical welds, all I needed was to pass the overhead welding test, and I would apply for a job.

By this time, two girls lived with me, my girlfriend Sally and a friend of hers, Sara. All of us enjoyed dancing, so I took them to a dance on Saturday night. During the dance, we split up, and another girl Kala asked me to dance, so since I could not even see Sally, I danced with her. During the dance, she started talking to me about God and his love for me. I found this conversation intriguing so, I continued talking to her for hours, forgetting all about my girlfriend. We ventured out to her car and proceeded to talk about faith, Jesus, and the Bible. The dance hall closed, and I could not find my girlfriends. I drove home, and the new friend Kala followed me, and we continued to talk until the sun came up. She left, and I never saw her again, but our conversation never left me.

When I went into the apartment, both girls were understandably angry with me. I told them I was sorry that nothing had happened. I was just talking all night long. Sally did not believe me. She said that she was going to stay out all night too, which she did.

Contents

Chapter 4
God works in mysterious ways

One-night Sally and I took some acid together. The strangest thing happened, we both were looking out the second-floor window, and we were sharing the same vision. We both saw people running and screaming and fires everywhere. I cannot remember anything else, but it scared us.

The next morning, I had to get to work. I went to my car, and it would not start. During my time in the Navy, I hitched rides a lot, so I went to the main street and put up my thumb. An older man picked me up and told me he was going right by where I worked.

During our trip, the first thing he told me was that the end of the world was coming. Now forty-eight years later, I have to smile, understanding how God moved His hand. God had brought this man to me. God had him say the words that would rock my world. Remember Sally, and I took acid the night before, and we saw this vision together. Therefore, when he told me that the end of the world was coming, I said, "I know we saw it happen last night." During the ride, he told me that God loved me despite all the bad things I did and that Jesus wanted to show me how to live. Looking back, I understand what he meant. Since that day, I have served God on many continents of the world.

The man asked me to go to his Church on Sunday. He picked me up and took me to his church. After about ten minutes, I got up and walked out of the church. It was just too much for me. Their worship style was hard for me to take. I was raised Catholic and went to Catholic Church "twice a year." In the Catholic Church, the sermons were in Latin, and I would sit there and get bored. This church was excessively aggressive in their worship style. Thinking that all Churches must use that style of worship, I did not try to find another Church.

By this time, I had shared with Sally and Sara what had happened to me. Neither one was Christian, so this caused many problems in the home, and we split up. I found another apartment.

I continued going to school and working two jobs. One was selling clothes in a clothing store on Saturday. The other was test driving new cars and new tires on Friday, Saturday, and Sunday nights from midnight to five in the morning. The company would give us new vehicles with new tires to road test and send us out. Sometimes we were told to take it easy and other times to tear them up. I'll leave it to your imagination on which test we like best. This, by far, was the coolest job any twenty-two-year-old man could want.

Since accepting Jesus, I enjoyed talking about God, but I was too busy to take time to let it go any further. One afternoon about two months later, I went to a Laundromat to wash my clothes. Doing my usual routine, I would go around the room, asking others to play chess after putting my clothes in the washer. To my surprise, I saw three people reading the Bible. I had bought a Bible after praying to receive Jesus in the car ride, but could not understand what I was reading, so I just stopped reading it. I asked them, "Do you people understand what you are reading"? They answered, "Yes, please sit down." After we talked a while, I shared what had happened to me with the man in the car. They read the Gospel of John Chapter 3 to help me understand what happened to me in the car.

This opened my understanding. It thrilled me to see that everyone needs to be born spiritually if we want to understand the Bible. We continued to read the Bible together for the next three hours. I felt as though I was being fed not physically but spiritually. My mind had been enlightened, and my spirit fed. I loved it.

When our clothes finished, they told me they had to leave. I asked, "where are you going." They replied, "We have to find a place to stay. We are traveling from Chicago". My enthusiastic response was, "you could stay at my apartment." They agreed and stay with me for three weeks. I gave them a key to the apartment. Our daily schedule was they would go out to share the Gospel in the morning, and I would go to school or work. In the evening, we would cook dinner, eat, pray, and read the Bible together. On the days I was free, I would go with them to share the Gospel, and I saw God move in peoples' lives, as He did in mine. My experience and understanding started to change. I realized that God is alive, and He wants to reach the world with His truth and love. The best way for Him to do it is if we share Him with others.

Three weeks went by fast, and they told me they were leaving. I asked, "Where are you going"? They told me they were going back to The Jesus People's Mission in Chicago. I said, "and me, what about me"? They responded, "What about you"? I said, "I want to go with you." They called the Mission and asked if they could bring me back with them. I am so thankful to say the answer was yes.

The next day my life began to take a significant change. I had a  yard sale and took things to the pawnshop. I told my mother, siblings, and old girlfriends what happen to me. I told them that I now know that God is real and that we can have a relationship with God through Jesus. I told them that I was going to Chicago to serve God. They tried to talk me out of it, but I knew God was alive in me. I knew that Jesus changed my life forever. I knew Jesus gave His life for me, and I wanted to give my life to Him. I wanted to tell everyone about Him. I packed my Volkswagen bug with their things and my things, and off we went.

It still amazes me how God changed everything that day. I stopped smoking cigarettes, marijuana, and drinking in one day without even trying. I had no withdrawals and very little desire to smoke. In less than a month, there was no desire at all. The schedule in the Jesus People Mission was close to what Teen Challenge Programs are today. We were up at six am, breakfast at six-fifteen, chores from seven to eight, Bible studies and memorization of Bible verses until eleven, break time, then lunch. After lunch, back to Bible studies, then at around four, we would prepare to go out to share the Gospel until seven or later. Then back to the Mission. I would be there for five months. During the five months, I memorized twenty verses on Salvation, nine verses showing that Jesus is the Son of God, twelve about the Holy Spirit. In the years to follow, I was able to memorize hundreds of Bible verses. As David in the Bible said in Psalm 119:11 Thy word have, I hid in my heart, that I might not sin against thee. And in Psalm 119:105, Thy word is a lamp unto my feet and a light unto my path. King James Version (KJV)

When leadership realized that I knew plumbing, electrical, and carpentry trades, they wanted to use my abilities. So, I was sent to Syracuse, New York, as it was ancient and needed work. I was in N.Y. for a month or so, and I told them my desire to go to a foreign field to share the Gospel.

A small Mission in Toronto, Canada, offered me a position in outreach. After being there for a month or so, I met a brother in Christ named Denny. He wanted to open a Christian theater in downtown Toronto. We spent hours working out new skits and theater productions. After a couple of months of work, the costumes were made, and the actors were chosen. The theater opened. On the day of the theater, we put on our costumes and parade up and down Young Street with guitars and signs saying that the free show would be starting at seven-thirty pm. We would fill the upper room where the show/skits were put on. Right after the show, all the actors would mingle with the viewers and share the Gospel. It was an excellent way to share the Gospel one on one. Many people came to Christ in the six months it ran. The finance ran out, and we had to close the doors.

God works in mysterious ways. During the time the theater was opened, a couple asked us if we wanted to care for a place in the mountains of Montreal for a few months. They told us it would be great for a team to go for studies and a retreat. We had to go somewhere, so when Marty, another brother, and I remembered their offer to go to this place, we jumped at it. Well, little did we know the house was a log cabin in the middle of nowhere. There was no electricity, no running water, no heat except for a log-burning stove and a small, poorly built outhouse. H.A., the only store, was a four-hour walk through the woods. Accepting the challenge, we stayed there for four months.

During this time, I was able to study the book of Acts, Romans, and Revelations. At night, the cabin would get cold, so we would take turns cutting wood and getting up in the morning to get the fire going in the stove. The other person could stay in his sleeping bag until the place heated up. It was winter, and we would walk about a mile to get to a stream to fill the buckets with water. We'd put a bucket on each side of a pole, lift it on our shoulder and carry the water back to the cabin. We would stock the cabin with enough food for a couple of weeks. Then when we had to, we would take the all-day walk through the woods to get enough food for the next couple of weeks.

I grew to love it in the mountains after a month or so. Life was all around us; squirrels, birds, and many other animals kept us company. It seemed that my mind was clearer than ever. I could visualize the writings of the early disciples of Jesus. I could take the time needed to slowly read their writings, letting them sink deep within my heart and mind. They came to life for me.

One of the times when we were walking back from town, after walking most of the way, the sun was going down, and the light in the woods became dim. We usually tried to leave early enough not to be in the woods at dark, but this time we had taken too long in town. We had come to know and enjoy talking to the shop keepers. While we were walking, we picked up some limbs. They were straight and perfected to hook the bags on so we could rest the pole on our shoulders with the bags hanging behind us.

I heard a rustling of leaves, and then deer started jumping across the path we were on, one then another and another five or six in all. We thought that is nice, but we did not think it was nice for long, as the lead wolf stopped right in front of me. Every hair on my head stood up. I did not know what to do, but I remember as a young boy, you never turn and run from a dog, so I stood my ground, staring right at him. I slammed my walking stick to the ground, and the bag of groceries fell to the ground. The next thing I knew, the lead wolf seemed to look both ways, then ran off. Then we saw the other three behind him. I think they thought the deer was easier prey. We praised the Lord for keeping us safe, and we kept going.

The months we were in the cabin were some of the best months of my life. (You will hear that a lot in this book). When the owner returned four months later, as we agreed, we went back to civilization. I began talking to Denny and writing to different Christian works and youth homes. I received an invitation to go to a home in Cleveland, Ohio.

This Jesus people location had eight people in it. They were living as it says in the book of Acts, as they had all things common. Any money coming into the home was placed in a common pot. Bills and needs were taken out of these funds. I found this to work very well, as we would pray for our needs, and somehow God would fill everyone's needs. Of course, nothing elaborate, but we did not feel we needed elaborate things. We worked together to reach

Cleveland with the Gospel. We would also share in the many chores that needed to be accomplished, like dishes, cooking, and cleaning. It was amazing how there were extraordinarily little bickering and complaining. We all wanted to please God and each other. We would have witnessing teams going out every day. Our goal was to reach the world for Jesus. The verses we used to open our conversation were John 3:1-8 and Revelation 3:20. People were open to us, and we prayed with many people during our daily witnessing.

While sharing the Gospel, we met a man that had a small farm in Louisville, Kentucky. He needed someone to take care of it for a few months. Since I had such a great time in Montréal, I volunteered and took off for the farm with the owner. He told me all the ins and outs of caring for the farm. He gave me the key to the house and the truck and left me to it. This farm had a lot more than the one I was at in Montreal. It had a big mule whose backside was as high as my head. His name was Red, because of his deep black/red coat. There were chickens and a dog named Judy. Being raised in the city, I was not used to going out to the chicken pen to get breakfast, but it did not take long to get used to it. Big Red and I would ride out to the mailbox every day, and Judy would run right beside us. One day Judy ran off and did not come back. I was distraught after she did not return that night. The next morning Red and I went everywhere looking for Judy, but she was nowhere. A few days went by, and Judy came home. A snake bit her, and she was not doing well. I prayed for her, and, thank God, she got better in a few days. After my time on the farm, I returned to Cleveland. The Pastor offered me the Copastor position, after praying about it, I accepted.

During one of our outreaches, we met a young girl named Sandy, sitting alone in the subway. Her clothes were a bit dirty, and she looked a little stoned, but she listened to each Word while we shared the Gospel. She prayed with us to receive Jesus into her life. After talking with her, I found out that she was a runaway. She was sixteen and lived in another state, and she was on heroin. I told her that we would help her, but to do so, we would have to call her parents.

When we got back to the Mission, we called her parents. I talked to her father for an hour or so. I told him she wanted to stay with us, but I needed his permission. He spoke to her, and she said she wanted to stay. She gave me the phone again, and he told me he did not know what to do with her anymore. I said she could stay with us, and I guaranteed she would not do any drugs. He agreed to let her stay, and we exchanged addresses and phone numbers.

Sandy stayed with us for three and a half months. During this time, she joined our regular schedule. Up at seven-thirty prayer time, breakfast, and then Bible study, afterward out, we went to share the Gospel. She experienced the Holy Spirit using her to help other people, and she was ecstatic. At the end of her stay, we put her on a bus back to her parents. A week later, her father called me and asked me what he could do for me and the Mission. I told him I needed a sponsor to help me financially as I wanted to serve God in a Home Church Plant in Brazil. He said, just let me know what you need, and I will cover it. He funded me to get there and gave me a startup fund, but I took the long way to get there and learned a great lesson.

I knew I felt the Holy Spirit leading me to go to Brazil. I started writing letters to a list of missionary homes in Brazil. Still, after writing many letters, I was getting impatient. I wanted to go into all the world to reach the lost.

I got to the point when I doubted my leading to go to Brazil, so I wrote one letter to Argentina. In a few weeks, a letter came inviting me to join them in Buenos Aires. Excited and ready to go, I booked a flight and was there within three weeks. The flight was long and bumpy. On more than one occasion, I thought the plane would fall out of the sky, but thankfully, it did not.

A brother who was bi-lingual picked me up. The small church was in a small house. There were six men and two women there, but no one spoke English except for the brother from Puerto Rico. I found out later that he was not in the church I was going to be but was asked to pick me up. I was discouraged.

My first six months were brutal, as I had a great desire to talk to the brothers and sisters in the church but could not. The schedule was up at eight, breakfast, devotions, Bible study, chores, then out we went to Share the Gospel. After about a month of not being able to communicate my faith, I had a revelation. I wrote verses on flashcards like John 3:16 and Romans 3:23 and Romans 6:23 also first John 4:8. I painted my face like a mime as I did in Toronto. My Afro went to the streets of Buenos Aries, Argentina, with two or three other brethren. I would signal with my hand for the person to stop, then lift the flashcards one by one to share the great news of Salvation. I did this for months, and little by little, was able to speak with the flashcards until I could share the Gospel in Spanish.

When President Juan Peron suffered a series of heart attacks on 28 June 1974. Isabel, his wife, was summoned home from a European trade Mission and secretly sworn in as acting president the next day. Juan Peron died on 1 July 1974, less than a year after his third election to office. As vice-president, his widow formally ascended to the presidency, thus becoming the first female in the world to hold the title of "President," although she was not the first female to lead a country. She was popularly known as *La Presidente*. I landed in Buenos Aries in 1976. During that same year, the Argentine military overthrew the government of Isabel Peron. The 1976 Argentine coup d'état was a right-wing coup that overthrew her as President of Argentina on 24 March 1976. A military junta was installed to replace her. This was headed by Lieutenant General Jorge Rafael Videla, Admiral Emilio Eduardo Massera, and Brigadier-General Orlando Ramón Agosti. It was part of a more extensive series of political coups called Operation Condor.

The military dictatorship that resulted called itself the "Process of National Reorganization," or "Proceso," and dubbed its activities the Dirty War. But the war wasn't with outside forces; it was with the Argentinian people. The war ushered in a period of state-sponsored torture and terrorism. The junta turned against Argentina's citizens, whisking away political dissidents and people suspected of being aligned with leftist, socialist or social justice causes and incarcerating, torturing, and murdering them.

Their takeover was not received well by many, including many of the university students. Soon the revolutionaries were blowing up government buildings and police stations. Often some of the revolutionaries were university students that we would be witnessing to. Our church of young men and women loved to reach our age group, and when we did, we would be in the parks, streets, and other public places sharing the Gospel. Therefore, if a military police wagon would come by, they would stop and ask us tons of questions. Many times, they would throw us in the police vehicle and take us to jail. I went through this type of ordeal thirteen times during my time in Argentina.

After I was in jail in Buenos Aries a few times, we prayed, asking the Lord to raise enough funds so we could move. The Lord was faithful, and some of us moved to Santa Fe, Rosario, and some moved back with their families. We moved to Santa Fe because some of the brethren knew some Christians there, and they were willing to share their three-bedroom house with us. It made things easier for all of us as money was short. The schedule was again similar to the other Home Churches up at seven-thirty, breakfast, devotions, and personal Bible study. Then we would make up teams and out to the Harvest fields of God. We knew we did not know much and had not gone through seminary, but we knew we knew the King of Kings, who gave us His Holy Spirit, Jesus. We wanted to let everyone know about it.

One day while out sharing the good news, we met a young man named Juan; he was about thirty years old. We shared the Gospel with him, and he gladly prayed with us to receive Jesus as his Savior. Afterward, he asked if I like to fish. He knew I was American, and he wanted to show me around his town. I said, "sure, I'd like that." He told me that he would pick me up at our house. I agreed, so we set the time for 9 a.m. Saturday. On Saturday morning, I heard a knock at the door, and it was Juan. He said I didn't need anything, so I just went with him to the fishing location. I was surprised to see he only had a small paper bag. I thought we'd pick up the rods and other equipment on the way. We got on one bus, then another and a few more. During the ride, I was wearing shorts, as it was a scorching day. He did not say anything about it, but people were looking at me strangely. Later I found out that people did not wear shorts in Rosario in 1976. Ha, just another thing I did not know, but it all worked out.

We arrived at the location, and there was bamboo all over the field. We started our way through them and arrived at the riverbank. The river was about thirty yards wide and flowing beautifully. I still did not see the fishing rods, etc. but he still had the small paper bag. Juan started digging a little six-inch-wide, long, and deep hole. Then

 he dipped his hands in the water a couple of times and filled the hole with water. He opened the little bag and pulled out a small hook, then an eight-foot-long fishing line. He gave them to me and told me to wait that he would be right back. When he returned, he had a bamboo pole about three feet long. He tied the string to it and

then the hook.

He reached in his bag again and pulled out a plastic bag, and when he opened it, I saw it was a piece of meat. He put it on the shore close to the hole and left. When he returned, he had a flat piece of wood. By this time, there were flies on the portion of meat. He hit the meat and the flies with the flat board. Then he picked up a fly and put it on the hook. He tossed the hook and bait in the water close to the shore. Within seconds, he had a minnow on the hook. He pulled it out, took it off the hook, threw the minnow in the six by six-inch hole with water, smacked the meat with the flat driftwood again. Put a fly on the hook, and in the water, it went. A few seconds again and, yep, there was another minnow. He handed me the small handmade fishing rod. He told me to continue the minnow fishing, and off he went.

This time he came back with a bigger bamboo. He reached in his little paper bag and pulled out another larger hook. In fact, it was a hook big enough to catch a whale (not really, but it was big). Into the bag, his hand went again. This time he pulled out a fishing line that was about thirty feet long. He tied the fishing line with the large hook to the bamboo pole, took out a minnow, placed it on the hook, and threw the line in the river.

Not more than ten minutes went by, and he was pulling in a Boga fish that I believed weighed at least six pounds. He took it off the hook, tied the Boga's tail onto the line of the small bamboo pole, put the fish back in the water, and then started all over. Again, in a brief time, he gets another one. The next two were Dorado weighing about the same. By this time, the sun was going down, so we packed up. H.A., we really only had to take the fish and the hooks back with us.

Juan took me to his house and showed me an incredible way to cook fish. He poured water into a cast iron pot that was thirty inches high and forty inches round. Then he put logs under the pot, lit it, and left it to boil. He cleaned and scaled them, stuffed them with garlic and herbs and wrapped each fish individually in aluminum foil, and then tied all of them by the caudal fin with a thin rope. There was a tripod above the pot. He tied the fish, so they were hanging over the boiling water. We talked about our lives and families and the Lord while the fish steamed. Not long afterward, he took them down and placed them on a plate, and I must say they were delicious. I had never seen fish cooked this way, but I sure want to do it again.

Everyone in our small home Church liked Santa Fe, Rosario. The people were genuinely friendly, but the revolution started reaching there too. The police began checking people when there were too many gathered, especially people our age. After being put in jail a few times, we prayed to ask the Lord to lead us as we did not want to cause this family any legal problems. So, we decided that one of the families could stay with the original family and just lay low while the rest moved on.

We contacted a small mission in Cordoba, Argentina, and they said a few could come. A sister and I moved there. Cordoba is a college town, so we thought we might blend in and still do what the Lord called us to do, share the Gospel. We tried to keep a low profile, but the devil was fighting our every move.

One morning at about 3 a.m., The police raided our house. I was sleeping on the second floor, and I was awakened by someone pushing through the shutters on the window. Man, that scared me. I jumped out of bed and was standing naked against the wall. The young man was holding a rifle and demanding me to go downstairs. His hands were shaking, which was making me even more frightened. I kept telling him that I was not a revolutionary, and I did not want to hurt him. I pointed to my clothes, he shifted his rifle, allowing me to get dressed, and we went downstairs.

When downstairs, I saw that everyone was up against one wall. We were all frightened and praying that the Lord would save us from this situation. The police officer in charge told us that we were under house arrest and would not be allowed to leave the property. Then they left the house, leaving guards to make sure we did not go without their escorts. For the next few days, we prayed that the Holy Spirit would touch the hearts of whoever oversaw the investigation. The military guard kept us under house arrest for three weeks as they checked us out. We were only allowed to go to the store with an armed officer. After the house arrest, we were told that we had to leave Cordoba. Again, it was time to seek God on what to do and where He wanted us to go.

I went to the city of Salta in the north of Argentina with a few others. We found a pension, and within a day, we were able to witness to the owner. When she found out that we were Christians and we wanted to reach the city with the Gospel, she was overjoyed. She was a wonderful Christian woman, and she wanted to reach her town with the Gospel too. She offered to do everything she could to help us. She gave us a couple of rooms to use and even served us mate (the regional tea) and biscuits in the morning. We were a small team of five, so this worked just fine for us. She allowed us to have devotion in the open area of her pension and pretty much let us do as we pleased. After our mate and biscuits breakfast, and personal Bible study, out the door we went, going two by two into the city of Salta. Salta was a small city, so we had to go on what we called road trips to surrounding pueblos.

On our road trips, we would share with everyone, as we shared the Gospel, we would also let them know that we needed a place to stay if it was too far to return to the pension. In these little towns (pueblos), there were no hotels and no lodgings anywhere. I remember on one trip. The Martina family kindly asked us to have dinner and spend the night in their home. We were very grateful and accepted. They did not have a bedroom or a bed, so they gave us each a couple of blankets and allowed us to stay on the porch. That night was freezing. Being on the blanket on a concrete floor, I had a tough night. The next morning, I had extreme back pain. The pain made it so I could not stand up. I push myself, and somehow, we were able to get back to the pension in Salta.

The next day my back was even worse. Every time I tried to get up, the pain would be too bad, and I could not stand. This went on for a couple of weeks. The owner of the pension did not know what to do, so she called a local doctor. He was not sure what was causing my pain and told me to rest. The other four brethren kept going out and sharing the Gospel each day, leaving me behind at the hotel. One day I could not take it anymore. I had been praying the whole-time asking God to help and heal me, with no change.

One day I started to claim a hand full of Bible promises and standing on them. I kept claiming them repeatedly. I stood on them. Quoting Bible verses to God like; Exodus 15:26, Psalms 34:19, and 107:20, Isaiah 53:5, Jeremiah 30:17 and 32:27, Matthew 4:2 and 18:19 James 5:14-15. Luke 17:14 says, as they went, they were cleansed. I stood up with tears of pain streaming down my face as I kept claiming these verses. The pain did not go away for four days, but I kept going out sharing the Gospel, and I kept claiming His Word and promises. On the fourth day, it happened, God did it. He healed me. I woke up on the morning of the fourth day, and I had no pain. I praised the Lord then, and I still Praise the Lord now, for His grace and healing that day.

I thankfully kept going out again to share the best news we can give the world, that Jesus is God, and He came to earth and won the battle over sin. He offers to take our sins if we allow Him to do it, and if we do allow Him to cleanse us of all our sins, our eyes are opened to devote ourselves to Him both now and for eternity.

The event that made us leave Salta was when Antonio and I were picked up by the police and thrown into a small dark cell. There were no seats, no beds, just a hard-concrete floor. We were in there for about twelve hours. There were no windows, no lights, only a steel door. The cell was so dark. We could not see our hands. We could not see each other. We talked and prayed the whole time.

Something happens in the prison cell that I have a hard time believing myself, but I know it happened. After being in the dark, cold prison cell for about eight hours, we were hungry and cold. We had stopped talking and were praying silently. Sitting on the concrete floor for so many hours was hard on us. I tried to adjust my position and leaned back. My hand touched something, and I moved my hand away from it as quickly as I could. It was warm and felt funny, so I was afraid to touch it again. After praying and talking to Antonio, I built up enough courage to reach out and touch it again. It felt like Aluminum foil. I pulled it close to me and lifted it to my nose because it was so dark, I could not see it. It smelt like a Milanese sandwich. I opened the foil, and sure enough, it was a warm chicken Milanese sandwich. I told Antonio, and we could not believe it. The cell room door had not opened, and there was no other opening to the prison cell. Yes, we ate it, and it was good. The only way that sandwich could have got in the cell was with God doing a miracle. Amazing, I love seeing God do these little but, at the same time, great miracles.

Our total time in the cell was about twelve hours, but it seemed like days. We shared the Gospel with the police chief, but he did not want to pray with us.

When the police let us go, we went back to the pension and found the other brothers and sisters were desperately praying for us. We started making calls to friends, Christian homes, and other home Churches looking for a place to move to as soon as possible. We laid low because the town was too small, and the military police would see us again, and more than likely return us to the police station.

We all loved the people in Salta as they were very nice, but the revolution against the Military government was too strong there for us to continue in this city. The police were picking up people when there were three or four gathered, especially people in their twenties and thirties like us. They would put them in the police van and take them to the police station to interrogate them.

I stayed in the pension, made calls, and wrote letters to Paraguay and Brazil. Paraguay answered, so off to Asuncion, I went. It was a new home church, and as always, the goal was to share with as many as possible about the gift of eternal life that God gave us through the blood of Jesus.

There were two families and four singles, me being one of the singles. There was a couple from Argentina, an American couple, two singles from Argentina, a young man from Germany, and me, the American single.

While sharing the Gospel in Asuncion, Paraguay, we met a young woman named Cielo, which means Heaven in Spanish. When we were witnessing to her, she told us that the Lord healed her of Polio. When she saw how we were going into the cities and towns sharing the Gospel, she wanted to do it also, so she asked us to take her with us. She was still a bit unstable, so we took it easy.

On one afternoon, we had an incredible experience that I have to share. I went out with Cielo, and as we usually did, we prayed and asked God to lead us to the area where He wanted us to go.

I felt the Holy Spirit was leading us to go to downtown Asuncion. We got on the bus, and halfway there, I felt a strong leading of the Holy Spirit to get off the bus. I rang the bell, and the bus driver stopped the bus. We got off, and I told Cielo, "I do not know what God wants us to do, so let's pray." I sensed the Holy Spirit leading me to go two blocks south. When we got there, we stopped and prayed again. I sensed the Holy Spirit leading me to go right another half a block. We ended up in front of an old house. There was an open gate, so we went up to the door and knocked.

A woman, about ninety years old, open the door and said in Spanish. "WHAT DO YOU WANT? It is siesta", so why are you bothering me. I told her that we did not know why; all we knew is that after praying, God led us to your door. She screams, "I do not need you; he might need you, but I do not need you." She points to a closed door, so we walked over to the door and opened it. We saw a man about the same age, but he could not have weighed more than seventy pounds. He, too, started yelling in Spanish, "WHAT DO YOU WANT." We told him the same thing that we were on our way to Asuncion, and God told us to get off the bus, and then God led us to you. He wants you to know that He loves you.

He calmed down, and I began sharing the Gospel. He listened to everything I said, and at the end, when I asked, would you like to know for sure that you are going to heaven. He responded, yes. I said in Spanish, all you have to do is repent of your sins and ask Jesus Christ to forgive you. He wanted to ask for forgiveness, so we prayed with him. Amazing, Praise the Lord. We gave him some Christian literature before we left, and when we were leaving him, he was smiling and thanking us for coming. His wife was still murmuring and complaining, but we had accomplished what God had led us to do. Praise God.

We were not in Asuncion long as the Catholic Cardinal heard about our non-denominational Christian home Church and had the authorities close the home and deported everyone. I was there for about four months. When the authorities came to our house, they gave us two weeks to get out of Paraguay. I was so grateful that after talking with the brothers and calling other Christians, a door opened for me to go to Porto Alegre, Brazil, as I did not want to go back to the USA yet.

I will never forget the difference between the cultures of countries. To help you see what I mean, in Argentina, when you asked someone how you are. They would say bad (Mal in Spanish) the government is bad, the economy is bad, and the business is bad. In fact, everything is just bad. On the contrary, when I asked someone in Brazil, how are you? They would say everything is good (Tudo Bom in Portuguese), and the answer would be everything is good back (Tudo Bien in Portuguese). This amazed me because many of the people that were saying that everything is good were eating rice and beans for lunch and dinner, and cornmeal for breakfast. The Brazilians attitudes were uplifting, even when Brazil's economy was much worse than Argentina's. To help clarify this, in the grocery stores, there were, let us say six employees, four jobs would be changing prices daily to keep up with the inflation, and the other two were cashiers.

The people, in general, were very happy. I really loved this, but they were, so none committed when it came to dedicating themselves to follow Jesus. They would listen, but their Christianity was so mixed up. Other religions and traditions were mixed in with their Christian faith. I found it extremely hard to open their eyes to the truth.

In the seventies, they may have called themselves Catholics, but millions of Brazilians also practice Macumba (a homegrown version of voodoo). With a population of more than one hundred and fifty million, Brazil is a multi-cultural melting pot. The two main African religions practiced in Brazil are Umbanda and Candomble.

I moved in with a family that had a small outreach on the outskirts of Porto Alegre. They had four children and wanted me to weld rooms on the bus they bought so they could travel and share the Gospel as they went. We had the same schedule as most Home Churches. Up at seven-thirty, breakfast, then devotions, personal Bible study, and chores. My job was to get his bus setup for trips. The bus was in the yard of our neighbor. He was a banker with four children.

I started working on the bus, and during this time, I found myself dehydrated three times. The first time I felt terrible and did not know why. Roberto, the neighbor, after looking at me, told me that I needed to drink two liters of water a day. I started doing it, and sure enough, I started feeling better. We became good friends over the next few months. One day he told me that he was going to his farm where he raised sheep and invited me to go. I thought it would be a great idea and talked it over with the others in the Home Church. We all thought it would be a good way for me to be able to share Jesus with him, so I agreed to go.

I had no idea what the trip would be like. He drove us in a beat-up Jeep, and after about a six-hour drive, we arrived. It was a tough trip, and when we arrived, we found out that the cabin had hundreds of honeybees flying around in it. Roberto told me it was nothing to worry about as they were docile and would not bother us. So, I went to sleep, but with reservations.

The next morning the cabin was still filled with bees. They were everywhere, on the bed, on the floor, on the table, even on the cups. We tried not to accidentally eat one as we drank our coffee. By this time, I had to agree that they were docile, and they did not eat much, Ha.

After breakfast, we started the search to see where the honeybees were. On the drive up, he told me he had honeybee boxes, so I thought they might be coming out of one of them. After going out the door, it was amazingly easy to see where they were, as there were hundreds of them flying all around the roof eaves.

Roberto put on protective clothing and a headcover he used for extracting honey from honeybee boxes. We had to look up under the roofing to see how deep the hive was. After smoking the hive, we found that the honeycomb was so giant he had to reach his whole arm in to bring it out. We saved the honeycomb and honey. It had a wonderful taste of eucalyptus and flowers.

The reason he asked me to go with him was to help build a cabin for his farmworkers. The first morning he took me over to where the workers were living, I saw why they truly needed a cabin. They lived in what was no more than a metal roof, leaning on a stack of wood. They had already placed piles into the ground so that the floor would be about three feet off the ground level. We built the floor and walls, but we did not get to the roof on this trip.

Yerba mate is a traditional drink in South America, especially in Argentina, Paraguay, Uruguay, Chile, and Brazil. This drink contains mateine (an analog of caffeine). It's made from an infusion of dried leaves of Yerba **mate** (Ilex paraguariensis). The tea is typically served with boiling water in a dried gourd and sucked out with a metal straw with a flat bent end that has holes in it.

The workers were sitting all together, drinking mate when we arrived. They would fill to gourd with boiling water, as is custom, drink from it, then pass it to the next person who would fill it again with boiling water, drink from it, then pass it to the next person.

The first time I drank Yerba mate was in Buenos Aires. It was somewhat challenging doing it at first as it just seemed like colds and other diseases could be passed on so easily, but I got used to it and even came to enjoy it with friends. The difference this time was the impoverished worker's teeth were half missing, and it was evident that some of their teeth were rotten. Their poor mouths were showing a great need of care.

Nevertheless, there was no way I could say no to sharing tea with them, as it would be an insult. I had shared mate with my neighbor earlier in the cabin, and he was sharing it with them now. I also wanted to be a good sample of God's love and friendship for him and them. So (by God's grace) when it was my turn, I took it, filled it, drank it, and passed it on. This went on for about an hour. I continued drinking mate with them for the weeks I was with them and Praise God I did not get sick.

We spent three weeks building the cabin. During this time, we drove around his property and looked over the hundreds of sheep, a few horses, chickens, and pigs.

One day we heard the windmill making a lot of noise. We knew we had to check it out because it supplied our water. He asked me to go up to where the tank was. I found it needed an adjustment that did not take too long. Just having to go up and down to get the required materials for the repair was tough, but we fixed it. The trip went very well, and I found out something about his faith. Like many Brazilians, he was Catholic, and he had many misgivings about the Catholic Church. I shared that Jesus did not come to give us a religion, but a relationship with God and others. He liked that.

When I returned to Porto Alegre, I continued working on the bus and going out to share the Gospel for another month or so. The time there was ending because the family doing the bus project ran out of money. He called a small Mission he knew that was in Rio de Janeiro and told them I was looking for a place to serve. I thank the Lord they offered me a position which I took. I was going to work as the school handyman. The first project was to build a treehouse for the children. It was only about three feet off the ground, but the kids loved it. I really enjoyed doing it, and I do not mind saying it came out real nice, although I did have another bout with dehydration.

Contents

Chapter 5
Love and Brokenness with an answer

I met a Brazilian girl name Chuva, and it was love at first sight. We worked at the same school for about four months before we knew we just had to be married. We went to the Civil Registry Office and found out we had to comply with the Brazilian Law, which meant I had to have a lot more money than I did. I had to have thirty thousand dollars in the bank. After even more investigation, they saw that my visa was almost up. At this point, they saw that I had a multi-entry Visa, and they would not extend it. I had two weeks to leave Brazil. We tried to get her a passport, but it would cost two thousand dollars. Our hearts were broken.

We knew we would not be able to stay together and get married. The Pastors at this Home Church knew another Home Church Pastor in La Paz, Bolivia. He gave him a call, and he said he could help me with a place to stay until I could find a longer-term position to fill. My fiancée was watching as my bus pulled out, and both of us could not stop crying. While in La Paz, Bolivar, we wrote weekly, but after three months, we found it impossible to get back together. I never saw her again. To this day, I think of and wonder about her and what became of her life. I believe if things were different, I would have continued living in Brazil and would have missed God's higher calling for me. I came to understand this, as it says in Proverbs 3:5-6 New International Version (NIV) [5] Trust in the LORD with all your heart and lean not on your own understanding; [6] in all your ways submit to him, and he will make your paths straight.

A new Mission said they could use my help in Lima, Peru. The Pastor in La Paz talked to the Pastor in Lima about my acting experience, and they wanted to start giving open-air shows sharing the Gospel. The connection was made, and I was offered the job. When I heard about it, I jumped on it. I loved the time I was in a Christian acting crew in Toronto, so I was excited about this new possibility.

On the way, I stopped for three weeks in Montevideo, Uruguay, to visit an American Christian Missionary home. During that time, we had a surprise visit by the president of Uruguay. President Aparicio Mendez had met the brothers from this home a few months prior to my arrival. They had asked him to come by for dinner. When he arrived, I was surprised to hear that he was concerned for his well-being. There had been threats on his life. The brothers asked if he would mind if we prayed for him. He was pleased to hear this and agreed to let us pray. His special forces waited, and he left after we prayed.

I continued to Lima, Peru. After arriving, we started rehearsing the show, and again to my disappointment, the vision for the shows stopped shortly after that. The acting crew was offered other opportunities; mine was to become a handyman for a small school outside Lima. The school was located right outside of a town called Chiclayo. I was amazed to see that after driving out of Lima for a while, the overcast of clouds disappeared. The sun was shining in Chiclayo. It was beautiful. The school had thirty children and eight staff. I found that within a day of travel that I had contacted contaminated food, which gave me hepatitis A. My eyes started to turn yellow, as well as my skin. I was immediately put in isolation. For the next six weeks, I was quarantined to this ten by ten room that had a half bathroom.

The weeks started going by incredibly slow. All I had was a Bible. Now do not take me wrong. I had become very attached to my Bible. I loved reading the Bible (and still do), but I was not reading it for sixteen to eighteen hours a day for six weeks. God knows what He is doing because, for six weeks, all I could do was study it.

I started with the Gospel's then the book of Acts, Revelations, and Daniel. It turned out to be a fascinating six weeks. I prayed, then studied, then prayed and studied again. This turned out to be one of the best times of my life, crazy as it may seem. The only interruptions I had was when food was brought to me. The food did not interrupt my studies either, as it was so bland. I could not have anything on my whole-wheat grains, which I received three times a day. No butter, salt, or any other herbs, etc. could be put on my food according to the doctor. After the six weeks, I healed completely, felt better physically, and spiritually. It was exactly what I needed. My broken heart was mended, and it was back on the Lord.

There were 30 children, a cook, four teachers, a Provisioner of food and other needs, two running the office, and me the handyman. The schoolhouse looked like it was a converted chalet. It was beautiful, and it even had a pool. I was in the school for five months, and things changed again. The school was forced to shut down. I went to live in a pension and was running out of money.

I called my brother Ron, and he was nice enough to send me the money I needed to fly back to the States. I stayed with him for a couple of months until I got a job working for my father in his plumbing business. Being the elder son, I thought I would have a better part of the company, but my Dad wanted me to learn from the bottom up. I became discouraged. Honestly, I wouldn't say I liked the plumbing service business anyway, so I looked for a way out.

I was able to find some Missionaries that were on leave in the Maryland area. I started studying the Word with them, having dinners with them, and before I knew it, they offered me to go with them to New Orleans. I accepted and gave my Dad notice, and off I went.

While in New Orleans, we met with another small Christian home.

While working with them, I met my wife to be Ruthie. Ruthie was a sweet 29-year-old woman from Texas. Her personality was very close to what Proverbs 31:10-31 says, which describes a woman who fears the Lord, "who can find a virtuous woman? For her, price is far above rubies". We were married in 1979.

We went back to Maryland and visited my family, then to Texas to see her family. We ended up in Houston and found a young man named Robert, who managed a large apartment duplex. He was a Christian that we met while sharing the Gospel. When he heard that we were trying to raise funds to go on a long-term Mission in Spain, he wanted to help.

Robert had an extra room in his apartment and offered it to us. Then he told us that he needed someone to paint the inside of the apartments when they vacated. We accepted the job. We got to the point that we were painting two or even three apartments a day. He was paying us eighty dollars an apartment. Therefore, within about five months, we had saved plenty to start our venture to Spain.

We had received an offer to come to a small Christian Mission in Andorra, Spain, about four months before getting the funds we felt we needed. Therefore, we thanked Robert and left for Spain. There was a plane flying from New York to London called the Night Train. It cost ninety-nine dollars each. We had to get from Houston to New York. We took a Greyhound bus to New York and arrived many hours early. We sat in the airport for hours until the time of the flight. The flight itself only took about seven hours to arrive in London.

We had to take a train from London to Paris, France. We got to Paris early in the morning. We were so tired we could barely walk. We found out we had another fourteen hours wait for the train from Paris to Andorra, Spain. We found a coffee shop and flopped down with our bags beside us. It was noticeably clear that the waiter was not happy about us being there with our bags, but came by and asked us what we wanted, in French. I do not speak French but tried saying it in Spanish with a French accent. I said, "Coffe con Leche Y media Lunas, por favor." The waiter just turned around and walked away without taking our order.

About eight students were sitting next to us, and they asked if we were Americans? I said we were, and right away, they ask us what we wanted to eat. We told them coffee and media Lunas. When they found out what we wanted, they yelled at the waiter and got our order for us. While we were eating, they asked why we were there. I told them that we were missionaries, and we were on our way to Andorra, Spain. We told them we had a fourteen-hour wait. They said, come to our apartment and stay with us and we will make sure you get back in time. We accepted their offer.

When we got to the apartment, we saw it was in an ancient building. I believe they told us it was built in the eighteen hundreds. The walls in the hall and bathroom were wet and moldy. It was a shared bathroom with the other apartments on that floor. The bathroom was so small; only one person could get into it. However, all that to say this, we were so happy and thankful for their hospitality. They got out a guitar and started to sing traditional French songs and some songs by the Beatles. We began to fall asleep, so they took us to the only bedroom, which was just a curtain dividing the room, and told us they would wake us when it was time to go to the train. Sure enough, they fulfilled their promise. We had a wonderful time with them, and we were able to share the Gospel with them too.

When we got to Andorra, we were so tired we slept for a day. We stayed with them for a few days and found out that we disagreed with their lifestyle. We asked if they knew of any other missions or Christian homes that may be needing assistance. They told us about a single Christian woman in Valencia and that she had four children and was asking for people to come and help her. We worked out the travel plan and took a bus to Valencia. On arrival, we found that we did not fit in well, so we traveled through other cities, praying that God would lead us to a place of service. We went to Alicante, then Malaga, and finally to Marbella. The Christian woman in Valencia gave us an address to some friends who lived close to downtown Marbella. We were exhausted and were praying that the Lord would provide us with some relief from all this traveling, so we went to see them.

To our surprise, they were gay. We had run out of money, and they were genuinely kind and told us we could stay with them for a while until we could get situated. They believed in Jesus but thought their sexuality was something they were working out. They knew we believed the Bible's definition of marriage. It is that marriage is a solemn and public covenant between a man and a woman in the presence of God, intended by God for their mutual joy; for the help and comfort given one another in prosperity and adversity; and, when it is God's will, for the procreation of children and their nurture.

I heard a few years back; one of them married a woman and is doing very well. Praise God. When I reflect on that now, it's truly a demonstration of Romans 3:23, which says, we all have sinned and fallen short of the Glory of God, Romans 6:23 For the wages of sin is death, but the gift of God is eternal life through Jesus Christ our Lord and Titus 3:2-7, To speak evil of no man, to be no brawlers, but gentle, showing all meekness unto all men. For we ourselves also were sometimes foolish, disobedient, deceived, serving divers lusts and pleasures, living in malice and envy, hateful, and hating one another. But after that, the kindness and love of God our Savior toward man appeared, Not by works of righteousness which we have done, but according to his mercy he saved us, by the washing of regeneration, and renewing of the Holy Spirit, which he shed on us abundantly through Jesus Christ our Savior; That being justified by his grace, we should be made heirs according to the hope of eternal life. God loves the world and wants to clear out the sins that divide us from Him, so His love and light can shine through us.

I found a job working to maintain an apartment building. Then some months later, met Sam, the owner of a real estate company who needed a site manager who was bi-lingual. He was from England and did not speak Spanish. For the next three and a half years, I worked for him. The biggest job was tearing down a small house and building a larger house on the hillside overlooking the Mediterranean Sea and the Rock of Gibraltar. The landscaping was terraced, making the pool, garden areas, sitting benches all have fabulous views.

My job as a site manager was to make sure the construction was moving. The men were all Spanish, so I would also interpret for Sam and his brother. The Laborers had a tradition, which I came to love. Each day at the end of the workday, they would talk about who would bring what ingredient for the next day's paella. The next day, about a half-hour before lunch, the cook would gather the ingredients from every man, then he would gather firewood and cook everything in a giant paella pan that sat on three rocks. It was a great experience and great food.

While living in Marbella, we met two different Christian group homes. They had the same desire as we did. They wanted to share the Gospel with people in the Marbella and the surrounding cities. During the second year in Marbella, we were asked to be district overseers for the three independent home Churches. We accepted and carried that responsibility for about two years.

Our visas were coming to the end date, so we knew it was time to move on. We prayed and felt led to write to the Home Churches I had served in Argentina to see how things were there now. We heard Carlos Menem was president and the government was more stable. We had to leave Spain, so we ended up in a pension in Lisbon, Portugal, awaiting news. A letter came, and we were offered a job with a home Church in Buenos Aries. Sad to say, my wife ate something that made her extremely sick, so we had to stay another three weeks until she was strong enough to travel.

Our flight to Argentina was about sixteen hours. There were some very rough times of turbulence, which drove us to pray. Thankfully, we arrived but shaken up. Foolishly, I misplaced the address and directions to the home Church. We were in an excessively big city of Buenos Aries and knew nobody, and we had no way to connect with them. Back in the eighties, we did not have cell phones.

We found a pension and slept for a day. The next day we were desperately seeking the Lord. I went to exchange some US dollars and got food. We wrote to the brethren; I knew years prior and to others who might have known this Home Church. Two weeks went by with no reply. We started to fast and pray. For the next five days, I fasted. We ran out of money, so we did what we knew we could do. We went out and shared the Gospel, expecting God to do a miracle as we went. After a few hours of witnessing, it was midafternoon, and we were hungry. We walked into a Chilean restaurant and asked to talk to the owner. We shared with him why we had come to Buenos Aries and then shared the Gospel with him. Both Carlos and his wife, Lorena, received the gift that only Jesus gives, and then they fed us. We did the same thing for a week; we would go sharing the Gospel, then around two or three pm. We would go by the restaurant to have fellowship and share the Word and eat. When we found out where the home Church was, we went by to say goodbye to Carlos and Lorena, and they asked us how much we owed at the pension. We told them, and they paid for our pension and gave us some money for our bus, etc. It's life events like this that the early Christians lived too. God is alive and on the throne. Glory to His Name.

When we arrived at the Home Church, we found that the sewage system had backed up, and there was an awful odor. It took almost two weeks to get everything back in order.

Besides our times for sharing the Gospel and personal study, we also had jobs in the home. My wife started working in childcare, and I worked as a handyman. During this time, we met another couple who wanted to pioneer and plant a Home Church in Posadas, Argentina. We pray about it and sought counsel with the Pastor of the home church. We decided to go and were asked to lead the mission and Pastor the church plant. The couple who had the vision for Posadas had six children. My wife and I prayed about it and accepted the challenge.

Our first step was having someone to go ahead of the small team and find a temporary location to live. The brother who invited us took the job of traveling from Buenos Aries to Posadas, Argentina, about a six hundred and twenty-five-mile trip by bus. He found a ridiculously small six hundred square foot two-bedroom house that we could afford with our joint finances. It had underground water storage, which would fill when it rained, and a septic tank for wastewater, as city water and waste service had not reached this part of the city.

When his wife and their six children, my wife Ruthie and I arrived, we were thankful for the house but knew we had to find another home to rent as soon as we could. Our daily routine was the same as most Home Churches, up at seven, someone cooked depending on the choice of the day while others would clean up and take personal time in the Bible. Then we would eat and have united devotions, pray for the day, organize the day, and go out to share the Gospel. We started going to the local businesses, letting them know that we were opening a small mission outreach. We found that many were Catholic and believed in Jesus but had not come to understand what Jesus did. We shared the Gospel with them, and many started supporting us right away. They would give whatever produce they produced and finance. Where God guides, He provides. Praise the Lord.

We prayed every day that the Lord would do what only He could do, lead us to a larger house that we could afford. Every day we would find people who were not sure about their eternal destination, and we would show them that Jesus promised us eternal life with Him if we would receive Him into our lives. Jesus wants everyone to repent from doing the things that they knew He does not like. We would share what Jesus said in the Gospel of John in Chapter three, that we can be born spiritually. Making sure they understood that the Holy Spirit wanted to lead their lives. If they allowed the Holy Spirit to guide them, they would not want to do things that displease God. We always left them short Bible studies and continued praying for them. It was difficult to connect them to a Bible-teaching church because there were no other churches at this time in the areas and towns we'd go to, besides the Catholic churches. The services were given in formal Latin, which most did not understand, so we would provide them Bible study materials and ask them to buy a Bible and study it. On these faith trips, we took buses and walked for hours, so because of the distance and travel times, we could not do more than this.

One day after three months of living in the very small six hundred square foot house, we saw an abandoned house behind a construction supply business. It was all boarded up, and the grass and weeds were as tall as we were. We asked the neighbors who owned it and were told the construction business owned it.

We went over and asked to talk to the owner and were led to his office. He was a genuinely nice person, and we had a great conversation with him. I shared what we were doing in Posadas and our vision to reach the cities near Posadas and Encarnacion, Paraguay also Foz do Iguacu, Brazil, with the good news of what Jesus has done for us. I offered to clean up the abandoned house at our cost if he would let us stay there for doing it, but he was not willing. We were heartbroken as it was getting to be hard living in such close quarters, and we were not getting water in the small house because it had not rained for weeks.

We continued with our home church's mission of sharing the Gospel. God did many miracles and supplied our every need, fulfilling the promise that if we asked, it would be given. We continued going to local markets and stores sharing what we wanted to accomplish in their city, and more owners who loved the Lord would sponsor us by giving goods, food, clothing, and the finance we needed to pay the rent. We also continued to pray that God would supply a larger house.

About three weeks later, I sensed the Holy Spirit leading me to go back to the owners of the abandoned house. We prayed again, asking the Lord to touch the heart of the owner. Then I went back to the owner and asked the same thing, even offering to pay rent. He shared with me that he had lost a stepson the year prior to suicide and that his wife thought it was not suicide but that he was murdered. He told me that if I could help her, then he would help me. We agreed to move forward, and we moved in the next day.

It took weeks to get the house fixed up, cutting the weeds and grass, cleaning the windows, floors, and bathrooms. The house had six bedrooms and three bathrooms. It had a small kitchen and living room and marble floors throughout the first floor. It was wonderful to see how God had answered our prayers.

I started working with his wife at the business part-time. She prayed and asked Jesus into her life. Some months later, she came to the point of giving the death of her son to the Lord, but to this day, she still believes he was murdered. We were there for two and a half years until he needed the house to store materials again. When we found this out, we were in a desperate situation again, so we prayed again.

The Lord opened the door to another house much quicker this time. It had four bedrooms and two bathrooms, with a beautiful garden in the back yard. There were even fruit trees, with a guava tree, fig tree, and wild apple.

We were in this house for about two years, and the volunteers at the home Church grew to six adults and eight children. We had a teacher and a person who would be in charge of the daily needs of cleaning and cooking, and all the rest of us would be sharing the Gospel daily. One day we found out the owner's wife was diagnosed with cancer. We prayed for her, and we saw the Lord do a great thing, He cured her. Praise the Lord.

After being in this house for almost two years, one of the children came to tell me there was a big bug outside. I went to look, and it was a scorpion. I killed it and searched through some wood that had been donated a few days earlier to see if that was where it came from, but I did not see any. A few weeks later, another one of the children showed me another scorpion. I saw it was coming out of a crack in the rocks, and I killed it. Thinking I wanted to kill the nest of scorpions in the rocks, I went to the store and bought a can of insect killer. I went home and sprayed it into the rock's crack, and I could not believe what happened. Thirteen scorpions came out of the crack. My hair stood on end each time I had to kill one.

I knew I had to talk to the owner of the house to see what he could do. When I did, he said that having scorpions were typical in Posadas. We saved up some money and got an exterminator. When he sprayed in the house, we had a total of forty-three dead scorpions. They were all over the inside of the house. I knew we had to get out of the house as there were children and our teacher was a frail woman. After reading up on the sting of a scorpion, I found that they will make a person ache all over for months and can even cause issues with organs. The study said a frail person could even die. Over the next couple of weeks, we were praying desperately and looking for a place to move. It was harder this time because of the number of people in the home Church, fourteen, so we needed a bigger house and fast.

I met with the owner four or five times, asking him to return our deposit so we could put a deposit on another rental. He refused every time. I was getting more and more anxious. This was one of the times in my life that I needed to get desperate with the Lord and not the man, but sad to say I was losing it. The last time I met with the owner, we met in a small restaurant in the center of town. After about thirty minutes of conversation, I blew up. I just yelled at him, telling him that he was putting lives in danger and that God would hold him accountable if any of the children or teachers were stung. What if they died? It would be on him as we had no place to go. Then I walked away.

On the way back to the home, God was convicting my heart about my actions. My argument was, "Lord, you know he is in the wrong. He is putting Your children at risk". This conversation with the Lord went on for three days. Finally, I surrendered to the Lord and went to the owner's house to ask for forgiveness. This was, without a doubt, one of the hardest things I have done in my life. I had to humble myself by asking someone for forgiveness when I knew he was wrong. We had fixed the house up so much that he should have paid us for doing it, but he would not even give us back the security deposit. I was still totally convinced that he was wrong, but God looked at my actions and not his. I am the child of God, and I needed to act like it. I had shown a very bad example of a Christ-follower. So, when I got to his door, I had many emotions. I was mad, sad, humbled, and convicted of my sin. When he came to the door, I could see he was angry; in fact, he did not want to let me in.

When I started to talk, tears began to fall down my cheeks. At this point, they were caused by humility and pride at the same time. When The owner saw this, he opened the door and let me in. I told him with humility that I still did not think he was right, but I knew I was wrong in blowing up on him. That I was going to trust God to do what we needed Him to do, which was helping us get into another house as soon as possible. That God would protect us until He moved us.

When I left his house, it felt as if a three-hundred-pound weight was taken off my shoulders. I felt happy and free of any guilt or pressure of our situation. I knew God was going to do what I could not do.

Sure, enough two weeks later, one of our sponsors made sure we got out of the house. She gave us the money we needed to move to another place. It was too small, but at least we were out of the scorpion filled house. We stayed there for four months until the Lord opened a home on the outskirts of Posadas.

The new rental home only costs two hundred dollars a month. It had sixteen acres and a pond and a swimming pool. We tried to get the pool to work, but it had too many problems, and it would not hold water. The house was strange. It had four floors, but the rooms on the second and third floor had stairs going through the room below it. HA, but the kids and single guys loved it. It had one bedroom on the first floor, a living room and kitchen combination, and the servant's quarters where I stayed. To get to it, I had to walk outside the house because there was no door to it from the main house. It had its own ridiculously small bathroom. There were pine trees all around the property, and it had ant hills that stood about three feet in diameter and two to three feet tall in about thirty percent of the land.

There was an old tractor with a pull behind mower. It would take me about four hours to cut the grass. We planted vegetables and took care of the owners' pigs. He had two pigs that weighed about two hundred pounds each. We fed them the scraps from the table.

One day a neighbor gave us a couple of puppies, which made the children incredibly happy, but about six weeks later, they started to whimper. This lasted for ten hours or so, and I knew I had to do something, so I went to the veterinary, and he told me that they had a sickness that might be cured with charcoal, but he thought they would not make it through the night. I stayed up all night with them, giving the Charcoal tablets as instructed, but sad to say they died during the night. It was rough on the children, me, and everyone in the home.

One day the owner of the property and his young son came to the house and told me he had to burn the surrounding fields because it was easy for them to catch fire during the summer heat. He had planted pine trees all around his property, and he did not want them to get burned. While he was burning the field, I heard his younger son yelling for me to come and bring a hoe with me. I grabbed a small four-foot hoe and followed. When I got to the fire, they both pointed to a snake. It was trying to get back into its hole in the ground. It looked like a big snake, about three inches thick. I swung the hoe and missed him, then swung again and hit him once, then sung one more time, and it was dead. I picked him up with the hoe, and it looked to me to be a garter snake, so I told them, and they replied, "no, no," it is a Carbajo, and it has a deadly bite. I looked at it again and said, no, it's not. I carried it back to the house on the hoe. When I went to show the owner's son that it did not even have fangs. I took a stick and the hoe and forced its mouth open. To my great surprise, venom was dripping off its fangs. WOW, I started thanking the Lord that I did not do something stupid like pick it up. His grace has saved me so many times in my life.

During a spring month, we saw a beehive growing daily in a tree by the pond. It got to be about three-foot round in just a few weeks. I became concerned because the children would play in the yard. I talked to the property owner about it, and he told me to get up early, just before the sun comes up when it is cold. He said I could cut it down at that time of the day without getting stung. So, one morning I got up early as I was told and put on a long-sleeved shirt, long pants tucked into my socks, a hat, a scarf, and gloves. I picked up the saw and went to the pond. Our two puppies (this was before they died) were about three weeks old, and they followed behind me. My plan was to saw off the limb and let it fall into the pond. I stood on the edge of the water and reached as high as I could and started sawing the limb. Things were going well; the bees stayed asleep during the whole time I was sawing until the limb fell. It did not do what I had envisioned. The limb fell before the bark was cut through, and it hung to the tree by the bark. It swung over and hit the land and not the pond. The bees woke up and started going after the puppies and me. I think the closest neighbors who lived a half a mile away heard me yelling and the puppies yelping. The bees were not able to sting me in many places except for my face, which swelled as big as a watermelon. It took three days for the swelling to go down. Again, Jesus kept me, sparing my life again. I laugh about it now.

After being in Posadas for five years, my wife became very homesick. Sad to say, I was so busy with things that I was not taking the time I should have with her. She had her duties, and I had mine. The things we learn from our mistakes. She moved back to a missionary friend's home in Buenos Aries to help with their children and to raise funds to go back to Mexico. She wanted to be somewhere where she could visit her mother more often. My heart was still in the mission of reaching Posadas with the Gospel.

I was training a couple to take my position at our mission. They would care for the mission when I went to visit Ruthie in Buenos Aries. I would leave them in charge of our home Church and property while I was away. The trip to Buenos Aries took twelve hours each way, so I would go for an extended weekend and spend time with my wife then head back. On the last trip to Buenos Aries, a brush fire broke out in the fields. When I returned, I found the pine trees had been partially burned, and the property owner was furious. I promised him that I would stay and trim the trees and take care of the property. The rental agreement was in my name, so I knew I needed to stay. My wife continued with her plans and moved back to Mexico and eventually back to Texas.

It took some months to close the Home Church, but when I did, I moved to a pension, then a small apartment, and finally to a big enough apartment where I could separate it into a bedroom and a small office space. I did not feel it was time to leave Posadas, yet as I had a few people, I was discipling. I started giving English lessons and Bible studies. The classes were going well until I heard my mother was dying. I tried to raise funds to return by offering English classes and doing handyman jobs. I also asked friends and family to help me to get back in time to see mom before she died. Nobody responded as they were not in agreement with what I was doing with my life. They thought I would use the money for the mission and not for the flight home. They were wrong, but I understand now as they really did not understand what I was doing.

The average wage for a laborer was twenty dollars a month, and I had to get seven hundred and fifty dollars for the plane fare. I gave it my all to get back before her death but could not. When I received the news of her death, it hit me like a ton of bricks. I had been trying for five months to get back. So, when I heard she died, I just stopped everything.

I stopped the English classes and Bible studies. I stopped all social events and just shut my doors for three weeks. This is how the Lord brought me out of it. One summer day, while I was trying to write this book (many years ago), it started to hail and not some standard hail. The hailstones were the size of a quarter. The hail started coming into my apartment windows as there were no screens in the windows. I jumped up, ran to the windows, and shut them. I had three windows and a back door, which I had installed so I could go out to the rooftop to sunbathe and hang clothes to dry. I also had a copper wire running across the rooftop so I could hear BBC radio. So, I shut every window and the door and went back to writing the book.

A few minutes later, I heard a knock at the door. The apartment was on the second floor over a garage, so I went down the stairs to answer it. When I opened the door, there was a young boy, about nine years old. He was holding a small bird in his hands. He told me he had to go to school and asked me if I could help the bird. It looked like it was dead, but I told the young boy that I would be glad to help the little bird. I reached out my hands and allowed him to put the bird in my hands. As soon as he did, he ran off.

I took the little bird upstairs, put it in a plant box, got some breadcrumbs and some water, and put them in the plant box then went back to what I was doing. While I was typing, I saw the bird move a little, then a little more, and in about thirty minutes, it started to fly. Now, do you know what happens when a bird is in an enclosed room? It flies until it hits a wall, then another wall, back and forth until it either gets knocked out or dies. I jumped up, opened a window, and out it went. Wow, I just started praising God and thanking Him for allowing this little bird to fly away. Right after I began to praise God for it, God spoke to me as clear as if someone were standing next to me. He told me, "why aren't you praising me for your mom? She has flown back to me too. Wow, I just stopped cold, fell on my knees, and asked Him to forgive me. I was broken, but at the same time, I was incredibly happy and thankful, knowing that my mother was in heaven. I would see her again. This changed my life.

I started up the English classes and Bible classes again and continued working with the wife of the construction business. We met once or twice a month, and it seemed no matter what I did, I could not get her or her husband to understand the importance of studying the Word of God, the Bible. She helped me with finance when months were slow, and I did not have the finance to cover the bills.

Contents

Chapter 6
Returning to the USA

Months after my mother died, I received a letter from my older sister with a five thousand six-hundred-dollar check in it. She said it was from the will of my mother. I used it to come to visit my family and to see Ruthie in the USA. When I got back to the States, I called my wife, and she told me that she had met someone and wanted to move on. It broke my heart when I heard she wanted a divorce, but I did not blame her, and I still do not. I blame myself for not caring for her better. (Just a short note, we are great friends now. I write to her and her husband monthly. She prays for the mission work I do now and financially supports it monthly). I have married again to a wonderful woman with whom I love dearly. We genuinely enjoy life together.

That same day I found out my father was in the hospital and was scheduled to have open-heart surgery. When I asked to see him, he told my family members that he did not want to see me. You see, I had not seen him since nineteen seventy-nine, making it fourteen years. My father wanted me to take over his business, as I was the oldest son, but as I brought out earlier in the book, I did not like the plumbing business, and we did not see things eye to eye.

When I understood he was having a life-threatening surgery, I asked again and received the same reply. The surgery went well, and my father went to live with my younger brother in his house. I was permitted to live in my father's building. It had his restaurant on the first floor and his plumbing company on the second floor. The building had an apartment and two other rooms also on the second floor. My younger brother, who had taken over the plumbing business, moved the plumbing office out of a room into the apartment, so I was given a small room to stay. I had no money, no credit, either bad or good, and no vehicle. I wanted to stay in the USA to be close to my father, so I stayed, leaving everything I own in Posadas Argentina except for a suitcase of clothes.

My younger brother felt threatened by me thinking I would want the business, but he did not realize that I had no desire to take it. I felt out of place. I was used to studying the Bible and sharing the Gospel every day for twenty years. Now I was around him and his partner, who would take advantage of anyone they could to make money. Their cussing and cursing were nonstop. I felt as if I was back in the Navy; it was terrible. I started looking for work and a Church to attend.

I could not find work, but I found an excellent Bible-teaching Church called Forcey Bible Church. I started volunteering and meeting other Christians. Knowing I could do just about all repairs needed in a house, I put an ad on the Church bulletin board that said, "Handyman services call this number." Well, sure enough, people started giving me jobs to do. I joined the singles group and met the youth Pastor (this was years before I met my wife, Susie). We hit it off well right away. He took me out on his speedboat to do some water skiing and other things. He was indeed a blessing. After he found out that I was taking buses and caring my toolbox to do small jobs, he offered me a small Toyota pickup to use. This was an answer to prayer. I started getting more and more business. Eventually, he offered to sell me the truck for two thousand dollars. This was a great deal, as it was worth more. I still did not have credit and could not buy any vehicle. I am still so appreciative for his brotherly love. John 3:35.

My father got better, and he offered me a job in the restaurant. I'd do my handyman jobs during the day and stocked the cooler at night. This was no small task as I had to bring up six to ten cases from the basement cooler to the second floor most every night. Then sweep and mop the floors, clear off the counters, and clean the glasses. This took me till about one-thirty at night. Then I'd get up the next day and worked the small jobs that I received from the Church Bulletin board.

This went on for about a year. I was trained in the Church to talk to newcomers and to see if they truly knew what Jesus had done for them and if they knew they had eternal life. 1 John 5:13 This was a true blessing for me as I felt I was back in the service of the Lord. One Sunday, a couple came into the Church, and I was asked to talk to them to see the condition of their faith. I found out they believe that Jesus was the Son of God, but they did not understand what that truly meant. I was able to help them see that Jesus paid for all sin when He died on the cross. Isaiah 53:6. He offers complete forgiveness of all sin to those who believe that He has all power in Heaven and on earth. All He asks us to do is repent, meaning to stop doing the things we know are not pleasing to God. Read His Word, the Bible, so we can understand God's view of what is right and wrong. Then trust Jesus to cleanse us of all sins, even when we are not perfect because no one will ever be perfect. They both prayed to receive Jesus's forgiveness and asked for the gift of eternal life.

Afterward, the husband looked me straight in the eye and said, I really could use someone like you in my company. He owned a Mortgage business. He told me he would train me if I would come and work with him. I prayed and thought it over. I called and said to him that I had to make sure my father had the position I was doing filled before taking his job, but I wanted the job.

I told my father, and he was not happy about it. I knew I did not want the plumbing business or the restaurant business. I did not see myself running those businesses for the rest of my life. He had another person take over the night cleaning and re-stocking, and he retook the register. He was now healthy enough to do it. We did not part in peace. I moved to another apartment and began my new job.

When the owner found out that I had computer knowledge, he had me run that department and sell loans simultaneously. He put me in a big office, and off we went. The first loan he showed me how to close was one that the client was charged a high percent. I had no idea that this was way too much, and I pray for the family to this day, some twenty-four years later. I started little by little understanding how loans worked. I helped set up the network for the computers in the office and just monitored them after that.

When I understood loans, I changed the manor I ran the loans. At this time, the mortgage companies and Fannie Mae offered loans up to 125% of their home values. I thought this was great because a lot of people had run up debt. Many had credit cards with fourteen percent or even up to twenty-one percent. With these loads, we could roll their debt into their home loan, saving them hundreds of dollars a month.

After I got the clarity of how I could help people, I started being the two percent, loan man. I loved helping people get back into a place where they were not under so much pressure with their debt. I would share the Gospel with some people but not as many as I would have liked because I was on company time. I showed them I cared by getting them the best loan, with the lowest percentage price that I could. After a while, I went from the large office to a smaller office than to a cubical. After a year or so, I changed companies. This did not help much because I was not willing to lie to the client, saying that because of their credit, I had to give them a higher percentage rate on their loan. You see, at this time, the lenders would give the mortgage companies a kickback if the percentage of the loan was higher than it needed to be. I got fed up with the whole mortgage racket, so I went back to the renovation business.

My younger brother offered me a job as a sub-contractor. He offered me a salary at first, and then it went to where he would keep eighty-three percent of the job and give me seventeen percent. This was after all the cost of materials was deducted. I got into some bad habits as I was hanging around him and his other employees.

I saved enough money to put down a deposit on a house. It was a house that needed a lot of work, so I got it cheap. I told the younger brother I was working with that I found a house I wanted to buy, and I found a loan that would allow me to purchase it. The loan was a no documentation loan that was being offered to self-employed people. Since he was using me as a sub-contractor, I fit in the category. He told me yes, go for it, and I will back you up. I bought the house and moved in. It needed tons of work. It was a true fixer upper. But I knew this when I bought it. Two months later, my younger brother told me he had to let me go. I was mad and sad, mad because he told me he had my back and to buy the house with no fear of losing my job. Sad because I was on a path of losing the house. I have to say he helped me learn the renovation business, and without him, I might not have started my own business.

I told my stepbrother Ron. He has always been a great and faithful brother to me. He got me out of Peru when that home Church closed, and I had no money. He was the brother that took me into his home until I could get on my feet. I told him what had happened, and he offered me a loan to cover things until I could get back on my feet. I was incredibly grateful, and I told him that I would get it back to him in the next few months. Sure, enough, Jesus allowed me to get enough work to pay him back in the time we agreed, two months.

I knew I had to get a contractor's license to do more extensive renovations and not just handyman jobs. I started to study for the exam. Ron's wife, Terri, did something incredible for me. She read the complete home improvement book on cassette tape for me to listen to when going from job to job. I will always be grateful to her. I studied and listened to her tapes for three months, then I took my Home Improvement License test and passed it the first try. I opened a renovation business and made it an LLC. I created a website and called the company A Plus Renovations, with the website called the same. I ran the company for seventeen years. I would share the Gospel and about the beauties and realities of heaven with clients as often as possible. During this time, I worked on the fixer-upper while living in it. My brother Ron helped me on the back foundation and the roof. He has always been a blessing for me. I truly am thankful for him and love him dearly.

I started dancing again. I always loved dancing even as a young boy. I would cut grass, shovel snow, and serve newspapers, so I had the money to go to the teen club and dance. As an adult, I found that most of the dance communities were not Christian. When I would bring up Jesus, it was not something that was a topic of choice for them. The dances were always fun and a lot of exercises. We would dance for three hours without a stop on many occasions.

I met my second wife, Susie, at a dance. One evening she came to the dance with her boyfriend. He was a big man, about six feet tall. He told her if you want to learn how to dance, then dance with these three men. He named each one, and I was the last one. When we danced, she was so easy to lead, which makes dancing flow. I told her that I really enjoyed the dance. She, too, said she really enjoyed our dance. I saw them at dances occasionally, and one night I asked her, what is with you and the big guy? She told me she was not sure if it was going anywhere, so I gave her my card and told her to call me when she knew. I did not want to step between a good dating relationship.

About two months later, I received a phone call from her. She said that they had broken up and she wanted me to know. I was happy to hear from her and that she was free to date now. I immediately asked her if she was free the next weekend. She said she was, so we made a date. We both enjoyed the date enough to make another one, and before you knew it, we were a couple.

In Genesis 29:23, there is a history of what happened to Jacob. Jacob served her father seven years to marry Rachel, but the seven years seemed like only a few days to him because of his love for her. Well, that is kind of what happened to me, but I did not have to serve anyone. I asked Susie to marry me within a year, but she made me wait seven years. To celebrate our seventh anniversary of being engaged, I found an evening cruise on the **Selina II** sailboat, that gave evening tours of the Miles River in St. Michaels, MD. We went with two other couples that we did not know, as they signed up online as we did. During the cruise, we found out that the other couples were married. Susie and I are demonstrative with our feeling, holding hands, and hugging. The Capitan seeing this said, you know a Captain of a sailboat can give a legal marriage ceremony. I saw Susie was thinking, and sure enough, she looked at me and said, I am ready. I was stunned that she wanted to marry me now and replied, what do you mean. She said I am ready to get married. Three weeks later, we were married on the same ship, Selina II. She has been the joy of my life and has been with me through thick and thin. I will always love her.

We both are self-employed, carrying our separate businesses. Susie does custom sewing, and I am a missionary to the USA. Our lifestyles allow us to be together a lot. She has her office in the basement, and I have mine on the second floor. I really loved this from the start, but it took a few years for her to see this as a blessing. She had never had a relationship where they were in the same location day and night. On the other hand, I have lived this way for the many years I was on mission. She has come to enjoy this type of closeness now.

In 2016, I turned sixty-six, and I retired from the renovation business. I started serving God full time again. My new mission is to go to Churches and train them in Evangelism. I don't just give Evangelism in a classroom, but I take them out to share the Gospel of grace. The salvation of God that comes through Jesus Christ. I have met many wonderful brothers and sisters in the Lord while serving Pastors and Churches. We are so blessed when we share the Gospel of Jesus without fear, but with compassion and love, learning how to listen to others and lift up Jesus at the same time. I'm so thankful to be back to renovating lives full time instead of houses.

Please understand I have not been to seminary and did not go to college. I have studied the Bible and many other Christian materials for the forty-six years since coming to Jesus, so I do my best to humbly share the Bible with others. The gift of God is eternal life through Jesus Christ. We all, every person who has ever lived, have fallen short of the perfection that Jesus lived, taught, and commanded us to live. Jesus told us He was with God from the beginning. God and His Son Jesus created the world and everything in it, including us. He loved us so much that Jesus placed Himself in the womb of a virgin. God, through His Angel, told Mary to name her son Jesus. He then lived a perfect life on this earth, showing us how we are to strive to live. No one has been able to live as Jesus did. This is why He has offered everyone who accepts His offer, the total removal of their sins. We receive this gift through faith. True faith is trusting Jesus, trusting that He did what He said He did. Jesus said he came to take the sins of the world. When we trust what He said, then Jesus leads us through His Holy Spirit into His Kingdom. This does not mean we become perfect. It means He guides us, corrects us, and makes us His children.

Jesus commanded everyone who believes in Him to "go into all the world (This also means the part of the world we live in, the USA too) and preach the Gospel to all generations." If you are a believer, this means you. It does not mean you have to go to the Seminary or become a full-time missionary. All we need to do is understand the verse John 3:16 and be willing to say it to people. Then tell them what happened to you, how you fell in love with Jesus. Then get together with them and read the Bible. Start with the Gospel of John than go through the rest of the Gospels. When they are ready, inviting them to your Church. In the 17 years on the mission field, our Lord allowed me and our teams to share the Gospel with over 200,000 people one on one, person to person, and about 35,000 prayed, asking Jesus to come into their lives and give them the spiritual birth that only Jesus can give. John 3:1-21 and Revelations 3:20.

If God could use me, He can use anybody.

Here are some of the wonderful things God allowed me to see and do for Him and His Kingdom.

I am so grateful for the Pastors of these Churches. They allowed me to give training in Evangelism since I been back in the USA.

Calvary Burmese Church, Church of Philippi, Chinese Christian Church of Baltimore, Nazarene Church of Alexandria, New Creation Bible Church, Middle River Baptist Church, Faith African Methodist Church, Forcey Memorial Church, and Fil-Am Community Church. I gave a six-hour Evangelism Workshop to these churches and members in them. By His grace, they have reached hundreds more for Jesus. The Holy Spirit has given us the power and boldness to share the Gospel. By His grace, they are now working in the Lord's harvest.

The Lord can and will guide us through His Holy Spirit anywhere.

In a Church service, I noticed that a woman sitting next to me did not take communion. After the service, I introduced myself and asked her why she had not taken communion. She said she did not come to church service the prior week, so she did not feel worthy to take communion. I shared with her that communion is a demonstration of what Jesus did for us. He told us in John 6:29, "the work of God for us is to believe in the One He has sent. Jesus's only command for us is that we are to love God and our neighbor as ourselves. When we believe that Jesus was God and that God came to the world in the body of a human being and that person was Jesus the Christ. By coming to earth and dying on the cross, He fulfilled the many prophecies given about Him. To help you understand this, please read Psalms chapter 22. It is one of the prophecies that tells us of the death of Jesus on the cross. This prophecy was given hundreds of years before Jesus was born.

You see, when Adam and Eve rebelled against God by eating the fruit of the "knowledge of good and evil," they fell away from God because they did not listen and obey God. We, too, continue to put knowledge before the love of God and before faith in God. This world has continued to eat the fruit of knowledge of good and evil ever since the beginning. Most of the world judges others by the good and evil they do, but this is not how God judges us. If we are not seeking Him, we are living in sin, because everything that leaves God out, everything that leaves Jesus out is evil. God wants us to find Him by believing in Jesus and following what He said while He was here on earth. That is good.

First, by accepting that God loved us so much that He came to earth in the body of Jesus. (see John 1:1-14) He fulfilled all the prophecies and gave His own life to save us. He made a way for us to be cleansed of our many sins.

What is sin? It's anything we do that is not loving Jesus first. It's being unloving and not uplifting to others. Sin can be in things we do and something we do not do, things we say, and even all our thoughts. If we are honest with ourselves, we all have committed thousands and thousands of sins during our lives.

Jesus said He could forgive our sins in many places, one of the locations where He makes it truly clear is in Matthew 9:1-8 and Luke 5:17-26.

A few days later, Jesus went back to Capernaum. And when the people heard He was home, they gathered in such large numbers that there was no more room, not even outside the door, as Jesus spoke the word to them. A paralytic was brought to Him, carried by four men. Since they could not get to Jesus through the crowd, they uncovered the roof above Him, made an opening, and lowered the paralytic on his mat. When Jesus saw their faith, He said to the paralytic, "Son, your sins are forgiven." "But some of the scribes were sitting there and contemplating in their hearts, "Why does this man speak like this? He is blaspheming! Who can forgive sins but God alone? "At once, Jesus knew in His spirit that they were considering this within themselves. "Why do you question these things in your hearts?" He asked. "Which is easier: to say to a paralyzed man, 'Your sins are forgiven,' or to say, 'Get up, pick up your mat, and walk'? But so <u>that you may know that the Son of Man has authority on earth to forgive sins</u>..." He said to the paralytic, "I tell you, get up, pick up your mat, and go home. And immediately the man got up, picked up his mat, and walked out in front of them all. As a result, everyone was amazed and glorified God, saying, "We have never seen anything like this!"

After sharing this Gospel with her, she prayed, asking Jesus to take all her sins away. Then we took communion together.

We all have that same choice; we can believe what Jesus said or not. We can ask Jesus to forgive all our sins or not. If we want to gain a relationship with God, we must choose to accept that Jesus wants us to not only ask for forgiveness but also be willing to change whatever we know is not pleasing to God. This is the only way we can grow into men and women of God. It is faith in Jesus that drives us to be like Him. If you want to be like Jesus, you have to study His Words. If this is not a reality, if your faith is not changing your life, rethink it. The whole reason Jesus came was to show us how children of God should strive to live. I have a wonderful church that I attend, but Jesus did not have a building. He had a walking relationship with God. We need both.

Contents

Chapter 7

Heaven, what is it like?

Isn't it amazing how technology has changed our lives for the better in so many ways? We can circle the globe in no time, or virtually visit our friends or loved ones in an instant online no matter where they are. People's lives are being saved every day in ways that just a few years ago would have been impossible. People like you are finding new and innovative ways to accomplish more.

Wouldn't it be tremendous if you could continue to discover new things without end, or even go back anywhere in time to learn what really happened and see what we as a human race could learn? This, in itself, could take thousands of years. I think heaven is going to be filled with technology, or should I say things we had never thought existed, amazing, powerful, things beyond what we can even dream of now.

I have found heaven to be a topic that nearly always stirs people's interest. Even if a person does not believe in heaven, just hearing of the fantastic descriptions of how it is there Biblically is usually enough to keep them interested and engaged for some time.

I believe that heaven will be an extension and enhancement of everything good in our lives. This will compensate for every lack, wrong, and pain we have faced in this temporal world. This life lasts less than one hundred years, but heaven will have no end. Hearing about heaven can bring comfort to those who are at the end of their rope at the bottom of their game, those who have no hope for a better future in this life. When someone is feeling down and out, a reminder that there is so much more than this moment, something infinitely better than what they are facing right now, can make a big difference. It can be the ray of hope they need. It can be a sign or a reminder that God loves them, and an appealing reality that may lead them to salvation.

Heaven is a place where everything will be made right. Understanding a little of God's nature from the Bible and reading what He says about the place He has prepared for us helps us to know that there will be some impressive and amazing things in the next life. God is a loving Father and desires to give His children everything that is good. He loves to fulfill our desires when they are good for us. Considering all this, should we not thank Him for allowing us to seek Him first, even glorify Him for the wonders He has created and the eternal life He offers us as a free gift. To live in this incredible new creation, He has waiting for us.

Here are some thoughts and reflections on how I imagine heaven. The Bible says in 1 Corinthians 2:9 (KJV), "Eye hath not seen, nor ear heard, neither have entered into the heart of man, the things which God hath prepared for them that love him."

Our human understanding and imagination fall truly short when it comes to picturing the wonders of heaven. The following points give an idea of the incredible variety there could be in heaven. Our lives there will be filled with purpose, love, and unimaginable joy.

I believe these are some of the realities in heaven.

1. Other people will fully understand you and not let you down.

2. You will be able to communicate with and befriend animals that were wild beasts on earth as Adam and Eve did in the Garden of Eve.

3. You will be able to walk through history, seeing the full reality of those who went before you. Time is something in

this world. Time never existed in heaven.

4. There will not be any boredom in heaven. There will be new adventures unfolding for all eternity.

5. There will be no more loneliness. Love is part of the heavenly atmosphere, and love brings union with others.

6. You are guaranteed exciting and fulfilling relationships with those of common interests and those of interest that are new and unique to you, broadening your horizons.

7. Your uniqueness will always be yours, but your ability to connect with others will be enhanced by God's Spirit of love.

8. You will see how important you are in God's overall plan. How you are not just a small, insignificant person, but one of great value to God throughout all eternity.

9. There are going to be new challenges to meet and new ways to be a blessing in the lives of others. There will be no limit to the joy of doing things for others.

Heaven is not the final destination, but a launching pad to greater usefulness, new horizons, new experiences, and dreams to reach for that you haven't yet envisioned. Heaven is not the end; it is only the beginning.

If you want an engaging subject for conversation. If you're going to give comfort to those who are at the end of their rope without any hope, or impoverished, or victimized, or fed up with their lives. If you want to offer them a fresh vision of what can be theirs through a relationship with God through His Son, Jesus, what better way to do it than through speaking about heaven?

I think in the depths of the hearts of most people, there is a desire to have an assurance that there is something good beyond this world. 1 Corinthians 15:19 (KJV). Puts it this way, "If in this life only we have hope in Christ, we are of all men most miserable." The Bible says that God has placed eternity in our hearts, and it is a common yearning of the human heart for a better world to come. Ecclesiastes 3:11 (NLT), Yet God has made everything beautiful for its own time. He has planted eternity in the human heart, but even so, people cannot see the whole scope of God's work from beginning to end.

Heaven is the full reality of the life that God has prepared for humankind. It is real, vibrant, and full of everything good. It is beyond a person's dreams for the future, and yet it fulfills every yearning a person might have. Joy and abundant life are what Jesus offers us in John 10:10 (KJV). "I am come that they might have life and life to the full.

This life on earth has many sorrows. Jesus knows them intimately. He lived through what we face. He knows firsthand what people everywhere experience. The life beyond this one will be so full, so overflowing with joy and purpose, that there will not be room to dwell on the sorrow of the past. The negative, the suffering, the loss and pain, and sorrow will be left behind.

If your understanding of heaven has become like a treasure that you have buried somewhere for safekeeping, maybe you'll want to get it out, dust it off, and proclaim its beauty and value to others. It is there for you to use to help others and to meet the burning need in people's hearts to find hope, comfort, and truth that will carry them through to the next life.

The choice is yours. If you desire to stop the things you know offend God (repent), then reach out to Jesus right now.

Romans 10:13 says, "Everyone who calls on the name of the Lord will be saved."

Read this prayer, say it believing that God hears,

I know that I have done many things wrong in my life. I have said things that hurt others. I have done things that have hurt others. I have not lived the life of love Jesus taught. I know that I cannot change things of the past. I understand that the Lord Jesus Christ came to remove my failures, things that God called sins. I now take Jesus Christ as my Savior. I am ready to turn from my sins and trust Jesus alone for the gift of eternal life. I ask Jesus Christ to deliver me from sin's power. I now give Jesus Christ control of my life. From this time forward, I will seek to trust Him and obey Him in all areas of my life. In Jesus Name, Amen.

If you said this to God, then print this page, sign it, date it, and know that you have eternal life and will be in heaven with Jesus. We are perfect in Gods' eyes because He sees Jesus in us. You will continue to make mistakes because you will continue to live in this fallen world. The verses I continually hold on to is; Titus 3:5-7 "Not by works of righteousness which we have done, but according to his mercy he saved us, by the washing of regeneration, and renewing of the Holy Spirit; Which he shed on us abundantly through Jesus Christ our Savior; That being justified by his grace, we should be made heirs according to the hope of eternal life."

If you accept this and claim it, sign, and date this, it is your spiritual birthday.

Signature _____

Date _____

While walking around the Church, I was praying that the Holy Spirit would lead me to His divine appointment. He directed my eyes towards a man sitting alone at a table. I told him, "I really do not like eating alone. Can I sit with you?" He said I could, and we started to talk about the sermon we heard on that day. A few minutes later, his wife and child came and sat with us. I found out that they were new to our Church. Amy shared how, after the sermon, she had doubts about her Salvation. I asked, "what part of the sermon gave you these doubts?" After hearing her comment, I felt led to share the Gospel with her.

As you know, only God can touch the hearts of His children and lead them to the understanding of what He did for us on the cross. After sharing, she asked God to help her and to give her the assurance that Jesus did it all. When we parted, she said, I now understand that it is by trusting in Jesus Christ alone that assures us that we have eternal life, trusting in His sacrifice, what He did on the cross.

My wife and I went to CVS to buy some items. We heard someone yelling, screaming, and cussing. The Holy Spirit led me to talk to the person and find out what was going on. His name is Emerita, and he was from Eritrea. His clothes were soiled, and it looked as though he might have been homeless. He told me the reason he was so upset was, he was trying to return some birthday cards, but the manager would not allow it. Asking the manager for the cards, I looked them over. I told him I would buy the cards. He said, "Why are you doing this?" I said because God loves you, and so do I. Then I shared the Gospel with him, and he prayed for Jesus to cleanse him from all sin and to lead him in his life. A few minutes later, the police came in, but before they started asking questions, I told them that everything was okay, that the man was leaving, and I looked at the manager asking if that was right. He said, "as long as he leaves." When Emerita was leaving, I told him I had something for him in my truck. We walked over to my truck, and I gave him a Gospel of John and a Gospel tract. I asked him, "if I give these to you will you read them"? He promised he would. All Glory to God.

When finishing an Evangelism training at the University of Maryland, we had a get together for the last time for the semester. We asked the students who had completed the training to bring friends who would like to take the next semester of training. Praise the Lord. Many did pledge to take the next Evangelism training. I am excited about the thought of getting back to the University of Maryland. Forty thousand five hundred students from all over the world are going to school at this university. We can reach the world with the Gospel by sharing it on campuses.

A Veteran called me and told me he wanted to get Evangelism going at the VA Medical Center in Perry Point, Virginia. He has ten men who want to learn how to share their faith in Jesus. He had taken Evangelism training some years ago and believes we need to train Christians on how to share the Gospel. He is trying to use the Chapel in the VA hospital to give training. I love seeing the Holy Spirit move in the hearts of God's children.

A 29-year-old Evangelism director contacted me to see if he could be trained in Evangelism. While sharing about the different training materials, the Holy Spirit led me to ask George if he would be willing to answer two questions. He agreed to the first question: "Do you know for certain that you will be in heaven when you die, or is that something you would say you are working on? He told me that he was not sure he was going to heaven. I asked a second question. "Let us say your turn comes and you are standing in front of God, and He asked you, why should I let you into My heaven?" How would you respond? He said he had been to seminary and that he was doing all he could to serve God. I shared the Gospel with him, showing him that once someone genuinely believes that Jesus has all authority in heaven and earth. He has the power to forgive all sins, and they willing to repent of things they know are not pleasing to God; they are going to heaven. George prayed for his complete assurance of salvation. When I asked him the second time, he told me he now knows for sure he is going to heaven. He said he would share with his Pastor how, after our time together. George, now come to know for sure he is going to heaven. All Glory to God.

I am so grateful to have the knowledge and confidence of how to lead someone to understand the true Gospel of Jesus Christ. As it says in 1 John 1:3, "That which we have seen and heard we proclaim also to you so that you too may have fellowship with us, and indeed our fellowship is with the Father and with His Son Jesus Christ."

I met Daisy in the lobby of the Church. She came up to me with a question. I answered her question, and I noticed that she had an accent. I asked her where she was from, and she said she was a student from Brazil. I told her I had lived there for four years, and after some small talk. I asked if she knew for sure she was going to heaven. She said she did not know a person could know! After sharing the Gospel with her, with tears in her eyes, she prayed to receive the gift that only Jesus can give eternal life. We went over to the computer room and signed her up for some youth ministries. Praise the Lord for His grace.

I went to the Freedom Festival as they asked me to come and give a presentation for Evangelism. There were a few leaders from different Ministries coming. North Korean Freedom Coalition, Little Lights, Awana, and Teen Challenge. I was delighted to get together with them all. Not many people visited the festival, but I was able to talk to Sam, who runs the Teen Challenge in our area. I asked if I could take his guys to a small hall where I was set up to give a Gospel presentation. He said I could, so I ended up giving a one-hour Workshop on how to share the Gospel to seven Teens. I was pleasantly surprised to get together with a Christian music artist and Guest Performer Michael Card. Praise the Lord for His little surprises.

During one of our training at the University of Maryland, we only had 45 minutes to find God's divine appointment. We prayed, and the Holy Spirit led us to Daniel. He is 20 years old and was sitting on a bench. When we asked if he knew for sure, he was going to heaven; he said I am trying to make sure of that now I just had open-heart surgery a couple of months ago. We were all amazed; he was searching to know God, and the Holy Spirit led us to him. We shared the Gospel, and he really wanted to pray and received Jesus as his Lord and Savior. His searching is over. God is incredible. I love seeing the Holy Spirit move.

While browsing around the campus with three students, we saw Brenda sitting on the sidewalk. She was waiting for runners to come by so she could direct them. We asked if she could help us by answering a questionnaire. She agreed to help us until the runners arrived. When asking her if she knew if she would be going to heaven when she died, she said that she wanted to go to heaven, but she was not sure she would be. We shared the Gospel with her, and she prayed with us to receive the assurance of her Salvation. All this before the runners came. Love God's timing. <u>All Glory to God.</u>

We met a student named Yat as he was eating lunch in the cafeteria. When we asked if he had a faith that he followed, he said he was a Buddhist. We asked him if he could share with us about Buddhist beliefs, he said, in reality, that was something that his parents believed, and he had not come to his own conclusions on his personal faith. We shared with him what Jesus did and that He did it for the whole world. That in truth, the Christian faith is more about a relationship with God through Jesus and His Holy Spirit and not being religious. That Jesus died on the cross but then He rose from the grave three days later. Then God sent His Holy Spirit down from heaven unto the whole world to lead and guide us. That all God asks us to do is accept the gift of eternal life through Jesus His Son. I still praise God that Yat believed our testimony and chose to become Christian. He received Jesus as his Lord.

When I got home from Church and my wife Susie told me as soon as I got in the door that our new neighbors John and Janet's roof was leaking, and the drywall was sagging in. I grabbed a drywall saw and a flashlight, put on my raincoat, took an umbrella, and went to their house. When I got there, they told me the leak was upstairs. To my surprise, the leak was exceedingly small, only getting a 4-inch spot on the drywall wet. It turns out that God had a plan. They were so grateful they kept thanking me for coming over to help. I told them that the last owner had the metal roof painted and that they might have bent it while walking on it. I told them they might want to give the contractor a chance to repair it, but the contractor would not fix it that they should call the Home Improvement Commission. I asked if I could ask them a question, and they gave me permission. I asked if they knew for certain that they were going to heaven. They told me they did not. About 20 minutes later, they understood that they could ask Jesus to take away all their sins. They prayed, asking Jesus to take all their sins away. I am so thankful I yielded to the Holy Spirit, and my wife, (Smile).

I got together with Mark, who had just finished the Evangelism training with me. We went to McLean Bible Church. Afterward, we went to lunch. He is living with his dad and going to the University of Maryland. He told me he had devoted himself to praying and staying in the Word daily. Praise the Lord.

I went out with Jim last week at the University of Maryland in College Park. He just started going to the Baptist Christian Ministry there.

He was raised in the Church and now wants to start sharing the Gospel. We talked to three people, all of which were open to talking about God. The ground of their hearts was broken, and seeds were sown. I am praying that Jim commits to Evangelism training. I told him that every person who claims that Jesus is their Savior is called to stand up for Christ in a considerate and compassionate way, as they share with the world what He did for us. Jesus said He is the only way to God in the Gospel of John 14:6. With broken and loving hearts, we are to share this with our friends, family, and everyone we can. I have been out sharing the Gospel with the Chaplin about five times now. We have talked about getting Evangelism training going, but as of now, she thinks it would be an overload of the students. She tries to take her students out, but she does not bring others to Saving Grace as she hopes their friendships will be long term, sad to say since there are forty-five thousand students on campus, she rarely, if ever, sees them again. I have seen it is better to bring them to a decision each time, if possible, then follow up.

It has been a challenging month. My father is in-home hospice care now. My wife just had shoulder surgery and cannot drive. I have a disk disorder in the L4 L5 location, and it is sitting on a nerve. I have doctor appointments to see what can be done to ease the pain. During all this, our water was shut off twice, and our furnace went out while it was 10 degrees and the engine light came on in the vehicle. With all this, I know we are more than victors in Jesus that it does not compare to the Glories, which is set before those who love God through Jesus.

During this time, I have been blessed to see what God is doing through those trained in Evangelism. After the service at McLean Bible Church, I saw Craig sharing the Gospel up by the stage. I walked up, and the Holy Spirit led me to stand a few feet away and pray. Craig has been training in Evangelism for months. He told me afterward that he was so happy to see how God could use him to lead someone to Jesus even when he was by himself. Beth, who also went through Evangelism training, told me that Mike and she led a taxi driver to Jesus this month. There are more testimonies of the many that have been trained in Evangelism training, but too many to list all of them. The Bible says that God's harvest of souls is always overwhelming, but people who are willing to give up their time and energy to work for God in their daily walks of life are very few.

I love seeing how our Lord can use us. Barb and her children came to the main auditorium when the service was ending. They seemed to be lost. I told them that the next service would start in about 35 minutes. They left to go to the lobby. I felt the Holy Spirit leading me to find them and to share the Gospel with them. I found them sitting down in the computer room. After talking to them for a while and finding out more about them, I shared the Gospel with them. Barb, Kelly, Andrew, and Amy prayed, asking Jesus to remove all their sins and give them Eternal Life.

I received a call from Jimmy. Someone gave him one of my tracts with my name and phone number. As soon as he told me this, I knew the Holy Spirit was up to something. We agreed to meet for lunch. Jimmy is a retired Capitol police officer. He gives tours in the Capital and attends prayer meetings there. He also works with a young adult mission. When ordering our meal, I told Don, the waiter, that we prayed for before our meals and that we could pray for him too. He told us that he would appreciate it and asked us to pray that he would have a better life. After finishing our meal, I was able to share the Gospel with Don, as there was nobody in the restaurant. He gladly received the gift of eternal life. Now he has started a journey in his better life. Praise be to God.

The Pastor of Trinity U.M.C. is one of the Pastors who came to an Evangelism training event. I gave an Evangelism Workshop at his Church on a Saturday. Nine wonderful women of God came, Nancy,

Carol, Wanda, Carolyn, Fay, Vicki, Joyce, Elaine, and Nan. We had a wonderful time. Lord willing, they will reach out to others that God brings into their lives. Before the workshop, the Pastor and his wife took me out to lunch. When the server Mary took our order, we told her that we prayed before our meals, and we would like to pray for her and asked what we can pray for in your life? She wanted prayer for her school studies. When we finished the meal, she brought the check. I asked if we could ask her a couple of questions, as they were no one else in the restaurant. When I ask if she knew for sure, she would be going to heaven, she said no. We shared the Gospel with her, and she prayed, asking Jesus to take all her sins away and give her Eternal life. She was so pleased after the prayer, and she smilingly said, now I know I am going to heaven. When we had finished, the Pastor told me the owner of the restaurant was sitting at the other table, watching the whole conversation. I went over to apologize for taking so much time with her waitress and that it was not her fault. The owner said I am so happy you shared the Gospel with Mary. I have wanted to do it myself. Thank you. I was amazed. Thank you, Jesus.

Last week two young women, Narabi and Medoini, prayed with us to receive the Lord's forgiveness and eternal life. Nairobi is from Columbia, and she is Christian, but she was not sure if she was going to heaven. She is now. P.T.L. Medoini is from India and is a Buddhist. She prayed, but in the end, she said she wanted to read the book of John (which I gave her) before she committed to Jesus. Let us pray she will.

I got together with Mark and Neil 3 times this month. They are part of the Baptist Christian Ministry (BCM) at the University of Maryland. They are now taking **Evangelism** training with me at the University of Maryland. Neil, Mark, and I went through the last week of training this week. They reviewed the Gospel with me, and they are doing exceptionally well. We share the Gospel on campus every week. Mark and Neil took their final examination for the Evangelism final. Both aced the test. Over the training period, we shared the Gospel with sixteen people, and five asked Jesus to take away their sins. I am praying God will lead them for the rest of their lives. The Lord has given Mark and Neil the vision to continue training so they can come to the place where they will train others.

I just returned from Harmony Church. The Church has a great Pastor and congregation. We had Pastors and leaders from all over, one from NY, another MI, another Florida, and others from NC. We went out to share the Gospel four times. Two people asked Jesus to come into their lives. Praise God. The Evangelism event was a great success. Pastor Craig, one of the Pastors who came, has already set up an Evangelism Workshop at his Church to be followed by Evangelism training. I will be going back to NC and giving the Workshop. Pastor Craig will be reaching out to invite other Churches. I love helping others to see that we all can reach out to the waiting world with the love of God.

The Holy Spirit led me to meet Camellia in the lobby of our Church. She is from Paraguay, and I told her I lived there for about a year. After talking with her for a while, I started sharing the Gospel with her. She was so ready to hear the Great News she had a desired to pray and receive Jesus's total forgiveness for her sins. Praise God

Praise the Lord, 26 people came to the Evangelism Workshop at Faith AME Church. It was so inspiring seeing the enthusiasm of the brothers and sisters at Faith Church. We will be starting an Evangelism training after the Holidays.

I took a flight at 11 am from Maryland to Atlanta, GA. I was arriving at 7 pm. We started setting up for the Evangelism training event at Belmont Baptist Church, and I received a call from my wife, Susie. She had to call the ambulance to take my father to the hospital. I canceled my return flight that was for two days later and got a flight out to be with him and my wife. I got up at 4 am and landed back in Maryland at 11 am. Our Lord wants us to honor our fathers and mothers by showing them His love. Praise the Lord; my father was doing okay when I arrived. It is wonderful to have a wife who stands behind you to support you—hugs to her.

God is faithful to lead us to those who desire to find Him and His Salvation. I was in the lobby at Church when Sara, a woman who has been through our Evangelism training, came over with her sister Lori. I asked if Sara had asked Lori our most important questions. She said she had not. I asked if I could and was given permission. Praise the Lord about 15 minutes later, Lori received the gift of Jesus. God is faithful to lead us to His lost sheep.

The Evangelism Workshop was incredible at the F & A Community Church. The devil tried to stop it by messing up the video equipment. We checked it two days prior, and it was working fine. The Lord had His way and got it working after forty-five minutes and after the Pastor prayed. Thank You, Jesus! Everyone was Intune and involved. The Pastor told me they are ready and planning to be in the Evangelism Launch training that we are planning.

Tara went through Evangelism workshop training with me two years ago. Her husband Jorge received Jesus as Lord and Savior two weeks ago. We are now in communication, and he is growing in the Word. Praise the Lord.

I talked to Jasmin about the problems with my father's computer. She is in her twenties, lives in Manila, Philippines, and is Catholic. Her grandfather died last year at 88. She asked Jesus to forgive all her sins when she was 16 but was not sure she was going to heaven. I shared the gospel with her. Afterward, I asked again if she was going to heaven, and she said she knew for sure now. I shared how important it is to read the Bible every day. Before disconnecting, she told me that she was so thankful for our conversation, that it was the first time someone shared the Gospel with her. She said it was amazing. It is such a fantastic event when a believer comes to the assurance of their Salvation and entrance to heaven. Both my father and I were amazed to see how the Holy Spirit used me to lead someone to the assurance of their salvation in Jesus all the way in the Philippines.

I got together with The Church of Philippi this month, and we went to the Arundel Mills Mall to share the Gospel. Joanie, Jeanie, and The Church of Philippi have faithfully taught their children with our Kids Evangelism program. I have been blessed to go out with them a few times. Hyun and I met with Antony, a young man, about twenty-four who was filling out a form for a job. We talked to him for about twenty-five minutes and found out that he believed and had already asked Jesus into his life. He needed to understand that he was going to heaven, not because of what he does, but because of what Jesus did on the cross. Anthony prayed for this assurance and was so thankful that the Lord had led us to him. Then we met Ros. He was Catholic and had the same understanding as Anthony. After about fifteen minutes with him, Ros also prayed and asked Jesus to come into his life. Ros thanked us, and when we said goodbye, he had tears in his eyes. During this outreach, the team talked to twenty-seven people, and nine people prayed to receive Jesus as Lord of their lives. Praise the Lord

We had an Evangelism training at a Church in North Carolina this month. There were Pastors from Washington State, New York, and North Carolina. We spent ten hours a day together for two days, training and taking the trainees out to witness to the waiting world in North Carolina. During one of our times out witnessing, we met Natalie and her son Cal. After about thirty minutes of sharing the wonderful news of what Jesus did for them, Cal and his mother, Natalie, came to know the Lord personally.

The Lord has opened the door for me to give a forty-minute introduction to Evangelism at the Noble Warriors conference in Richmond, VA. I am praying that the Lord uses this open the door to assist Pastors to see the need to equip their congregations on how to share their faith. I was claiming that Iron sharpens Iron. During this one-day event, there were featured national keynote speakers, worship leaders, and sixteen different equipping workshops—all having resources for the men. Around forty men took their time to be introduced to Evangelism. I am praying that they share with others about the importance of us standing up for Jesus in our daily lives.

Jerrie from the Watchman on the Wall event called to sign me up for the event. She was such a blessing and helped me to get into the already overbooked event. After a few phone calls, our Lord's Holy Spirit led me to ask if she knew for sure if she would be going to heaven. She thought she would but was working on it. After sharing the whole Gospel with her, we prayed for her assurance of salvation, that her sins would be forgiven, and that she could share this with others. It is such a blessing to see our Lord's Holy Spirit working in lives.

I went out with Joanie, Jeanie, and the Church of the Philippi kids again. While going out to the food area of the Arundel mall, we approached twenty people, and nine people prayed with us to receive Jesus as their Lord and Savior! So thankful for the Church of Philippi and Joanie, Jeanie, as they train up the Lord's children and reap His harvest.

I went to Dale City Christian Church to see how their Evangelism training is going. I thought I would listen to the service before talking to the Pastor. The Lord had me sit down behind Dan, Mary, and their son in the service. I arrived early, so, while waiting for the service to start, I started a conversation with them. They told me it was the first time at this church, and I said it was my first time also. I was able to share the Gospel with them. They all understood the Good News, and when I asked them if they would want to pray and received Jesus as their Lord and Savior before the service, they did so we prayed. After the service, we exchanged contact information. I talked to one of the Pastors. He told me that they were training four people to be laborers for the Lord. I shared that I would be happy to go out with them on a witnessing night. Then I gave him their contact info so he could follow up with them.

I went to Medical Mission, which was organized to deliver healthcare, dental, and social services to those who might not otherwise have access to these services. We were able to pray for many who were sick, as they shared why they were there, and many received Jesus as Lord. We also prayed with many who needed the assurance of their Salvation. Please pray for Antonio and Elmer as they came to the assurance of Salvation. Jerad, a man in his eighties who came for health issues, asked us for prayer. We prayed for his health, his son, and family, and then he prayed to receive Jesus as Lord. We also were able to share the whole Gospel with three medical interns. They are all from India and came from a Hindu background. After sharing the full Gospel with them, they all prayed to receive Jesus and His complete cleansing from sin. I am praying that when we follow-up with them that they are reading the book of John and have found a Bible preaching Church close to them to grow in.

I met Monic at the open MRI while doing some tests. When I asked her if she knew if she were going to heaven, she said that she would be going to heaven, but she thought she could get there by doing good things. I shared the complete Gospel of the grace of Christ with her. In the end, we prayed that Jesus would give her assurance that He had paid the price for her. She realized, no one will go to heaven because of how we lived, as none of us are perfect. We all have sinned, and those sins have to be forgiven. I asked the same questions for a second time, and she knew that only Jesus could get her into heaven. I gave her a book of John and a gospel tract. She told me that she would read it.

I went to the three-day Watchmen on the Wall Conference in Washington, DC. There were many excellent speakers, like Tony Perkins, Pastor Jack Hibbs, Anne Graham, and many more. We had an Evangelism Exhibit set-up for the three-day event. There were hundreds of Pastors in the conference, and many of them wanted more info on how to get Evangelism into their Churches. They want to get their congregants sharing the Gospel with those around them. Please pray that Pastors see the need for this to happen, so the world will know what Jesus did.

I went to the Home Depot to get some keys made. The Lord's Holy Spirit led me to share the Gospel with Abhor as he was making my keys. I knew it had to be a short version of the Gospel, but I knew I had to share it. After sharing the short version of the Gospel, Abhor said, "I knew there was a reason I had to come to work today." He now knows he is getting into heaven by the Grace of Jesus.

I went to the Glory Days restaurant around 10 pm. I had a tough day, and I was hungry and tired. I sat at the bar, as there was no wait to give your order. I started talking with Jessie and his friend Janet. We talked about food, then golf, dancing, and eventually, I could not help it. I had to share the Gospel. Janet said, "I love your questions. They make me think" when I asked her about the fullness of her life. We talked for about thirty minutes, and in the end, Janet asks Jesus to forgive all her sins. Thank You, Jesus.

I went to the Chinese Christian Church of Baltimore to begin setting up the pre-presentation to the youth group. There were thirty young people there. By God's grace, they will see the need to reach the harvest of our Lord. We then plan to set the date to give the Evangelism Workshop, followed by youth Evangelism training.

I was blessed to assist in giving the Evangelism Workshop in Spanish this month at MBC. Then four trainees continued with the three-day Spanish Evangelism training. We went out to train the trainees, and during these times of outreach, eight people heard the Gospel, and six asked Jesus to come into their lives and to give them eternal life. Praise the Lord!

I got together with Pastor Terry at his Church, and we worked on the Evangelism presentation that we planned to give at the Church of Pentecost. We shared a two-and-a-half-hour presentation. Pastor Terry has been giving Evangelism training for a long time, and he is a true blessing. Pastor Paul wants to take the next step of training, and he will be talking to three other Churches.

I assisted in giving a three-day youth Evangelism training in downtown Washington, DC. I went out with Stephany and Daniel. Stephany was having a hard time believing that person to person Evangelism really works. She thought that people would not listen to the Gospel and respond. Our Lord's Holy Spirit led us to Roberto, a man from the Philippines. He and his family were touring the Capitol grounds. While sharing with Roberto, his family wanted to leave, so Roberto asked them to go and that he would catch up with them, as he wanted to continue talking with us. My trainees Stephany and Daniel gave the full Gospel presentation, and at the end of the presentation, he did not want to pray. We asked if we could pray for him, and he said we could. I was asked to lead the prayer. I prayed just going over the Gospel. God, You loved us so much that You placed Yourself in the womb of a virgin, and she named her Son Jesus. You lived a perfect life, then died offering to take our sins on Yourself. I thank You, Jesus, for dying for our sins so we could enter Your Kingdom on earth and for eternity. Before leaving, Roberto told us he prayed the prayer with us in his heart, and he believed what Jesus did for him. While walking back to Stephany and Daniel, both said they could see how Evangelism can and does work today in our generation.

I was asked to help run the Evangelism display table at the three-day Values Voter Summit that was a Family Research Council event. When I was free, I attended some of the incredible speeches. People like Kirk Cameron, James Dopson, and many Governors, Congressmen, Senators, Generals, even Donald Trump, and Mike Pence spoke. In addition, the Lord led me to some of His wandering sheep. Caroline was working on a table with her father. After sharing the Gospel, she asked Jesus to come into her life forever. I also met Stephany, who was working on a food stand. She also asked Jesus to guide her life forever. Such a great day. I also shared the Gospel with Katy and Sandy, who were Christian lawyers. They were very responsive, and I know there were seeds of faith sown in their lives, but they would not pray with me.

I met nurse Jacin in the Veterans Hospital emergency room with my father. It was a hard week for him. He has COPD, and he was not doing well. While I was at the Hospital, I also met nurse Sally; both nurses love Jesus very much and love what we are doing. Both want to see if they can take our training, and Sally said she wanted to be a prayer partner.

I have been to the University of Maryland six times this month. I am so inspired by these wonderful young Christians. They understand the importance of becoming bold witnesses for Jesus. I know what it took me to come to the complete understanding of the incredible importance of God's harvest. I want to see them grow in their understanding of the need to reach the students around them with the Gospel of Jesus. Reaching the lost is a Commandment. Our Lord Jesus gave us this Commandment just before leaving this earth. We, the Church, need to come to the realization of how this is the reason we are still in this world. The mission of all of God's children is to seek and share the Good News with their lost brothers, sisters, friends, and everyone the Holy Spirit leads them to. Luke 15:3-7 says; So He (Jesus) told them this parable, saying, "What man among you, having a hundred sheep and losing one of them does not leave the ninety-nine in the wilderness and go after the one which is lost until he finds it? And when he has found it, he places it on his shoulders, rejoicing. Then when he comes home, he calls together his friends and neighbors, saying to them, 'Rejoice with me, for I have found my sheep which was lost.' Likewise, I tell you, there will be more joy in heaven over one sinner who repents than over ninety-nine righteous men who need no repentance. Let's go find them.

I went to witness at the University of Maryland (UMD) I witnessed to Jalon, a 1st-year economy student. He is a Muslim. He listened to the Gospel and responded with openness. I met Andrew He's Jewish and in his 3rd year of computer science. He heard the full Gospel and told me he had never heard it completely before and that it was clear to him now. I gave him my card and got his contact info.

After the 11 am Church service, the Holy Spirit led me to stand by the bookstore. I try to obey when I get these leadings of the Holy Spirit. About 15 minutes before the service, I met Mary. Her hairdresser invited her to Church, and she was waiting for her. We talked for a while, and then I asked her if she knew for sure she was going to Heaven. She said she thought she would. Then asking, what she would say if God would ask her why He should allow her into Heaven. I found out that she has a love for the Lord, but she had never asked Him to forgive all her sins. Therefore, she was not trusting in Jesus alone for her entrance into Heaven yet. We prayed, and she received total forgiveness. She said she would read the Bible, and when she fails to do the right things, she will get up and ask for forgiveness to both the Lord and the person she sinned against, then keep on walking with Jesus. She realized she needs Jesus because she will never be perfect. Without Jesus, nobody will enter into Heaven. After the service, Mary told me she was going to leave before meeting me, but she was so happy she did not, as the sermon touched her heart, and she repented of her sin of bitterness. She wants to be baptized. **Praise the Lord**

I am taking it slow with Tony at Pizzeria. I stop there for lunch after Church sometimes. So far, I have shared about Jesus wanting a relationship with us, and today I gave him a Gospel of John. He told me that he has read it before, but that he would reread it. I told him I read it at least twice a year, as it keeps me in God's heavenly vision, and I think it will do the same for you.

I went to Night of Hope at my Church. During the service, someone asked me to talk to Vic. He is from Lima, Peru, and I told him I lived there for eleven months. When I asked him if he was sure he was going to heaven, he said to me that he was not. After sharing the Gospel with him, I came to find out that he believes Jesus is the Son of God but had not come to the true understanding of what Jesus had done for him. I prayed with him that he would have the assurance of eternal life. I gave him my business card, and he said he would be in contact.

I met Algal at Church. She was crying as she came down for prayer at the altar call, so I asked if she would like to talk. We went to the prayer room and talked for about a half-hour. She is 18 and is gay. She told me that she was living in a very dark place and that she had tried to take her own life several times. She had asked Jesus to come into her life four years before starting her gay lifestyle and has not felt His presence in her life since. I shared the Gospel with her and shared that there are times in everyone's lives when we are not living right in God's eyes. When this happens, we lose our connection with the Lord. I asked her to honestly seek what God's Word says about her lifestyle, that God really loves her and wants to be a part of her life. A few minutes later, I met her father. We prayed that Jesus would lead her by His Holy Spirit.

During a time with family over Thanksgiving, I shared the Gospel with my nephew Phillip. He did not realize that Jesus died for all our sins. I took the time to share the scriptures where Jesus said He took away the sins of the world. He told me, "now I understand that I'm getting into Heaven because Jesus did on the cross" He paid the price of the world's sins. He prayed for the gift of God through Jesus. Glory to God.

At my church, we had a Christmas Program. I met Emmeline (19), Lia (19), Ashly (6), Rose (8), and James (11) at the Christmas show. They told me they were visiting from another Church and then asked me to pray for unity in their family. I asked them if I could ask them a question first. They permitted me, so I asked if they knew for sure if they were going to heaven. The youngest ones said they were going to heaven, but when I asked the second question, why they should get into heaven, none gave the correct answer (because Jesus paid the price for us). I asked them to come with me to the prayer room that I had a gift for them. In the room, I was able to share the Gospel with them, and all five prayed to receive the Gift of heaven and eternal life through Jesus. I asked them again if they were going to heaven, and they all said yes, because of Jesus. We prayed that the Holy Spirit would give them the unity they desired.

At the Christmas show, the Lord's Holy Spirit led me to Julie and Police Sargent B. After taking the time to get to know one another, I asked if I could ask them a rather personal question. They said that it would be fine to go ahead and ask. After discovering that they were not sure, they had eternal life. I shared the Gospel with them. Both received the best gift for Christmas (More Christ in Spanish is Mas Christ or Christ-mas), eternal life. Praise the Lord.

I was blessed to go to the Church of Philippi and their Kids Evangelism graduation. Jesus used them, as seventy-five people prayed, asking Jesus into their lives during their thirteen-week training. In addition, I was asked to share the Gospel with Geno. His wife is a believer, and she was genuinely concern for him, as he has not given his life to the Lord. The Holy Spirit led the conversation, and when I asked if I could pray for him, he gladly received the prayer for his life. I am praying that he surrenders to the Holy Spirit.

What an exciting month. We met with Pastor Eric, the pastor of a new Church. He has been giving Evangelism training for a few months to four of his members. Pastor Eric requested that we come and share with his Church. We shared the vision of how we can unite so we can train more witnesses who will then turn around and train others. He wanted us to give an Evangelism Workshop at his Church. We shared that we would like to give it to other Churches at the same time, so he got two other Churches to join us in the training. We gave it in two parts to make it easier for the two Churches to organize. Praise the Lord.

I went out to share the Gospel with Pastor Eric and two other trainees. The Holy Spirit led us to share with Joe and then to a young man from Vietnam named Vic. When we were finished, the trainees were excited and wanted to go out again soon—praying that the Holy Spirit will inspire them to continue training and raising up harvesters for the Kingdom of God.

At the reception for Senator James Lankford, I was able to share the Gospel in Spanish with Hugo. His friend told me that he was not a believer. He asked me to share the Gospel with him. After taking twenty minutes talking and sharing the good news with Hugo, he received Jesus as his Lord. We exchanged contact information. I am praying that he will continue to grow in the Lord and will be used to reach out to his country of Chile.

My Home oil distributor called to set the price of heating oil for winter. After talking about the oil, etc., Shari said, "Lord Help me." In *response,* I asked if she is a Christian? She said she was, so I asked if it would be okay to ask her a couple of questions. She said I could. I asked, "Have you come to the place in your spiritual life where you know for sure you're going to heaven." I was pleased to hear she knows she is going to heaven. When I asked what she would say to God if He asked why He should let you into His heaven, she said she does her best to be good. I realized that she was basing her entrance into heaven on her being good enough. I shared with her that it is right that she is doing all she can to be a good daughter of God, but that none of us will get into heaven by our good works. I shared the Gospel with her, and she understood that Jesus is the reason we are getting into Heaven. Sometimes we need to help people find the assurance of their eternal life.

Risa, a Verizon customer rep, called me after I had canceled their service. She was so nice helping me after three others had not been nice about me canceling the service, and sad to say I was getting upset, and my voice showed it with the other reps. After dealing with the cancelation, I asked if I could ask her a question. She said I could, so I asked her if she was going to heaven. She answered the second question with an "I'm working my way to heaven. She, too, like many others, said she does her best to do good things. After sharing the Gospel with her, she said it makes sense that heaven is a gift not received by works. She, too, found assurance of eternal life. I found out that her husband Hershey was going into open-heart surgery the next day, so we prayed for him. She called the following day to tell me that the surgery went very well and that her Jewish husband wanted to thank me for my prayers. Praise the Lord.

I went to the Washington Prayer Gathering at the Lincoln Memorial.  There were Churches from all over Maryland, DC, and Virginia. We prayed for many issues that our nation is facing today, for repentance, a renewed vision, and love of the Lord. We need to reach our country and the world with the saving message of our Lord Jesus and pray for a revival. I was able to share with and give my Evangelism business card to thirty or so people, letting them know about our training programs.

Please take note. I am not some great Evangelist, speaking to thousands at one time. I just took the challenge to reach the people around me with the wonderful news that Jesus loves them. This is something anyone can do, yes, even you with a hand full of verses from God's Word, the Bible, and the conviction of the Holy Spirit. There are many more people that I would like to share about, but all this to say, God's harvest of souls is always waiting to hear about how much He loves them. We just have to be willing to do our part, opening our mouths to share with them.

The verses I used for years while in South America were John 3:1-8 There was a man of the Pharisees, named Nicodemus, a ruler of the Jews. The same came to Jesus by night and said unto him,

Rabbi, we know that thou art a teacher come from God: for no man can do these miracles that you do, except God be with him. Jesus answered and said unto him, verily, verily, I say unto thee, Except a man be born again, he cannot see the kingdom of God. Nicodemus saith unto him, how can a man be born when he is old? Can he enter the second time into his mother's womb, and be born? Jesus answered, verily, verily, I say unto thee, Except a man be born of water and of the Spirit, he cannot enter into the kingdom of God. That which is born of the flesh is flesh, and that which is born of the Spirit is spirit. Marvel not that I say unto thee, you must be born again. The wind blows where it listeth, and you hear the sound thereof, but cannot tell whence it comes, and whither it goes, so is every one that is born of the Spirit.

Revelations 3:20 Behold, I stand at the door and knock: if any man hears my voice and opens the door, I will come into him and will sup with him, and he with me.

Many other verses will show others what Jesus did for us, but these break it down to the simple truth. There are two births for everyone. One of our physical birth and one of our spirit. Some other verses are John 1:12, John 3:16, John 3:36-37, John 10:28, John 14:6, Acts 16:31, Romans 3:23, Romans 6:23, Romans 10:9-10, 2 Corinthians 5:17, Ephesians 2:8-9, Titus 3:5, 1 John 5:12-13 and many more.

Contents

Chapter 8

Some Bible studies of my favorite chapters

The Word Became Flesh

Note: Verse 14 tells us; that the Word of God became a man. Verse 1 says; the Word was with God in the beginning. Verse 2 tells us; all things were created through the Word. Jesus is the Word and was with God before He came to earth.

Verse 4 tells us; we get life and light from Jesus, so we can understand.

Verse 5 Tells us, Jesus shines in the darkness. If we trust in Jesus, He will lead us into His light and love.

Verse 8 tells us; John the Baptist was not the light.

Verse 9 tells us; Jesus is the true light that gives light to all that seek it.

Verse 10-11 tells us; Jesus was in the world and He made the world, but the world rejected Him.

Verse 12 tells us; Everyone who trust in Jesus may become the Children of God

Verse 13 tells us; When we trust in Jesus, we are born of the Spirit

Verse 14 tells us; Jesus the Word became a man

Verse 17 tells us; Jesus gives us the grace of the Father Jesus came to give us eternal life as a gift

Jesus came from heaven where He live with God

John 1:1 In the beginning was the Word, and the Word was with God, and the Word was God.

John 1:2 He was in the beginning with God.

John 1:3 All things were made through Him, and without Him nothing was made that was made.

John 1:4 In Him was life, and the life was the light of men.

John 1:5 And the light shines in the darkness, and the darkness did not comprehend it.

John 1:6 There was a man sent from God, whose name *was* John.

John 1:7 This man came for a witness, to bear witness of the Light, that all through him might believe.

John 1:8 He was not that Light, but *was sent* to bear witness of that Light.

John 1:9 That was the true Light which gives light to every man coming into the world.

John 1:10 He was in the world, and the world was made through Him, and the world did not know Him.

John 1:11 He came to His own, and His own did not receive Him.

John 1:12 But as many as received Him, to them He gave the right to become children of God, to those who believe in His name:

John 1:13 who were born, not of blood, nor of the will of the flesh, nor of the will of man, but of God.

John 1:14 And the Word became flesh and dwelt among us, and we beheld His glory, the glory as of the only begotten of the Father, full of grace and truth.

John 1:15 John bore witness of Him and cried out, saying, "This was He of whom I said, 'He who comes after me is preferred before me, for He was before me.' "

John 1:16 And of His fullness we have all received, and grace for grace.

John 1:17 For the law was given through Moses, *but* grace and truth came through Jesus Christ.

John 1:18 No one has seen God at any time. The only begotten Son, who is in the bosom of the Father, He has declared *Him*.

The Testimony of John the Baptist

John 1:19 Now this is the testimony of John, when the Jews sent priests and Levites from Jerusalem to ask him, "Who are you?"

John 1:39 He said to them, "Come and see." They came and saw where He was staying, and remained with Him that day (now it was about the tenth hour).

John 1:40 One of the two who heard John *speak,* and followed Him, was Andrew, Simon Peter's brother.

John 1:41 He first found his own brother Simon, and said to him, "We have found the Messiah" (which is translated, the Christ).

John 1:42 And he brought him to Jesus. Now when Jesus looked at him, He said, "You are Simon the son of Jonah. You shall be called Cephas" (which is translated, A Stone).

Jesus Calls Philip and Nathanael

John 1:43 The following day Jesus wanted to go to Galilee, and He found Philip and said to him, "Follow Me."

John 1:44 Now Philip was from Bethsaida, the city of Andrew and Peter.

John 1:45 Philip found Nathanael and said to him, "We have found Him of whom Moses in the law, and also the prophets, wrote—Jesus of Nazareth, the son of Joseph."

John 1:46 And Nathanael said to him, "Can anything good come out of Nazareth?" Philip said to him, "Come and see."

John 1:47 Jesus saw Nathanael coming toward Him, and said of him, "Behold, an Israelite indeed, in whom is no deceit!"

John 1:48 Nathanael said to Him, "How do You know me?" Jesus answered and said to him, "Before Philip called you, when you were under the fig tree, I saw you."

John 1:49 Nathanael answered and said to Him, "Rabbi, You are the Son of God! You are the King of Israel!"

John 1:50 Jesus answered and said to him, "Because I said to you, 'I saw you under the fig tree,' do you believe? You will see greater things than these."

John 1:51 And He said to him, "Most assuredly, I say to you, hereafter you shall see heaven open, and the angels of God ascending and descending upon the Son of Man."

Verse 20 tells us; That John was not the Christ.

Verse 23 tells us; John the Baptist tells the Jewish leaders that he is voice telling everyone to prepare for the Lord's coming.

Verse 26 tells us; John the Baptist said he gave the baptism of water of repentance. We see later that Jesus would baptize us with the Holy Spirit.

Verse 29 tells us; John the Baptist prophesies that Jesus takes away the sins of the world.

(As Adam brought all sin into the world. Jesus takes all sin out of the world. We just must ask Him to take them and He does. Repent and be cleansed of you sins.)

Verse 32 tells us; John saw the Holy Spirit of God come on Jesus. God did this for our belief.

Verse 34 tells us; John tells us that Jesus is the Son of God.

Verse 35-37 tells us; John allows his disciples to follow Jesus.

Verse 38 tells us; The disciples of John ask to go with Jesus.

John 1:20 He confessed, and did not deny, but confessed, "I am not the Christ."

John 1:21 And they asked him, "What then? Are you Elijah?" He said, "I am not." "Are you the Prophet?" And he answered, "No."

John 1:22 Then they said to him, "Who are you, that we may give an answer to those who sent us? What do you say about yourself?"

John 1:23 He said: "I *am* 'THE VOICE OF ONE CRYING IN THE WILDERNESS: "MAKE STRAIGHT THE WAY OF THE LORD," ' as the prophet Isaiah said."

John 1:24 Now those who were sent were from the Pharisees.

John 1:25 And they asked him, saying, "Why then do you baptize if you are not the Christ, nor Elijah, nor the Prophet?"

John 1:26 John answered them, saying, "I baptize with water, but there stands One among you whom you do not know.

John 1:27 It is He who, coming after me, is preferred before me, whose sandal strap I am not worthy to loose."

John 1:28 These things were done in Bethabara beyond the Jordan, where John was baptizing.

Behold, the Lamb of God

John 1:29 The next day John saw Jesus coming toward him, and said, "Behold! The Lamb of God who takes away the sin of the world!

John 1:30 This is He of whom I said, 'After me comes a Man who is preferred before me, for He was before me.'

John 1:31 I did not know Him; but that He should be revealed to Israel, therefore I came baptizing with water."

John 1:32 And John bore witness, saying, "I saw the Spirit descending from heaven like a dove, and He remained upon Him.

John 1:33 I did not know Him, but He who sent me to baptize with water said to me, 'Upon whom you see the Spirit descending, and remaining on Him, this is He who baptizes with the Holy Spirit.'

John 1:34 And I have seen and testified that this is the Son of God."

Jesus Calls the First Disciples

John 1:35 Again, the next day, John stood with two of his disciples.

John 1:36 And looking at Jesus as He walked, he said, "Behold the Lamb of God!"

John 1:37 The two disciples heard him speak, and they followed Jesus.

John 1:38 Then Jesus turned, and seeing them following, said to them, "What do you seek?" They said to Him, "Rabbi" (which is to say, when translated, Teacher), "where are You staying?"

This was the first miracle of Jesus. It is interesting to note that Jesus and His disciples were so well-liked that they were invited to the wedding.

There was wine at the wedding and they ran out, so Mary, Jesus' mother, tells Jesus about this, expecting Him to help. This seems to show that He must have been performing miracles at home. Jesus tells His mother that it is not time to show the world who He is, but Mary instructs the servants to do what Jesus tells them to do. Mary know Jesus can create wine.

Jesus must have communicated with His Father, God, at this time because He asks the servants to fill the water jugs.

After He changes the water into wine, the servants must have been able to detect a change in the wine because they take it to the master of the feast. When he tastes it, he says, why did you hold back serving the best wine until now?

It was wine created by God Himself, so it must have been heavenly. ☺

It is thought that it took Jesus and His disciples four days to walk from Capernaum to Jerusalem.

Jesus was furious when He found people selling merchandise in the temple. I believe Jesus was angry because the priests were exploiting the needs of God's seekers to make a profit. I think, to compare this to our generation, there are preachers who are not explaining the Bible to their followers but are selling their thoughts to become rich.

The Wedding at Cana

Joh 2:1 On the third day there was a wedding in Cana of Galilee, and the mother of Jesus was there.

Joh 2:2 Now both Jesus and His disciples were invited to the wedding.

Joh 2:3 And when they ran out of wine, the mother of Jesus said to Him, "They have no wine."

Joh 2:4 Jesus said to her, "Woman, what does your concern have to do with Me? My hour has not yet come."

Joh 2:5 His mother said to the servants, "Whatever He says to you, do *it*."

Joh 2:6 Now there were set there six water pots of stone, according to the manner of purification of the Jews, containing twenty or thirty gallons apiece.

Joh 2:7 Jesus said to them, "Fill the water pots with water." And they filled them up to the brim.

Joh 2:8 And He said to them, "Draw *some* out now, and take *it* to the master of the feast." And they took *it*.

Joh 2:9 When the master of the feast had tasted the water that was made wine, and did not know where it came from (but the servants who had drawn the water knew), the master of the feast called the bridegroom.

Joh 2:10 And he said to him, "Every man at the beginning sets out the good wine, and when the *guests* have well drunk, then the inferior. You have kept the good wine until now!"

Joh 2:11 This beginning of signs Jesus did in Cana of Galilee, and manifested His glory; and His disciples believed in Him.

Joh 2:12 After this He went down to Capernaum, He, His mother, His brothers, and His disciples; and they did not stay there many days.

Jesus Cleanses the Temple

Joh 2:13 Now the Passover of the Jews was at hand, and Jesus went up to Jerusalem.

Joh 2:14 And He found in the temple those who sold oxen and sheep and doves, and the money changers doing business.

Joh 2:15 When He had made a whip of cords, He drove them all out of the temple, with the sheep and the oxen, and poured out the changers' money and overturned the tables.

Joh 2:16 And He said to those who sold doves, "Take these things away! Do not make My Father's house a house of merchandise!"

Jesus wants the Church to be a house of prayer and worship. When His people make it anything else the leaders are going astray.

Jesus was talking about His physical body. He knew He was going to die on the cross and that He would rise from the grave. Jesus was both fully man and fully God. Though His physical body suffered horribly, He endured it knowing that He would remove the sins of all who would allow Him to.

Jesus could read their thoughts. He knew at a glance without investigation Joh 6:64; Joh 13:1; Luk_6:8; Act_1:24; Heb_4:13).

He who would have Christ trust Himself to him must first trust himself to Christ. (*T. Whitelaw, D. D.*)

Although Christ knew all the evil that was in man by sin, He did not disdain to undertake the rescue. By assuming the nature of the fallen, and meeting the law in their stead, He received the curse into Himself and exhausted it.

Biblical Illustrator.

Joh 2:17 Then His disciples remembered that it was written, "ZEAL FOR YOUR HOUSE HAS EATEN ME UP."

Joh 2:18 So the Jews answered and said to Him, "What sign do You show to us, since You do these things?"

Joh 2:19 Jesus answered and said to them, "Destroy this temple, and in three days I will raise it up."

Joh 2:20 Then the Jews said, "It has taken forty-six years to build this temple, and will You raise it up in three days?"

Joh 2:21 But He was speaking of the temple of His body.

Joh 2:22 Therefore, when He had risen from the dead, His disciples remembered that He had said this to them; and they believed the Scripture and the word which Jesus had said.

Jesus Knows What Is in Man

Joh 2:23 Now when He was in Jerusalem at the Passover, during the feast, many believed in His name when they saw the signs which He did.

Joh 2:24 But Jesus did not commit Himself to them, because He knew all *men,*

Joh 2:25 and had no need that anyone should testify of man, for He knew what was in man.

John Chapter 3 with thoughts from Vince Varriale

Verse 1-3 Nicodemus came to Jesus by night. It is evident he did not want anybody else to know he was meeting with Jesus, but he knew that God was with Jesus because of the miracles He was performing. Nicodemus continues as a believer. In John chapter 19 verse 39, we see that he is with Jesus even to death.

Verse 3-11 When we understand that there are two births in this life, one of our physical body and one of our spiritual being, it changes our understanding of why we are on earth. The physical birth is temporal; we are here for a short time. The spiritual realm is eternal. We will be alive in God's kingdom forever. Jesus came to awaken our spiritual lives. He came to remove sins from all who allow Him. He asks us to believe, which means to trust that He can remove and has removed all our sins and made away for us to be with Him for eternity. Will you do it now? Say "Jesus, please take all my sins. Please become the master of my life. Help me to see the things as You do so I can change and be the person You want me to become. "In Jesus' name. Amen.

Verse 12 Our minds have a difficult time with heavenly realities.

Verse 13 Jesus was in Heaven and He was place in the womb of a virgin.

Verse 14-15 See Numbers 21. Because of sin, God sent venomous snakes, then healed those who believed.

You Must Be Born Again

Joh 3:1 There was a man of the Pharisees named Nicodemus, a ruler of the Jews.

Joh 3:2 This man came to Jesus by night and said to Him, "Rabbi, we know that You are a teacher come from God; for no one can do these signs that You do unless God is with him."

Joh 3:3 Jesus answered and said to him, "Most assuredly, I say to you, unless one is born again, he cannot see the kingdom of God."

Joh 3:4 Nicodemus said to Him, "How can a man be born when he is old? Can he enter a second time into his mother's womb and be born?"

Joh 3:5 Jesus answered, "Most assuredly, I say to you, unless one is born of water and the Spirit, he cannot enter the kingdom of God.

Joh 3:6 That which is born of the flesh is flesh, and that which is born of the Spirit is spirit.

Joh 3:7 Do not marvel that I said to you, 'You must be born again.'

Joh 3:8 The wind blows where it wishes, and you hear the sound of it, but cannot tell where it comes from and where it goes. So is everyone who is born of the Spirit."

Joh 3:9 Nicodemus answered and said to Him, "How can these things be?"

Joh 3:10 Jesus answered and said to him, "Are you the teacher of Israel, and do not know these things?

Joh 3:11 Most assuredly, I say to you, We speak what We know and testify what We have seen, and you do not receive Our witness.

Joh 3:12 If I have told you earthly things and you do not believe, how will you believe if I tell you heavenly things?

Joh 3:13 No one has ascended to heaven but He who came down from heaven, *that is,* the Son of Man who is in heaven.

Joh 3:14 And as Moses lifted up the serpent in the wilderness, even so must the Son of Man be lifted up,

Joh 3:15 that whoever believes in Him should not perish but have eternal life.

God loves You

Verse 16 God loves you so much that He came to earth in the person of Jesus. Jesus is the Christ, meaning the Messiah or Anointed One.

Verse 17 Jesus came to save anyone from their corrupt lifestyle and give them a full and joyful life both here and for eternity.

Verse 18 The choice is up to you. Believe and He will remove your debt of sin. If not, remember that not one sin will be allowed in heaven.

Verse 19-20 Do you like the worldly life so much that you will not submit to Jesus. All authority in heaven and on earth has been given to Him. Matt 28

Verse 21 When you come to Jesus and read His Words, you will be exposed to the truth; if you yield to His Words and seek to live them, you will go through a change. The world will see it and take note that you love Jesus.

Verse 22-27 John tells us all that a person cannot receive anything unless it has been given to them from God. John was talking about Jesus. This applies to all mankind.

Verse 28 John declares the he is not the Christ.

For God So Loved the World

Joh 3:16 For God so loved the world that He gave His only begotten Son, that whoever believes in Him should not perish but have everlasting life.

Joh 3:17 For God did not send His Son into the world to condemn the world, but that the world through Him might be saved.

Joh 3:18 "He who believes in Him is not condemned; but he who does not believe is condemned already, because he has not believed in the name of the only begotten Son of God.

Joh 3:19 And this is the condemnation, that the light has come into the world, and men loved darkness rather than light, because their deeds were evil.

Joh 3:20 For everyone practicing evil hates the light and does not come to the light, lest his deeds should be exposed.

Joh 3:21 But he who does the truth comes to the light, that his deeds may be clearly seen, that they have been done in God."

John the Baptist Exalts Christ

Joh 3:22 After these things Jesus and His disciples came into the land of Judea, and there He remained with them and baptized.

Joh 3:23 Now John also was baptizing in Aenon near Salim, because there was much water there. And they came and were baptized.

Joh 3:24 For John had not yet been thrown into prison.

Joh 3:25 Then there arose a dispute between some of John's disciples and the Jews about purification.

Joh 3:26 And they came to John and said to him, "Rabbi, He who was with you beyond the Jordan, to whom you have testified—behold, He is baptizing, and all are coming to Him!"

Joh 3:27 John answered and said, "A man can receive nothing unless it has been given to him from heaven.

Joh 3:28 You yourselves bear me witness, that I said, 'I am not the Christ,' but, 'I have been sent before Him.'

Verse 29 God showed John things to come, as Jesus had not yet shared with us this parable of the bride yet.

Verse 30 This applies to our lives too. We need to lift up Jesus more than ourselves.

Verse 31 John knew that Jesus came from heaven and became a man.

Verse 32-33 Jesus came to earth so that He could reveal the way things are in heaven.

Verse 34 The Words Jesus spoke came directly from God.

Verse 35 Jesus is in control of all things in heaven and on earth.

Verse 36 If anyone does not accept the authority of Jesus and submit to Him as their Lord and Savior then they will not be allowed into the Kingdom of God, Heaven. Jesus was willing to leave an incredible place, a place full of joy, peace and love, and come to this fallen world to show us how to strive to live ; He then fulfilled the prophecies of the Messiah's or Savior's dying on the cross (a form of killing that did not even exist in the age when Isaiah prophesied) for the sins of us all. After Jesus rose from the dead, He walked with His disciples for 40 days. He cooked for them. He walked through walls to visit them. He even appeared to them out of the thin air. Then Jesus rose to heaven right in front of them. He has been working through His followers ever since. Now it is your turn to choose. Call to Jesus now and ask Him to forgive all your sins, then commit to change your life so you may please Him and love others.

Joh 3:29 He who has the bride is the bridegroom; but the friend of the bridegroom, who stands and hears him, rejoices greatly because of the bridegroom's voice. Therefore this joy of mine is fulfilled.

Joh 3:30 He must increase, but I *must* decrease.

Joh 3:31 He who comes from above is above all; he who is of the earth is earthly and speaks of the earth. He who comes from heaven is above all.

Joh 3:32 And what He has seen and heard, that He testifies; and no one receives His testimony.

Joh 3:33 He who has received His testimony has certified that God is true.

Joh 3:34 For He whom God has sent speaks the words of God, for God does not give the Spirit by measure.

Joh 3:35 The Father loves the Son, and has given all things into His hand.

Joh 3:36 He who believes in the Son has everlasting life; and he who does not believe the Son shall not see life, but the wrath of God abides on him."

PAGE 1

Verse 1. Jesus is the vine and God is the vinedresser.

Verse 2. Vines and branches are not weeds. They need to bear fruit, and if they do not, they are good for nothing. If we are bringing people to Jesus, He works in our lives so He can use us even more. We are the branches of Jesus. The branches (believers) grow out of the vine (Jesus) and fruit (other people) grows off the branches (us) and become believers.

Verse 3. We are saved because we believe the Words of Jesus.

Verse 4-5 Jesus is the Word as John said in his 1st chapter. If we share Him (His Words, Verses from the Bible) with others we will bear fruit. Just saying our own words will not bear fruit, we MUST share the Words of Jesus to bear fruit.

Verse 5-6. We must abide in the Word, read it and memorize it so we can use it. Without the Word in us we can do nothing. If we do not continue to read the Word , we will wither away from the Lord when things get tough.

Verse 7. If we abide in Jesus and keep His Words with us daily, the things we ask for will be according to His plan and we will receive them.

Verse 8. We must be winning others to Jesus if we want to glorify God and be Jesus' disciples.

Verse 9. God loves Jesus and Jesus loves us. We are to abide in His love, meaning continue in His love.

Verse 10. Jesus commanded us to love one another and to tell the world about Him. If you are not doing this you are not abiding in Him or God.

Verse 11. When we share the Words of Jesus with others His joy flows through us. Our joy will be full. If we do not share Jesus' Words with others His joy will not be with us.

Verse 12. When we love Jesus it is impossible to not share what He has done for us. To love Jesus and tell others about Him is to love others as He loved us.

Verse 13. Telling others about Jesus is laying down our lives. We are not talking about our lives, we are talking about Jesus' life. This is the greater love.

John 15:1 "I am the true vine, and My Father is the vinedresser.

John 15:2 Every branch in Me that does not bear fruit He takes away; and every *branch* that bears fruit He prunes, that it may bear more fruit.

John 15:3 You are already clean because of the word which I have spoken to you.

John 15:4 Abide in Me, and I in you. As the branch cannot bear fruit of itself, unless it abides in the vine, neither can you, unless you abide in Me.

John 15:5 "I am the vine, you *are* the branches. He who abides in Me, and I in him, bears much fruit; for without Me you can do nothing.

John 15:6 If anyone does not abide in Me, he is cast out as a branch and is withered; and they gather them and throw *them* into the fire, and they are burned.

John 15:7 If you abide in Me, and My words abide in you, you will ask what you desire, and it shall be done for you.

John 15:8 By this My Father is glorified, that you bear much fruit; so you will be My disciples.

John 15:9 "As the Father loved Me, I also have loved you; abide in My love.

John 15:10 If you keep My commandments, you will abide in My love, just as I have kept My Father's commandments and abide in His love.

John 15:11 "These things I have spoken to you, that My joy may remain in you, and *that* your joy may be full.

John 15:12 This is My commandment, that you love one another as I have loved you.

John 15:13 Greater love has no one than this, than to lay down one's life for his friends.

WHEN SOMEONE TRULY KNOW JESUS, THEY BECOME A
BRANCH OF THE VINE.
PAGE 2

Verse 15. A friend understands you. For us to be Jesus' friend we need to understand the harvest of God as Jesus did. All who join Jesus in bearing fruit for Gods' Kingdom are friends of Jesus. To accomplish this we need to pray all the time, read the Bible daily, find a Bible teaching Church, Fellowship with others who are Christians and seek for lost souls. Allowing the Holy Spirit to lead you to them. Be ready to share with others about what Jesus did for you and letting them know what He can do for them. Memorize the Word of God so you can share His Word with them. Verses like Ephesians 2:8 & 9, we can't save ourselves and, Romans 3:23 we all made mistakes, and 1 John 4:8 God is love, and John 3:36 So they do not receive the wrath of God. John 3:16 God loves them so much He came to earth and died for them, and Rev. 3:20 Jesus is standing at the door of the life, they need to ask Jesus to come into their life.

Verse 16. He choose you to continue His work of telling the world of His sacrifice for them. If we do He will lead us and provide for us.

Verse 17. Jesus' command is to love one another. The greatest way to show your love is to make sure they do not go to hell.

Verse 18-21. Jesus promised that some people in the world would hate us when we talk to them about Jesus. This is because they are of the world and we are not, Jesus told us we would be persecuted if we talk about Him, because they do not know Jesus and they do not know God.

Verse 22-23. When we tell people about Jesus and they reject us and His Words. When they come in God's presence, they will have no forgivness for their sins.

Verse 26. The Holy Spirit will speak through you if you just start talking about Jesus. Jesus told us many times in the Bible that He forgives sins. He commanded us to tell everyone in the world that He will forgive their sins. Are you doing that? If not start today.

John 15:14 You are My friends if you do whatever I command you.

John 15:15 No longer do I call you servants, for a servant does not know what his master is doing; but I have called you friends, for all things that I heard from My Father I have made known to you.

John 15:16 You did not choose Me, but I chose you and appointed you that you should go and bear fruit, and *that* your fruit should remain, that whatever you ask the Father in My name He may give you.

John 15:17 These things I command you, that you love one another.

John 15:18 "If the world hates you, you know that it hated Me before *it hated* you.

John 15:19 If you were of the world, the world would love its own. Yet because you are not of the world, but I chose you out of the world, therefore the world hates you.

John 15:20 Remember the word that I said to you, 'A servant is not greater than his master.' If they persecuted Me, they will also persecute you. If they kept My word, they will keep yours also.

John 15:21 But all these things they will do to you for My name's sake, because they do not know Him who sent Me.

John 15:22 If I had not come and spoken to them, they would have no sin, but now they have no excuse for their sin.

John 15:23 He who hates Me hates My Father also.

John 15:24 If I had not done among them the works which no one else did, they would have no sin; but now they have seen and also hated both Me and My Father.

John 15:25 But *this happened* that the word might be fulfilled which is written in their law, 'THEY HATED ME WITHOUT A CAUSE.'

John 15:26 "But when the Helper comes, whom I shall send to you from the Father, the Spirit of truth who proceeds from the Father, He will testify of Me.

John 15:27 And you also will bear witness, because you have been with Me from the beginning.

Psalms 110

John Wesley

with notes from Vince Varriale

Verse 1. The Lord - God the father. Said - Decreed it from eternity, and in due time published this decree, and actually executed it, which He did when He raised up Christ from the dead and brought Him into His heavenly mansion. Unto His Son the Messiah, whom David designedly calls his (David's)Lord, to admonish the whole church, that although He was his (David's) son (in the lineage of David) according to his human nature, yet He (Jesus) had an higher nature, and was also his (David's) Lord, as being God blessed forever, and consequently Lord of all things. The Hebrew word Adon is one of God's titles, signifying His power and authority over all things, and therefore is most fitly given to the Messiah, to whom God hath delegated all His power Mat 28:18. Sit - Now take Thy rest and the possession of that sovereign kingdom and glory, which by right belongs to Thee; (Jesus) rules with me (God) with equal power and majesty, as Thou art God; and with an authority and honor far above all creatures, as thou art man (Jesus was both God and man). By My almighty power communicated to thee as God by eternal generation and vouchsafed to Thee as mediator Jesus is our mediator). All ungodly men, sin and death, and the devil. Footstool - Thy slaves and vassals.

Verse 2 The rod - Thy strong or powerful rod, and the rod is put for his scepter, or kingly power: but as the kingdom of Christ is not carnal, but spiritual, so this scepter is nothing else but His Word.

Verse 3 People - Thy subjects, shall offer Thee (Jesus) as their king and Lord, not oxen or sheep, but themselves, their souls and bodies, as living sacrifices, and as freewill - offerings, giving up themselves to the Lord, 2Co 8:5, to live to Him (Jesus), and to die for Him (Jesus). The day - When Thou shalt take into Thy hands the rod of thy strength and set up Thy kingdom in the world (Jesus's return). In the beauties - Adorned with the beautiful and glorious robes of righteousness and true holiness. The dew - That is, Thy (Jesus) offspring (the members of the Christian church) shall be more numerous than the drops of the morning dew.

Verse 4 Sworn - That this priesthood might be made sure and irrevocable.

Verse 5 The Lord - God the Son; the Lord, who is at Thy right - hand. Strike - Shall destroy all those kings who are obstinate enemies to him.

Psa 110:1 **Of David. A psalm.** The LORD says to my lord: "Sit at my right hand until I make your enemies a footstool for your feet."

Psa 110:2 The LORD will extend your mighty scepter from Zion, saying, "Rule in the midst of your enemies!"

Psa 110:3 Your troops will be willing on your day of battle. Arrayed in holy splendor, your young men will come to you like dew from the morning's womb.

Psa 110:4 The LORD has sworn and will not change his mind: "You are a priest forever, in the order of Melchizedek."

Psa 110:5 The Lord is at your right hand; he will crush kings on the day of his wrath.

Verse 6 (Jesus) the Judge - Condemn and punish them. The places - Or, the place of battle. Dead bodies - Of His (Jesus) enemies. Heads - All those princes who oppose Him (Jesus). But this and the like passages are not to be understood grossly, but spiritually, according to the nature of Christ's kingdom.

Verse 7 Drink - He (Jesus) shall have a large portion of afflictions, while He (Jesus) is in the way or course of His life (beatings and crucifixion), before He comes to that honor of sitting at His Father's right - hand. Waters in scripture frequently signify sufferings. To drink of them, signifies to feel or bear them. Therefore – He (Jesus) shall be exalted to great glory and felicity.

Pulpit sermons say, There seem to be no sufficient grounds for rejecting the traditional views of the authorship and the interpretation. The psalm belongs to the same class as Psalm it. It is wholly Messianic. David has had revelations made to him concerning the kingdom, the priesthood, and the ultimate victory of the Messiah over the entire power of evil. In a grand burst of song, rough and rugged, no doubt, but full of energy and genius, he addresses Messiah, and sets forth his praise and glory, the mighty offices which he holds, and the wonderful triumph which awaits him. Metrically, the psalm consists of two stanzas—one of three, and the other of four versos (verses 1-3, 4-7).

C. I Scofield said; The importance of Psalms 110 is attested by the remarkable prominence given to it in the New Testament.

(1) It affirms the deity of Jesus, thus answering those who deny the full divine meaning of his N.T. title of "Lord." Mat_22:41-45; Mar_12:35-37; Luk_20:41-44; Act_2:34; Act_2:35; Heb_1:13; Heb_10:12; Heb_10:13.

(2) This Psalm announces the eternal priesthood of Messiah--one of the most important statements of Scripture (Psa_110:4).

(See Scofield on Gen_14:18; Heb_5:6); Heb_7:1-28; 1Ti_2:5; 1Ti_2:6; Joh_14:6.

(3) Historically, the Psalm begins with the ascension of Christ Psa_110:1,; Joh_20:17; Act_7:56; Rev_3:21.

(4) Prophetically, the Psalm looks on

(a) to the time when Christ will appear as the Rod of Jehovah's strength, the Deliverer out of Zion. Rom_11:25-27 and the conversion of Israel; Psa_110:3; Joe_2:27; Zec_13:9; Deu_30:1-9 (See Scofield on Deu_30:3), and

(b) to the judgment upon the Gentile powers which precedes the setting up of the kingdom (Psa_110:5; Psa_110:6; Joe_3:9-17; Zec_14:1-4; Rev_19:11-21.

See "Armageddon" Rev_16:14 (See Scofield on Rev_19:17). "Israel" Gen_12:2; Gen_12:3. (See Scofield on Rom_11:26). "Kingdom" (See Scofield on Zec_12:8; 1Co_15:24; Psa_2:6; Psa_118:22). See Psalms 118, last in order of the Messianic Psalms.

Psa 110:6 He will judge the nations, heaping up the dead and crushing the rulers of the whole earth.

Psa 110:7 He will drink from a brook along the way, and so he will lift his head high.

TIME OF HOSEA 722 B.C.
COMPARED TO TODAY AND
THE CORONAVIRUS

Verses 2-13 Has Christians and the whole world come to a place were we see Gods' disapproval with the way we are living? Is He stripping the world of the things or gods that have taken the place of Him? Has the peoples of the world put the cares of this world before our Creator?

Have we shamelessly given ourselves to the love of food, clothing, and drinking and other things and events and forgotten God in the meantime?

Through this coronavirus God has block our path to these things and events! Why do you think God has changed our way of life.

Is Gods' desire that we conclude that we should return to Him through Jesus?

After reading Hosea chapter 2 should we come to the realization that God was blessing us with everything we had, but we forgot Him. That we were spending most or even all that He was giving us and not using it for His Kingdom?

Has God stopped our festivals and celebrations world wide?

Please read this side first. Then see the notes.

Hos 2:2 "But now bring charges against Israel—your mother—for she is no longer my wife, and I am no longer her husband. Tell her to remove the prostitute's makeup from her face and the clothing that exposes her breasts.

Hos 2:3 Otherwise, I will strip her as naked as she was on the day she was born. I will leave her to die of thirst, as in a dry and barren wilderness.

Hos 2:4 And I will not love her children, for they were conceived in prostitution.

Hos 2:5 Their mother is a shameless prostitute and became pregnant in a shameful way. She said, 'I'll run after other lovers and sell myself to them for food and water, for clothing of wool and linen, and for olive oil and drinks.'

Hos 2:6 "For this reason I will fence her in with thornbushes. I will block her path with a wall to make her lose her way.

Hos 2:7 When she runs after her lovers, she won't be able to catch them. She will search for them but not find them. Then she will think, 'I might as well return to my husband, for I was better off with him than I am now.'

Hos 2:8 She doesn't realize it was I who gave her everything she has—the grain, the new wine, the olive oil; I even gave her silver and gold. But she gave all my gifts to Baal.

Hos 2:9 "But now I will take back the ripened grain and new wine I generously provided each harvest season. I will take away the wool and linen clothing I gave her to cover her nakedness.

Hos 2:10 I will strip her naked in public, while all her lovers look on. No one will be able to rescue her from my hands.

Hos 2:11 I will put an end to her annual festivals, her new moon celebrations, and her Sabbath days—all her appointed festivals.

Hos 2:12 I will destroy her grapevines and fig trees, things she claims her lovers gave her. I will let them grow into tangled thickets, where only wild animals will

Contents

eat the fruit.

Hos 2:13 I will punish her for all those times when she burned incense to her images of Baal, when she put on her earrings and jewels and went out to look for her lovers but forgot all about me," says the LORD.

The Lord's Mercy on Israel

Hos 2:14 "But then I will win her back once again. I will lead her into the desert and speak tenderly to her there.

Hos 2:15 I will return her vineyards to her and transform the Valley of Trouble into a gateway of hope. She will give herself to me there, as she did long ago when she was young, when I freed her from her captivity in Egypt.

Hos 2:16 When that day comes," says the LORD, "you will call me 'my husband' instead of 'my master.'

Hos 2:17 O Israel, I will wipe the many names of Baal from your lips, and you will never mention them again.

Hos 2:18 On that day I will make a covenant with all the wild animals and the birds of the sky and the animals that scurry along the ground so they will not harm you. I will remove all weapons of war from the land, all swords and bows, so you can live unafraid in peace and safety.

Hos 2:19 I will make you my wife forever, showing you righteousness and justice, unfailing love and compassion.

Hos 2:20 I will be faithful to you and make you mine, and you will finally know me as the LORD.

Hos 2:21 "In that day, I will answer," says the LORD. "I will answer the sky as it pleads for clouds. And the sky will answer the earth with rain.

Hos 2:22 Then the earth will answer the thirsty cries of the grain, the grapevines, and the olive trees. And they in turn will answer, 'Jezreel'—'God plants!'

Hos 2:23 At that time I will plant a crop of Israelites and raise them for myself. I will show love to those I called 'Not loved.' And to those I called 'Not my people,' I will say, 'Now you are my people.' And they will reply, 'You are our God!'"

Chapter 9

Some thoughts and prayers

Reflections of a Missionary

After forty-eight years of walking with God.

Here are four years of thoughts that

I would like to share

Thoughts and prayers from 2015 through 2019.

Date	Time	Note
10/4/2015	13:40	I will grow if I am willing to listen to critical remarks about me genuinely. I believe this is an area most humans are still learning. The question is, are we even trying to listen.
10/5/2015	4:39	Jesus knew His mission, and although His flesh was in anguish, His Spirit kept it in check until He completed the will of His Father in heaven. We, too, have a choice daily.
10/7/2015	12:07	When Jesus, our Lord, said forgive them for, they know not what they do. He showed yet again the depth of love that no mere man could ever live. Jesus forgave them. After

having His hands and feet nailed to the cross. Our amazing Lord forgave them and us.

10/7/2015   12:17   The moment I received the Lord, I still remember that the Holy Spirit showed me the Lord hanging on the cross for me. I knew it was for me and my sins. He is so full of mercy. Even now, I know who I am and how imperfect I am. He continues to be merciful to me. I know the difference between my Lord and myself. His ways are higher than my ways, as the heavens are to the earth. By His Grace, love, and patience, He will continue to use my mouth, eyes, and hands to reach the lost and uplift the brethren.

10/7/2015   12:24   Correction that is Godly given, with meekness and compassion, makes it much easier for me to take. All corrections can and should be applied with prayer. Receiving correction is something that I continue to grow in daily. By the grace of our Heavenly Father and our Lord Jesus, I will continue to grow in this area. When thinking about this, not taking Godly correction is what took Satan down. I believe Satan could not follow instructions, as brought out in the Word. Satan wanted to be God. I am continually praying that I learn to receive all instructions and corrections well. Pro 3:11 My son, despise not the chastening of the LORD; neither be weary of His correction. Hard Truths

10/9/2015   12:06   We cannot boast. If we could be good enough for God in any sense of the word, Jesus would not have come. The only reason Jesus had to come is because none of us are good enough to get into heaven by ourselves. We will never reach God's perfect standard, but he still loves us and wants us to know it. God, see's Jesus when He looks at us.

10/9/2015   12:13   I have read the Bible many times, and I love it, but I can't say that I have come to a place where I live it out in my life all the time. I only wish I could say this. If I understand it correctly, even Paul did not count himself to have arrived at perfection. I believe that all we can do is strive for perfection and ask for forgiveness when we fall short of it.

10/9/2015   12:23   The only way we can become like Jesus is to treat Him as Lord, King, and Almighty God who came to earth and told us how to live life. Jesus told us what we could expect heaven. The truth is, if we Christians genuinely believe this, then it would, without a doubt, drive us to study His Word, the Bible. It would cause us to hide His Word in our hearts, so it would take hold of us and change us so that we could become children of God. Become like Jesus. You ask me why I am not more like Christ; well, I didn't say I would become God. I said I want to become more like Jesus. It truly is by His Grace we become more like Him, but to do so, we have to be willing to be disciplined by God and others, which will allow us to become His disciple.

10/18/2015   4:55   There are times when I'm yielded to the Precious Holy Spirit, and when I am yielded, He does what only He can do. I would like to be yielded to Him all the time, but there are times when I am not listening, and I miss the incredible things He wants me to do and experience. By His Grace and mercy, I will grow to be more like Jesus, listening to God's small still voice and acting upon it. Leaving myself behind and allowing Jesus to shine through me.

10/18/2015   5:01   I'm amazed and very thankful that the Lord has been so gracious to me, as He has allowed Jesus in me to shine sometimes. Others have come on board with the ministry that He has given me. I pray that I will be faithful to the Lord first, which will then make me be faithful to my sponsors.

10/18/2015   5:03   I am so thankful for my faithful brethren; because of their faithful sponsoring, I am driven to do the works of our Father in heaven.

10/24/2015   1:04   No one is righteous, no, not one; therefore, if our Lord were not full of grace and forgiveness, no one would be saved.

10/25/2015   15:55   At times, yes, it is hard to be a Christian, and at other times I flow with the Holy Spirit and live in His joy.

10/25/2015   15:59   There are times when God allows me to be used to bring others to the understanding of what Jesus did for us all. Times when He does not, but I put it in His hands and do what I can when I can for the Kingdom of God.

10/25/2015   16:03   I can say that I am the happiest when I'm walking with my Lord by my side. Yes, I know He's always there, but we, or at least I am not seeking to listen all the time. Still working on this

10/25/2015   16:06   It took many people in many ways to bring me to Jesus, too many to list here. But I can say in the forty-three years that I have known Jesus; He is and has always walked in front of me. I just try to keep up.

10/25/2015   16:09   The self-righteous do not think they are bad enough to need a Savior. As for me, I need a Savior daily.

10/25/2015   16:11   It is always a choice. Jesus walked among sinners, as I do at times. The choice is to look for times when you can lift up Jesus among sinners. Who's Holding You, I, and others Back?

10/25/2015   16:15   I know there are times when I feel I am not doing enough. This is, in some ways, me trying to be good enough and trying to get right. I still need to remember to seek a relationship with Jesus; then, He will lead me to His harvest.

10/25/2015   16:17   All true Christian brethren should have a strong desire to seek and find their lost brothers and sisters.

10/25/2015   16:19   The Lord knows how He has made us and what gifts He has given us. All Jesus wants us to do, is to use those gifts, His gifts for His Glory, and if we do, we will lift up His kingdom on earth.   Different Abilities

10/25/2015   16:29   There are many that desire to understand God's Word; this is discipling. Discipling without witnessing is not discipling. By His Grace, He will use me and help me take the time needed to help the lives He sends my way.

10/25/2015   16:38   So many people have received the grace and gift of Salvation. Our God and His Christ are so far above us; we can do nothing less than fall on our knees when we come into His presence.

10/25/2015   16:42   Why are we here? The reason for life is to Love God and love our neighbors as ourselves. This is the secret to living with joy.

10/25/2015   16:44   When we know and trust the reality that God loves us. Then we can believe that God placed Himself in the womb of a woman, Mary, to fulfill His prophecy of the Virgin Birth of Jesus.

10/25/2015   16:48   God is the creator of all things. He plans to raise up children. I am one of His creations and one of His sons. Amazing. All Glory to

God and His Son Jesus. Holy, Holy, Holy

10/25/2015 16:51 All that have ever seen God have trembled. I know I will tremble, stand, or kneel in awe. I will fall even more in love with my Lord Jesus and God when I see Him face to face.

10/26/2015 13:44 Unfailing love goes hand and hand with forgiveness. The Lord has allowed me to forgive everyone. I have no hate towards anyone. Being slow to anger is something I am working on.

10/26/2015 13:49 I do not consider myself lazy; in fact, I've worked very hard in my time on earth. I think the trick is to use your time wisely. The wisest time spent is time spent sharing the Gospel, and by His grace, some will come to know the amazing truth that Jesus will give them the gift of eternal life. A Lesson from Ants

10/27/2015 1:12 Jesus said if we look at a woman and allow lust to come into our minds, we have committed the sin of adultery. Covet, not your neighbor's wife or any other woman. Please be true to yourself; most people, men, and women have committed adultery in this way. Jesus's Holy Spirit will help you overcome this sin. In Jesus Name. Many temptations hit us every day. I honestly believe that the closer we get to the Lord, the more the devil wants to stop us, like David with Bathsheba.

10/27/2015 12:06 Even John had a hard time describing heaven after seeing it in Revelations. The eye has not seen, nor ear heard what God has in store for those that love Him. The un-repented sinners will not see the Kingdom of God, so let's admit our sins, repent, and ask Jesus to take all our sins away, and He will! Even if the battle continues.

10/27/2015   12:14   I should not be getting into heaven. Before knowing the Lord, I was a typical kind of guy. Although I did a lot of drugs, I had a foul mouth and smoked cigarettes. I considered myself a nice guy, although, in God's eyes, I sinned continuously. Now, I understand, forty-three years after receiving Jesus as Lord of my life, I sin much less. I do what I can not to sin but being human; I will always fall short of God's perfect standard. Does this stop me from trying to be like Jesus? No. In Titus 3:5, the Holy Spirit speaks through the author, and he writes; Not by works of righteousness which we have done, but according to his mercy he saved us, by the washing of regeneration, and renewing of the Holy Spirit. We as Christians will continue to be washed, regenerated, and renewed every morning.

10/28/2015   12:34   The most recent division I had with a Church Member was when a leader at Church told me that reaching out to the brethren with inspirational thoughts was overstepping her boundaries of leadership. I believe God allows this to help me learn to stay humble and submit to the authority He has placed over me. That the Lord has given to her, it is her God-given position. I put this division in His hands and seek unity. By our Lord's grace, I have grown in this area. Proverbs 15.

10/28/2015   12:40   There must be leaders and followers, whether in business or the Spiritual warfare. We are at war against the evil one, and someone must lead the battle. Proverbs 11:14

10/28/2015   12:43   The enemy loves to use our guilt. He builds fear onto it and uses it to separate us from God.

10/29/2015   4:12   Paul said in Romans 7:15; I do not understand what I do. For what I want to do, I do not do, but what I hate I do. (NIV) There have been times in my life that I do things I do not want to do. I believe it is memories of my life prior to coming to Jesus and the evil one tries to use those thoughts. We are in a spiritual battle; just remember Jesus has already won it for us. Repent and move forward.

10/29/2015   12:48   Moses got fed up with the Israelites. Instead of listening to the Lord and just talking to the rock as he was told, as he did when God opened the sea. As for me, at times, I get fed up with things people do and say, and it can drive me to lose it too. The answer is to seek the Lord in these conversations even when it costs money or time.

10/29/2015   12:53   Being a slave to sin is when you are driven by it. We all have things we are working on, shortcomings, a weakness that we know the Lord wants us to grow in. We have not and never will be able to always exist in the perfect standard of Our Lord and God, but we can always take steps to become the child of God that He wants us to become. Slaves No More

10/30/2015   12:06   Sin is always at the door knocking; I just have found if I keep a regular routine, sin can be kept at bay. Then by the grace of our Lord, we can reject the other temptations.

10/30/2015   12:10   The Lord has been good to me. I believe I have forgiven everyone who has ever done anything against me. Jealously hits me occasionally, but by His grace, it hasn't a hold on me.

10/31/2015   5:52   I remember when I was in the military, how older, more experienced men in the world led me in evil ways.

10/31/2015   12:39   Sex outside of marriage leads to hurt and harm, but sex within marriage can secure and strengthen our love and passion for each other. We humans need touch.

11/1/2015   5:15   We are God's hands, feet, and mouths in this world. In my opinion, the most important is our mouth. It's the only true and sure way we can let others know the reason our hands do things for them, and our feet go to aid them is because Jesus leads us to do what we do. Only our mouths can tell them that Jesus told us to do what we do. Giving written tracts, etc. are good, but there is nothing like a face to face conversation. All Glory to God.

11/2/2015   12:43   I respect the authorities, as God has set them up to protect us. If we stay within the law, we have nothing to fear. The only thing I will not respect is if they tell me I cannot love Jesus and spread His Gospel. Live Without Fear

11/3/2015   1:50   I was walking in the ways of the world for twenty-two years until I met Jesus. I still have friends who are walking in the ways of the world. They know I am Christian, and I have sought to share the Gospel with them but felt like a brick wall stop the words. I am praying the Holy Spirit will bring them into God's Kingdom through Jesus. Praying for Him to move in their lives.

11/4/2015   5:19   Only the Holy Spirit renewing us through the Word will give us the strength to live for Him and work in His harvest.

11/4/2015   5:21   , I have been working on controlling my temper. If I could do it myself, I would. I have found that only Jesus can change my characteristics. So, I seek Him first; then, He can change my old personalities and ways daily.

11/4/2015   5:28   I hate to say it, but there are some few

occasions when I fall into foolish talking. I truly want to control my tongue. Being joyful is not the same as foolish talk. By the grace of the Lord, I will be alerted of the difference.

11/4/2015   13:06   I can say that I seek to stop arguments. Still working on it. A meek and humble spirit the Lord loves. So, if I seek the Lord and put others above myself, I will overcome.

11/5/2015   13:34   I try not to gossip. I guess most of us do it without thinking, as we talk about people and things they are doing and saying.

11/5/2015   13:42   I always try to be honest when sharing with others. Sharing in meekness and kindness is how the Lord wants us to share, knowing that we too have our faults and weaknesses

11/6/2015   15:29   Just do not allow quarreling. I thank the Lord for by His grace; He has helped me grow in this area. My wife and I do not quarrel very often.

11/6/2015   15:31   One of the worst things we can do is withhold our bitter and even hateful feelings. These feelings hurt us more than the person we hold them against. Our Lord Jesus has shown us how to forgive. We need to share what is hurting us meekly and humbly, knowing that we are more than likely, fifty percent of the cause.

11/7/2015   15:00   I am working on knowing the difference between foolish mistakes and evil doing. Jesus taught us to pray for our enemies, even love them. This is something I am still working on. What a Savior. The Power of Overlooking Wrongs

11/7/2015   15:02   When we tithe and give to other causes, we are investing in the lives that are being touched. I know I could do more. Praying on how. Eternal wealth enhancers

11/8/2015   14:11   The Lord said in many places that He is married to the backslider. Jesus said love thy neighbor as thyself, and to pray even for your enemy, your wife is not your enemy, but it shows how deep the love of Jesus is. Unequal Partnership

11/8/2015   14:13   I walk, talk and live Jesus, but I fall short every day. I am so thankful for His mercy every day. Bath Spiritually Daily. **Titus 3:5** Not by works of righteousness which we have done, but according to his mercy, he saved us, by the washing of regeneration, and renewing of the Holy Spirit.

11/9/2015   4:48   Many are the affections of the righteous, but the Lord delivers them from them all. This verse at the age of sixty-five holds much more truth than when I was in my twenties, thirties, forties, and even fifties. So thankful for, it is a comforting truth.

11/9/2015   13:56   I thank the Lord He has allowed me not to hold on to anger. I have in times past, and when I did, it hurt me and not the person I was angry at. It is simply living and loving, as

Jesus said, putting others above yourself.
Not going to Bed Angry

11/9/2015 14:00 When I have my mind and heart on Jesus, I can easily control myself, but when I am not, I can lose self-control or should I say Holy Spirit control. That is what it is all about keeping our eyes on Jesus. He will never lead us wrong; He will always lead us to put others above ourselves. Think and Exercise

11/10/2015 13:45 Forgiving is the key to a happy life. To forgive, even while the issue, you must forgive is happening. Forgiveness wins every time   A Call to Love

11/10/2015 13:46 When I look at how Jesus lived, I marvel. Loving my wife as He loves the Church is my challenge and my joy. Heart guard

11/10/2015 13:47 Lazy people do irritate me. Although I do not consider myself lazy, I still miss the mark of God's highest calling by not staying busier for Him and the Kingdom of God. So, I should not be irritated, but inspire them to move.

11/11/2015 1:43 God wants a day to spend with us. It is not just a commandment; it is a human need; without taking a day a week with God, we rob ourselves of His peace, love, and joy. Our creator loves us and wants to give us His peace, love, and vision. Even all His creation understands that He created it. We should treat Him as our Creator, Father, and God. He can save us if we choose to let Him, but know this, He does not need us and will allow us to ignore Him and go our own path to Hell.

11/11/2015   14:15   I cannot think of a time that I was planning to do evil. Although anything that is pulling you away from Him, He counts as evil. By His Grace, I will listen to His Holy Spirit and walk in ways that are pleasing to our Father in heaven.

11/12/2015   13:11   I can think of a time where I was angry about someone else's good news while reading about Jonah anger, it's evident that Jonah was upset because Nineveh repented. Was he thinking of what the people would say about him? I can sadly say I have allowed my anger to come out when my pride is hurt. Thankful for the Word and God's grace through Jesus.

11/13/2015   13:05   God promised to comfort us. There are so many people oppressed both physically and spiritually. Both can be comforted by receiving Jesus. He gives peace that the world does not comprehend. His peace is pass human understanding. Lord helps us to do our part in supplying their physical needs and spiritual needs at the same time.

11/13/2015   13:22   There's both physical adultery and spiritual adultery. Both are stealing from the beloved. Both are wrong. Physical adultery is someone stealing a spouse and is punished by humans and God. Spiritual adultery is humans putting anything in first place instead of their creator, Jesus. The prophet Hosea was told by God to take a whore for his wife to demonstrate how Israel sought other gods. It is putting things and people before God. This is true for us too.

11/14/2015   15:08   God really knows the depth of everything. He knows our every thought, our wicked thoughts, and Godly thoughts. He alone can judge honestly.

11/14/2015   15:10   Wicked people will be destroyed because evil, by its nature, destroys itself. Our God has made it that way. His ways are right and true and never change. I praise Jesus and thank Him for His truth and His Holy Spirit that guides us into all truth.

11/14/2015   15:18   Riches tend to satisfy and remove our urge to need the Lord. Riches can distract us from Jesus. Many get so tided up by the riches and the desire to keep them that they put the Lord and His will on the side, and this is a disaster. They lose the joy of the Lord and, in many cases, do not use their riches to lift the Kingdom of God; therefore, their lives fall into despair, and they become separated from God. Satisfaction Breeds Complacency

11/16/2015   3:34   We do not know what tomorrow will bring, so how can we truly know how to prepare for it. The only way to prepare for the future is to put our total trust in Jesus.   Dying Hopes

11/16/2015	3:37	People have lost the understanding of God's temple. Jesus said we are His temple. We are to care for ourselves because Jesus lives in us.
11/16/2015	3:41	We are to flee from lust. Men and women were created to find their mate and marry so they can be fruitful and have children. These children are to be raised in the knowledge of the Lord and His Word. God warns all humanity to flee lust. If people do not flee lust, that same lust will destroy them. Flee lust
11/16/2015	3:44	God made us for one purpose, and that is to Love Him and others. If we do not live this eternal truth and keep it close to our hearts, we will have missed why the Lord God has placed us on this earth. True Worship
11/16/2015	13:46	God fulfilled many prophecies when He became a man in the person of Jesus. God planned that He would come to earth in His perfect time in the world's history.
11/16/2015	13:49	The closer I get to Jesus, the more I see how sinful I am. He is perfect, and I fall short in many ways.
11/17/2015	13:48	Jesus was totally man and totally God. His man's side had to suffer the heat, the lack of food, and many other hardships of all humanity. Jesus being God He knew when He came, He would live as a human, then He showed us by His life and His Words how we

are to strive to live.

11/18/2015	4:46	I take Jesus with me everywhere. By His Grace, I will get to a place in life where I can stop to share Jesus more, and at any moment of my daily life.

11/19/2015　6:06　Servants of the Lord. Free and Enslaved

11/20/2015　1:41　Pride is the reason all of us reject correction. It is much easier when correction is given with humility and wisdom, but sad to say most of the time, it's not. So, praise the Lord and ask Him to provide you with grace for the moment. My dear wife is exceptionally good at correcting me. ☺ Accepting Discipline

11/21/2015　15:03　Excess of anything will drag anyone down spiritually. By the grace of God, He allows us to find moderation in all things good.

11/21/2015　15:05　Anyone that wins souls will be as the stars of the heavens. I am just looking forward to seeing our Lord face to face. So exciting. I really want Him to say to me, well done. Expect Judgment

11/22/2015　1:07　As Jesus said, only God is good.

11/23/2015　14:56　Only through the Blood of Jesus can we be righteous in God's eyes because He sees Jesus in us.

11/23/2015　14:59　A wise person knows that this life is short, so they seek after the eternal.

11/25/2015	3:34	Pray and get into God's Word, the Bible.
11/27/2015	2:25	When I was running a business, I try to search out prices before making up a contract to do work for my clients. I wanted to make sure I was competitive and that I did not overcharge them. Leaning on a Scale
11/27/2015	2:28	As Christians, we want to be an excellent example to the world, so others see His love in us. Then we have an open the door to tell them about Jesus.
11/27/2015	2:30	The devil always sends temptations to Gods' children, but by the grace of God, we will stay strong. To remain strong, we must remain in prayer and His Word.
11/30/2015	14:03	Share with as many as you can about God's saving grace through Jesus.
11/30/2015	14:25	Faithfulness to our wife is not just about not fornicating; it is showing love and respect.
11/30/2015	14:28	God places people in authority for a reason. He commands us to obey them, knowing that He will remove them in His time if so needed. Respect and Honor
11/30/2015	14:31	Life really begins when we are spiritually born through Jesus. Every human being is born spiritually dead. Jesus told us He came to give us a spiritual birth and not a religion. He offers it to everyone. Finding True Life
11/30/2015	14:44	I can humbly say, last night, God's precious Holy Spirit led me to share with my sister's

boyfriend. He heard some of the witness but was not ready. Godly Messages

12/1/2015	1:05	I am trying to grow in the understanding that all my choices in life should be made with eternity in my mind first.

12/1/2015   14:03   God has commanded all of us to give both financially and spiritually. We are to raise up His kingdom here on earth. I have a portion taken out monthly automatically for Church, and other mission works. I can say I could give more. By His Grace, I will find a proper balance.

12/2/2015   1:14   The goal that needs to be in every child of God is to tell others about Jesus's gift of eternal life. We find so much joy when we know the Holy Spirit is using us. When we share about Jesus, it is always Him shining through us.

12/2/2015   14:35   There are times that I am just so tired it seems all I can do is watch TV. I need to get this under better control.

12/3/2015   1:15   Frist, I commit myself to Jesus, then I commit myself to stay close to my family members. God must always be first.

12/3/2015   13:30   The wicked are perverted because they do not seek the perfect one, Jesus. They fill themselves with evil thoughts and actions. They are led by themselves thinking only of themselves. When the Holy Spirit leads us, we leave our perverted hearts behind, allowing His perfect ways to pour through us. The more there is of Him, the less there is of imperfect us.

12/4/2015   1:14   Mere financial gain and the desire to be rich will lead to sadness and emptiness. Wealth without Jesus ends wickedly, but joy and satisfaction will come to all who put their trust in Jesus.

12/4/2015   13:10   Our Godly legacy is all we take with us when we go to be with Jesus and our Heavenly Father. I have labored in His fields for many years of my life, but I feel I could have done more.

12/7/2015   2:23   His grace has allowed me to stand firm in His truth. As long as I leaned on Jesus when the going gets tough, I'll be OK.

12/7/2015   2:24   Very sad to say, many more humans cheer when the wicked are successful in this world, compared to someone coming to the eternal riches. When someone receives the gift of eternal life. When anyone lifts Jesus, I celebrate.

12/7/2015   2:29   The flesh is weak, but the spirit is so willing. It is a constant battle, but Jesus has already won. Christ is the Beginning

12/7/2015   2:32   Being humble is yielding to the guidance of the Holy Spirit and putting others above yourself. Again, this is something I am working on.

12/8/2015	2:00	It amazing that God chose Paul to fulfill His will, knowing the terrible things he had committed. All God needs from anyone is for them to submit to Him, and He will use their life.
12/8/2015	13:33	His grace has led me to stop and pray for many people daily. We cannot stop praying, Prayer is the world's greatest Wi-Fi, or should I say God-fi?
12/9/2015	13:23	God, the Father and Jesus the Son are one. They created all things; therefore, they are the owners of all things. We are to Glorify God, and in return, God completes us.
12/9/2015	13:25	Some of the time, I find myself looking at the waves like Peter. He started with full faith while walking on water, but when he took his eyes off Jesus, he sunk. I lose the vision when I take my eyes off Jesus.
12/10/2015	3:56	For the Church to run as God wants it to, Jesus must be leading it. For the world to run as God wants it to, the Church must lead with love and truth. This is God's will. So, Church, we need to be united in Jesus.
12/11/2015	5:22	When the Lord God created the world, He knew we would be reconciled to Him. It was His plan from the beginning. So, He is doing what He planned. The Reconciliation
12/11/2015	5:25	Jesus has taken over my life and is making me the man He wants me to be. Titus 3:5. A work in progress.

12/11/2015	13:17	Our God is a just God, and He will judge everyone when we get to heaven with righteousness, but He will not let any sin into His heaven. This is why we all need the cleansing blood of Jesus.
12/12/2015	4:10	If it weren't for God's love lived through Jesus in us; the world would fall apart.
12/13/2015	1:31	Anyone who is living in this life without Jesus is living in darkness because Jesus is the only light. Rescue mission
12/16/2015	1:53	I remember that I was living a life far from God. I praise and thank Jesus that He allowed me to find His grace and forgiveness.
12/16/2015	1:56	I want to Prayerfully use money as it is the Lord's finance given to me to use rightfully.
12/17/2015	13:54	We don't Sic God on them because Jesus taught us to pray for our enemies. Forgiveness wins
12/19/2015	15:17	The father of lies is Satan.
12/19/2015	15:18	Evil is anything that does not Glorify God; therefore, there are things in all our lives that are evil.
12/19/2015	15:21	I can say with all sincerity, that I try to live a Holy life that Glorifies my Lord and King. By His grace, I will keep trying until I am by His side.
12/20/2015	14:29	They persecuted Jesus in His day, and He

told us the world would persecute us too if we live as He lived. We are His disciples, so understand this truth and stand firm when people who are worldly-minded hurt you.

12/21/2015   15:04   If it were not for His Grace and His love, I'd be lost, lonely and sad, living in a world and headed for a dead end. Thank you, Jesus, for your love and light. Captives of Christ

12/22/2015   13:40   I believe all human being rebel at times about something. I never want to rebel against my Creator God, His Son Jesus, or the Holy Spirit. I desire to hear the leading of the Lord through His Holy Spirit and do precisely what He is leading me to do, but at times I miss the mark, and that's sin.

12/24/2015   6:22   I genuinely want to inspire others and my sponsors, so I send monthly reports on what God is doing as I follow Him and His mission. Letter of Recommendation

12/26/2015   1:30   I know there are times when I grieve over my family and friends. I want them to know Jesus's love for them.

12/26/2015   16:14   I know God hears our prayers; the problem is, at times, we do not think He has because He does not do what we want. A time will come when we will know, He heard everything we asked for and did what was best for us.

12/27/2015   13:34   When I get stressed. I am learning to stop and be filled with God's Glorious Power through prayer and His Word.

12/27/2015   13:38   I am thankful for the many promises there are for our children. I pray for the poor and abused, and I tend to get angry with evil. I have been able to pray for them to see the light that Jesus taught.

12/28/2015   1:39   I try to stay away from words that hurt, but I know there are times when the old Navy man tries to slip out. Working on it. Bad Talk

12/28/2015   13:07   Jesus, I cry out to You. I love and need You.

12/29/2015   2:05   God's Not Happy when we leave Him.

12/29/2015   13:19   Guard your desires. The more our hearts desire the things of this world, the less we seek and serve the Lord.

12/31/2015   13:07   While living in South America, I was never beaten or physically hurt, but I was put in jail many times in Argentina for sharing the Gospel with young people my age. This was during the military takeover in 1976-77, when Mrs. Peron was pushed out of power.

1/1/2016   5:44   I have been angry, but by His everlasting grace, He forgives me.

1/2/2016   7:26   I believe God has given us a personal choice in our lives. The reason for this world, for creation, is to give all humankind the choice to follow God or not. We see God did that in the Garden of Eve. Since the coming of Christ Jesus, God has given us the choice to follow His example, to seek, to follow Him, or follow our own way, the way of all humankind. God has an eternal Everlasting purpose, and it is for His good pleasure He created all things. This is the whole reason for the creation. God designed it to bear children of God.

1/2/2016   17:53   Solomon said much joy comes from finishing work with our hands, but I will add our joy can come from the words we speak and the actions we take to help others.

1/3/2016   3:03   God will get His desired fruit from His harvest of eternal sons and daughters; these are those who love and trust Him no matter what. Satan and his demons rebelled against God and His Son Jesus. Now God will have children who saw the fruits of rebellion and, for this reason, never rebel against Him again.

1/3/2016   14:01   My goal in this life has been to always trust in God's unfailing love. John 3:16.

1/4/2016   13:47,   I strive to be a person with integrity. I do not like to have things in my life that I need to try to hide. I strive to do unto others as they would do to me. I am living with a desire to lift Jesus daily. To be an example of what it means to be a Christian. I do slip and fall from His wonderful Grace at times but seek forgiveness when I do.

1/6/2016   4:33   I see the Holy Spirit every time we go out and share the Gospel. We met Matthew and Precious, two homeless people. We started sharing the Gospel with them, and George saw that the security guard was coming towards us. George thinking the guard might try to stop us from talking to them, walked over before he got to us. George started talking to the security guard whose name was Jamel, and to our surprise, he was coming over to thank us for taking the time to speak to the homeless. We continue to minister to Matthew and Precious while George shared the Gospel with Jamel, the security guard. Matthew and Precious said they wanted to pray with us, so we prayed right there at union station train station that Jesus would come into their lives and give them eternal life. Also, that His Holy Spirit would guide their lives and care for them. I gave them some money before leaving. God is still on the throne, he does miracles, but many times we just do not See It.

1/6/2016   4:39   We find in the last chapters of Job; we have no reason to question God about anything. We are God's creation, and we need to seek what He wants when things go wrong. Lord, I pray for Your mercy in this area. We misread Your leading at times in our lives. By Your Grace, we will grow in this weakness.

1/7/2016   1:11   There are times when we cause our own problems, and there are times the devil causes them, but nevertheless, we can always learn to grow in His Love and peace if we choose to.

| 1/7/2016 | 1:14 | Jesus has and always will forgive all our sins. We will reap the rewards from all we do in His Name, but Salvation is a gift of God. I am so thankful for the gift of eternity. It excites me to think about it. |

1/7/2016   14:02   , Jesus already knows all things. He knows I am not perfect, and there are things I need to grow in, but one thing I know, Jesus knows my heart, and it is to reach the world with His Gospel. My weakness will come to light at times, but I will not allow the enemy to use them to stop me from sharing my faith. This is one of the Devil's favorite tricks. He loves to discourage us, and he intentionally tries to kick us down. I will do my best to live the love Jesus taught, long live love.

1/8/2016   13:07   All of us need to come back to Jesus in different degrees. This is a daily call to all. Some to come back to Him as they have turned away altogether, others it is missing the mark, not accomplishing God's task for today. For the largest portion of the Christian Church, is to be standing for Jesus by telling those around them what Jesus did for them. Personally, I have found family and friends to be the hardest to reach and strangers easier. Jesus told us in Luke 4:24 I tell you; no prophet is accepted in his hometown.

1/9/2016   16:22   When I heard Matthew 6:19-21 for the first time, I knew I had to give my life to serve God's Kingdom. It says; Do not store up for yourselves treasures on earth, where moths and rust destroy, and where thieves break in and steal, But store up for yourselves treasures in heaven, where moths and rust do not destroy, and where thieves do not break in and steal. For where your treasure is, there your heart will be also.

1/10/2016   12:48   God gives wealth to those who love Him and to those who do not, but eternal blessing lasts forever.

1/11/2016   13:45   Lord, without You, we are flesh and bones which exist to survive. We were made by you and for Your good pleasure. You wanted to give us a clear way to communicate with You, so You sent Your Son to die for our sins. You God, O Mighty, Great, and magnificent, you are life and love, without You we are nothing. Thank You, Jesus, for cleansing me of all sin and calling me to serve You in Your Kingdom. I am honored, so honored to be called Your son. Without You wonderful Savior, I can do nothing. I love and need You.

1/11/2016   13:48   Our hope is in knowing that we will be with Jesus forever. The wicked live for today, this life, we live for the life to come. Thank You, Father God, for sending Jesus. Praise You, Jesus.

1/12/2016   5:26   When we meet the Lord, we will be the same as when we came into this world. We brought nothing coming into this world, and we will take nothing going out of this world.

1/12/2016	13:31	Lord, I know, I strive forward in my effort seeking to do your will. I love you and know that it is You that move the hands and hearts of man, and not my efforts. You run the universe, you run the world, and it's You that control all things, including health and wealth. I have seen your hand so often but still, fall back in my own efforts to save myself. Lord, forgive me for my lack of faith. While you were in this world, it grieved You to see lack of faith. Lord, by Your Grace, I will stop grieving You with my lack of faith for finance and health. Open my eyes that I may see the wonders of Your grace. Allow me to be Your servant In Jesus Name Amen.
1/13/2016	5:53	Oh Lord, I want and need to do Your will. Only by doing Your will, will I be fulfilled.
1/13/2016	13:26	, I love to share the complete Gospel. Paul said I become all things to all people that I might win some. 1 Cor. 9:19-23
1/13/2016	13:33	Praise You God Almighty. Thank You that You uphold me and strengthen me in my weakness. Your everlasting grace overwhelms me. I am so grateful that You have allowed me to serve You, even in my weakness. Oh Lord, You are life, you are the reason we are here, Your will be done. In Jesus, amen.

1/14/2016	14:26	I freely offer my services, But in order to continue working towards the goal of training Pastors and leaders on how to train their members the share the Gospel, I need support, so I do ask for sponsors for support.
1/15/2016	13:33	All the Pastors and brethren I meet that have the vision to reach God's harvest inspire me to keep going.
1/15/2016	13:51	My Lord and King, it is only by Your Spirit that we can accomplish anything in this world, only by Your precious Holy Spirit can we reach out into this dark world with Your light. You, Lord, are the light of the world, and all we can do is seek You, seek to be filled with Your Holy Spirit, then and only then can we shine Your light, because it is Your light that we shine. Lord, please have mercy on me and use this flesh of mine to shine Your light, your truth, and offer Your gift of Salvation to multitudes. In Jesus Name, I Pray. Amen.
1/17/2016	1:47	Before I came to the knowledge of who Jesus is and how I could have a daily relationship with Him. I went to bars, seeking to fulfill my life with things and people. I now seek to fill it with Jesus and His Holy Spirit. I love to share Him with people anywhere and everywhere.
1/17/2016	5:31	Oh Lord, there is nobody like You. You are the Creator of all that is and all that will ever be. We are Your creation; we were made by You to be what You created us to be. You will

fulfill Your plan in this world, regardless of what humans do. Oh Lord God, please have mercy on me and make me be the person you want me to be. Allow me to fulfill Your plan for my life. Let me be a vessel in Your hands. My Lord, King, and Creator. In Jesus Name, Amen.

1/18/2016   5:45   Frist of all I know, I am nothing without Jesus. Jesus knows I know I am nothing without Him. There are times I catch myself seeking the praise of man; I am so sorry. I always want to give Glory to God through Jesus; by His Grace, He sees that. When I realize that it is Jesus that sets up all events in my life so He can shine through, then I'm on the right path. Jesus is Lord, and I am nothing without Him.

1/18/2016   5:48   Yes, I have suffered for sharing Jesus with the world. He gave me the grace for those times.

1/18/2016   5:55   Praise the Name of our Lord and Savior Jesus. He is the King of Kings and Lord of all. I bow down to Jesus; He is the Creator of all, Jesus Created the world with His Father as said in the Gospel of John Chapter 1. He deserves all Glory, so that is why I lift His Name high. Everyone will give Jesus the Glory He deserves when they stand in front of Him. Be wise and Exalt His Greatness now.

1/18/2016   13:55   The Bible says I am to love our Lord and

Savior with all my heart. I love it when His grace overrules my flesh.

1/18/2016   13:57   I am praying for family and friends. I praise the Lord as He is working in their lives.

1/18/2016   14:12   The Jews were slaves in Egypt. God promised to free them from slavery. He did this through many plagues, the last being an accurate prophecy of Jesus, the Lamb of God. The Jews painted the lamb's blood on the doors of their houses so that death would pass them by. Jesus died on the cross for us. Everyone who believes that His blood was given to cleanse us from all sin will be saved from the second death. His blood has been painted on our souls, saving us from eternal death.

1/19/2016   14:25   I'm Fighting to allow the Holy Spirit to change me to be like Jesus. By His Grace alone, I know I will be as Him when entering the Kingdom in Heaven. I am so thankful that Jesus is in me. I praise Him daily. Lord, you are my light and love without You, life is worthless. I look forward to serving you for eternity. You are my King, Lord, and Savior. Thank You, Thank You, Thank You. The Greatness of His Salvation

1/19/2016   4:53   God's mission for my life is to bear fruit for His Kingdom. My Evangelism ministry is to bring as many people as I can to the knowledge of the saving grace of God through Jesus.

1/20/2016	3:00	As for what the Lord has done during my life. It would take many more books to share. The years He cared for me while in South America on a mission. The countless times He supplied my housing, food, clothing. Now in the States, He has raised up Sponsors for my Evangelism Ministry. Our God is loving and merciful. Praise the Name of Jesus. The Greatness of His Provision
1/20/2016	3:25	The Old Testament was perfect; it shows God doing what was necessary to keep humanity connected with Him. Jesus said the Bible would be with us for eternity. In the New Testament, God sent His only Son Jesus. We are in a new age, the age of grace. I am so thankful to be living in this age.
1/21/2016	4:00	We must care for our physical bodies so God can use them as vessels that grow into His children.
1/21/2016	13:50	We need to live a life that will Glorify God.
1/21/2016	13:58	Our Great God has always been there for me. He has upheld me in my many trials and afflictions. He has provided all my needs. He has never forsaken me. He is merciful and compassionate.
1/21/2016	14:07	Praise the Lord, His mercy is forever, His Grace sees the way and guides me. He provides even when I am weak. His will be done on earth as it is in Heaven.
1/22/2016	4:54	I Run a business and an evangelism ministry.

I also take care of my 87 yr. Old father, calling him daily and running around for him and taking him to the hospital when needed. I am a husband and do the honey-do list, helping around the house. I look at the downtime, and it makes me feel lazy. Lord, I know I could do more. Help me to find the right balance. In Jesus Name

1/23/2016   5:30   I need Jesus so much. He gives me confidence. He could remove it, too, so I am so thankful for His everlasting mercy.

1/24/2016   5:32   We know that the body of Jesus was broken for us and His blood spilled for our sins. So grateful knowing we will be with Him at the wedding feast of the Lamb and then for eternity.

1/24/2016   16:02   The day I stand in front of the Lord will be the best day of my life, even for eternity... At Home with the Lord

1/24/2016   16:27   Lord, I know I could do more for you, help me to be more diligent with my time, help me to know when to read the Word, pray, work, play, and relax. Please help me to control my mind better. I pray that You help me control my mind. Please cleanse me of all sin, even the hidden sin that looks to destroy me, rebuke the devil in Jesus' Name. You have given me a sex drive; help me to keep it under control. Thank you for your self-control. Amen

1/25/2016	13:09	Jesus said that we would be hated in this world as He was, so don't be surprised when battles and difficulties come because you live for Him. Destined for Trouble amen.
1/27/2016	13:20	I know I will see things that I have done both good and bad, but I also know I will be with Jesus for eternity. Standing Before Christ
1/27/2016	13:22	Grace T.Y.J saves us.
1/27/2016	13:24	So many times in so many lives, including mine, I have seen God use us for His Glory's sake.
1/28/2016	1:19	By Your Grace Lord, please use me to complete Your purpose for my life.
1/28/2016	1:27	In these last days, we must stand firm for Jesus in all areas of our lives. By His Grace, we will stand firm for our Lord till the day we go to be with Him for eternity
1/29/2016	4:36	Honesty pays Honest Witnesses
1/29/2016	4:37	Pride comes before a fall. Be Ordinary
1/29/2016	4:53	It is true that the leadership of any Church must be in the Word, and the Word must be in them. Teach the Word.
1/29/2016	17:03	The power of Prayer never stops to amaze me. Jesus is still the King of Kings, Lord of Lords, Ruler, and God of the universe. They knew that when Jesus walked the earth and we as God's Church must know it now. Lord, have mercy on our unbelief.

1/30/2016	5:34	We all go through tests, things that are hard to go through. It takes time for us to see and understand why God allowed them, but God is faithful, and He will not tempt us above what we are able to take. 1 Cor. 10:13
1/30/2016	16:49	Lord help my words to be Your Words. Please give me Your Spiritual and Physical strength to do Your will.
1/30/2016	16:55	Without You Lord, we are nothing. Help me to grow ever closer to You through prayer. One of my weaknesses is when things get tough, I go to my mind first then pray. Lord, please help me first to seek You in tough times so You can give me the strength I need to get through. This gives You the Glory.
1/31/2016	17.35	There is only one day in the life of anybody that counts. Days of births, baptism, graduation, career, marriage, and retirement are all important, of course, but the critical day, the most important day, is the day of our salvation—the day when the grace of God saves us through Jesus Christ.

My goal is to assist Pastors. To encourage their congregations on how to articulate the Gospel and articulate it with joy and conviction. They then will know the Holy Spirit can and will speak to others through them. It is beautiful when I see others learn that Jesus, through His Holy Spirit, wants to use our lives daily, allowing Him to use our lives to lovingly, relationally, and intentionally reach others without fear. The day of salvation is the only day in life that truly counts for all of eternity. Anyone can share about God's love, children, young adults, adults, and even prisoners.

2/4/2016	14:36	But the fruit of the Spirit is love, joy, peace, forbearance, kindness, goodness, faithfulness, gentleness, and self-control. Against such things, there is no law. Gal. 5:22
2/4/2016	14:44	We need to complete the task God has given us.
2/6/2016	16:31	It is wonderful when the Lord's Holy Spirit leads us to a Divine appointment to meet someone. We can be used by God to do His will. We are so blessed when the Lord uses our mouths the speak to those whom He sends us to. We get to see the Kingdom of God being established on earth. Those who receive Him through our witness come into the eternal Kingdom of God.
2/6/2016	16:42	When I was running a business and serving as an evangelist, it was tough. I had to give lots of time to work; even though I told people about what Jesus did for me while working, I could because I own the business. I closed the company so I can devote full time to training Churches and their members on how to share their faith daily. We need to reap God's Harvest as it is ripe and ready to harvest. Luke 2

2/7/2016	13:43	God has been incredibly good to me. He allowed me to find thousands of true Christian brothers and sisters to walk by my side in this life. We will see each other for eternity.
2/8/2016	14:10	The Lord called me forty-four years ago, and He led me to go into His great harvest field. To harvest souls for His Kingdom so His wedding feast would be full. Till this day, I believe when someone truly comes to Christ, they should be faithful in their study of God's Word—sharing His Gospel. Romans 10:9-10 says, if we confess with their mouth the Lord Jesus and believe in our heart that God has raised Him from the dead, we would be saved. The belief grows when the confessing happens. It is all or nothing at all. Just studying the Word without confessing is nothing. In fact, it is hiding their gift. Matthew 28:16-20 and 25:25 His Great Commission.
2/11/2016	4:56	By the Grace of Jesus, He will keep me going strong as He pours out His Holy Spirit on me, which is Gods' Spirit. May He take over every fiber of me and use it for the Glory of God the Father, God the Son, and God the Holy Spirit.
2/11/2016	5:00	I know it is the Lord's will that we reach out to everyone that the Lord's Holy Spirit sends our way. This is why we are still living on earth. We are living to give Glory to God as we bring His sheep into His Kingdom. The Great Power for the Great Commission.

2/11/2016   5:02 When the Holy Spirit leads me to share the Good News, The Gospel with someone and I do not do it. I feel as though I missed the mark. Every time I do not yield to the Holy Spirit to open my mouth, it is brought to my conscience that I miss something He wanted me to do. By His Grace, I will be a yielded vessel for His use always.

2/11/2016   14:31 There's nothing more important, nothing that can be done that comes close to the call upon each Christian, who has understood the Gospel. To do what Jesus did and taught, Luke 19:10, to seek the lost, Matthew 20:28, minister to others, Luke 4:43, preach the Gospel to everyone the Holy Spirit leads us to, John 3:17, that Jesus came to save them and John 10:10, to give them life to the full, that Jesus does not condemn them, John 12:47, or judge them He came to save them "If they believe Him and receive Him as their Savior, If they hear His truth John 18:37, Then they will be saved. His Great Compassion for the Lost.

2/15/2016   5:54 Jesus gives me enthusiasm for You daily.

Contents

150

Chapter 10

Let's spread the news

God's Word declares that this world and our lives are not all that there is. This life is only a portion of our existence, and our spirits continue to live after the death of our bodies. It also teaches that it is only possible for us, as humans, to be in God's presence in the afterlife if we are first reconciled with Him.

In His great love for the world and each of us, God made it possible to bridge the gap between Him and us through Jesus, who gave His life for our misdeeds, wrongdoings, or what the Bible calls sin. Because of this great act of love, our sins have been forgiven, and we can live in God's presence both now and in the eternal life to come. This is the profound truth that you and I, as Christians, believe; what a tremendous comfort to know that because of Jesus' sacrifice, we will live with God eternally.

There is also a sad part of this: not everyone has this information, and many people either do not know or do not understand that eternal life with God is available to them. Most of *us* did not know this either, until we heard it from another Christian, either personally, through written material or via the media. Because we were told, we believed, and we inherited eternal life.

My life has been completely changed. I was searching, seeking for answers, someone took the time to share with me about God's love. I imagine my life might have taken a hugely different direction had someone not spoken to me about Jesus the Christ.

Most Christians have similar stories. Someone told them about

Jesus. Maybe it was their parents, or perhaps a preacher, or someone witnessed to them at school, or on the street, or in a restaurant. Perhaps it was a friend, a relative, or someone at work, or someone sitting next to them on a bus, train, or plane. Most likely, God used someone to tell you how much He loves you and to tell you about Jesus. If this happened to you, I bet you are glad they did.

What I have written about in this book, hopefully, is showing and speaking to you about Jesus' love and compassion for others. How God's Holy Spirit draws people to the Lord and the lives we live, the love we show, the light of God's Spirit within us, is often what attracts the interest of others. But at some point, words of explanation also become necessary. There is a time for words to be spoken, for faith to be expressed verbally. It is essential to walk the walk of a Christian life, and it is also necessary to talk about the Lord, salvation, and faith to those with whom you connect.

Christians telling others the Gospel is key to conveying the understanding that there is life beyond this life and that because of God's deep love for humanity, He has given us the gift, the opportunity, of living with Him forever. If Christians do not do the "telling," then people will miss the opportunity to hear this wonderful news.

> *"Everyone who calls on the name of the Lord will be saved."*
> *But how can they call on Him to save them unless they believe in Him? And how can they believe in Him if they have never heard about Him? And how can they hear about Him unless someone tells them? Romans 10:13-17*

I know that many of you have witnessed to others throughout your life, and what I am telling you is not new information. It is instead a reminder to continue to share the Gospel. No matter what our situation, the call to share this news is always before us. Jesus said in John 15:16

As the Father has sent Me, even so, I am sending you. I chose you and appointed you that you should go and bear fruit.

Each of us has received the free gift of salvation, free for us but costly for Jesus. He gave all of Himself to redeem humankind, but He depends on us Christians to share the message with others. And if we do not, there is no guarantee they will hear it some other way.

The apostle Paul expressed how important sharing the Gospel with others is when he stated in 1 Corinthians 9:16

For necessity is laid upon me. Woe to me if I do not preach the gospel!

Other translations of this verse say: "An *obligation* is laid on me" (NRS), "I am *compelled* to preach" (NIV). Another expresses it like this: "Indeed, a *compulsion* weighs upon me to do that. How *horrible* it would be for me were I not to preach the gospel" (MIT).

We have been given the greatest gift anyone can be given. We have found the pearl of great price. We have the privilege of the entrance to the kingdom of heaven. Multitudes are searching for what we already enjoy, whether they realize it or not. Because of God's love and mercy, we are privileged to know the truth, the purpose, and the meaning of life. We have connected with God and have been granted eternal life. Others are seeking for the answers and purpose that God, in His love, wants to give them.

People need the life-giving water of God's Word. How sad, how deeply regrettable it is, when those of us who are so richly blessed do not share it with those who are desperately in need when Jesus's directive to share the good news with others is ignored.

Regardless of nationality, country, color, or creed, the heart of man is the same the world over, and his heartaches and sorrows and sins and pains and fear of death are the same. His longings, and hunger for God and His truth, for joy and happiness and peace of mind, are God-created, and the same in men the world over.

Even though many people are seeking genuine love, they seldom, if ever, find it, for there are never enough of God's people who are willing to show them His real love.

"Go ye into all the world and preach the Gospel to every creature" is not an option. It is a commandment. The message is clear. There is no denying it or excusing ourselves.

[Witnessing] is not just a nice thing to do when we feel like it or can find the time, but it is the God-given job and responsibility of all His faithful children.

As Jesus, Himself said, "The harvest truly is plenteous, but the laborers are few. Therefore," He commanded, "pray ye the Lord of the harvest, that He will send forth laborers into His harvest." His vast harvest of multitudes of frozen, cold, hungry people, wandering around in darkness without God.

We have been given the privilege of being called out of that darkness into God's marvelous light, and it is incumbent on us to do what we can, when we can, to help others connect to God through Jesus.

It most definitely can be challenging to do this with the busy lives we all lead. It is hard to make or take the time for it. I am saved because someone took the time for me. You are saved because someone put in time and effort to share the Gospel with you, someone who probably felt they did not have time either. Jesus sacrificed Himself on the cross for you, and another Christian sacrificed time and effort to connect you with Him. As has been said, Christ alone can save this world, but Christ cannot save this world alone. Someone must tell people about Jesus and salvation, and when God brings a person across your path, that someone is you.

When, where, how, and with whom we share the message will differ for each of us. But if we genuinely recognize the deep love and concern God has for each person, and that Jesus gave His life so they can possess eternal life, then we should feel compelled to tell those whom the Lord leads us to or brings across our path even if it's inconvenient, difficult, costly, or humbling.

We are directed by the Savior of our souls to present the opportunity to know Him to others. To bring the awareness of the great gift that was freely given to us to those who have not yet heard about it. Are we willing to do what is asked of us? Do we pray for souls, and then put feet to our prayers? Do we pray for laborers who will share the message with others, and are we willing to be those laborers ourselves? Do we pray for the Lord to bring those who are searching across our path? Do we ask the Holy Spirit to lead us to those who will respond to God's love? Are we willing to give some of our time, effort, thought, prayer, and action toward the commission Jesus has given us? When faced with someone in need of eternal life, do we act by sharing the message with them?

When we realize that the Creator of the world and all things became a man, our maker and designer put Himself in a virgin and became a man than lived a life that we can strive to live with the assistance of His Holy Spirit. If we are committed to doing what Jesus has asked of us, we will become the children of God. When we realize the eternal effect, it will have on someone's life and future if we will share with them what Jesus has done for us. If we are trying to be like Jesus, we will share His Words with them. If we love our neighbors as ourselves, as Jesus taught us, then we will be compelled to let them know how deeply God loves them and to show them how they can enter the kingdom of heaven through believing in Jesus. Jesus told us this; I am the way, the truth, and the life, no one comes to the Father but by me.

So, let us spread the news.

Contents

Chapter 11

I dedicate this to my wife, Susie

WOMANHOOD AND THE WISDOM OF GOD

Proverbs 31:10-31

Amidst a Confused Culture (and Church)

Here are the characteristics of the Christ-like Woman… W.O.M.A.N.

W = She is **_wise_**

Because she fears God, her value cannot be **_measured_**, her future has no **_fear,_** and her beauty will never **_fade_**

O = She honorably **_oversees_** her home

Her husband **_trusts_** her. She promotes his **_good_** and protects his reputation. She lays down her life so they might **_live_**

M = She is **_mighty_** in her work

She has willing and skillful **_hands_** with an innovative and

Industrious **_spirit._** She has a **_sharp_** mind and a **_strong_** body.

A = She is **_attractive_** in all the right ways

Her words are kind, and her **_works_** are admirable.

Her dress is tasteful, and her demeanor is **_delightful_**.

N = She is **_a neighbor_** to the needy

She **_gives_** generously and serves sacrificially.

She trusts God's Word, and God affirms her **_worth_**.

Women: Seek to become a Christ-like woman. God's grace covers your past, empowers your present, and guarantees your future.

Married men: Love and nurture your wife like Christ.

Single men: Pray for and seek out a Christ-like wife.

Single Women: Pray for and seek a Christ-like husband.

Church: Praise your Christ-like women. Promote Christ-likeness in women

Contents

Chapter 12
More thoughts and prayers

2/16/2016 17:45   By His grace, I will have complete confidence in God's Word the Bible.

2/19/2016 6:10   I ask two basic questions before sharing the Gospel, 1. Do you know for sure you will be going to Heaven when you die? Or is that something you are working on? 2. Let say your turn comes, and you are standing in front of God, and He says to you, " Why should I let you into Heaven? " What will you say? If they say anything else, then because Jesus paid for all my sins, then share the Gospel. Heaven is a free gift. Ephesians 2:8, and 9. I will know, depending on the answers to these questions, if a person is trusting in the Grace and Gift given by God through Jesus, or if they do not understand what Jesus did on the Cross.

2/19/2016 16:01   let's Love Jesus so much that we love to tell others about Him.

2/20/2016 6:03   We are the representatives of Jesus on this earth.

2/22/2016 4:54   We need to go into the highways and the byways and unto every house to share about the wedding feast of the Lamb. Mat. 22:1-14

2/22/2016 4:59   I know I can do nothing without the Lord, I know Paul knew he also could do nothing without the Holy Spirit.

2/22/2016 16:57	I do pray for all the Churches that I would like to get Evangelism Training into, as the harvest is still white and ready to harvest.
2/22/2016 17:01	Romans 10:15, KJV: "And how shall they preach, except they be sent? As it is written, How beautiful are the feet of them that preach the gospel of peace and bring glad tidings of good things!".
2/23/2016 5:23	2 Tim 2:15 Present yourself to God as one approved, a worker who does not need to be ashamed and who correctly handles the word of truth.
2/23/2016 14:41	By the Lord's Holy Spirit's help, I try to show empathy.
2/24/2016 4:29	No one can boast; we are all sinners falling short of God's Glory.
2/24/2016 14:24	We are to have a giving heart and spirits.
2/24/2016 14:33	God wants our hearts. He is our Creator; we are His creation. We will only come to full peace and understanding when we give ourselves back to Him with all our hearts.
2/25/2016 5:43	This is a daily battle in America. We are continually being hit with worldly things. It is only by His Grace that He allows us to go forth and lift His Word and Salvation.
2/25/2016 16:28	We strive to bear fruit for the Lord, Some 30

some 60 and some 100.

2/26/2016 3:03	Many people make up their own truth and do not follow the Bible. They create their God of choice. Sad to say, this describes a high percentage of the world today. They never read God's Word, the Bible, so they do not know Him. Jesus told us He is the Word in John Chapter 1. If someone does not study His Words, they will never know Him. By His Grace, I will study to be approved by God and follow His truth.
2/26/2016 16:09	There is nothing more important than obeying Jesus' commandment to go into all the world and preach the Gospel. All the world means everyone around you every day. By His Grace, I will serve Him till I go back to be with Him. Giving to God
2/28/2016 3:58	Mathew 6:19-34 tells us to lay up treasures in heaven. Wisdom and Money
2/28/2016 3:59	We must judge each case by its own merits and, according to God's Word, the Bible.
2/28/2016 13:44	Getting stronger. His grace is enough.
2/28/2016 13:48	For years, I was striving to get set up for my old age, I worked so hard towards that goal, and I ignored my Lord and His harvest for years. He is so merciful. He never left me, even using me at times during these years.
2/29/2016 4:17	Speak with others with a humble heart.

2/29/2016 15:03	Live a Godly life. Be a man or woman after God's heart. Be a disciple of Jesus, our Creator, God, and Savior; without Him, I am nothing. Sent to Proclaim
2/29/2016 15:27	God, by His extraordinary Grace, will lead us.
3/1/2016 12:52	I am in the midst of raising my support for the mission the Lord has given me. Month by month, I see Him supply sponsors. It amazes me to see God, by His grace, lead me daily to evangelize the area of the world He has placed me. I found that His grace is enough. The Lord is giving me the grace to witness to His lost sheep. Depending on God's Grace
3/1/2016 13:24	God is calling Israel to return to him by accepting and receiving Jesus as their Messiah. Put away the abominations. The Lord wants us to live in truth and justice and righteousness. So, He can bless us. That is what he's talking about when he says break up the ground and do not sow among thorns. We are to live righteously in God's sight and repent of anything that is not right in His view. By His grace, we will grow to be the people he wants us to be. Take to the Plow.
3/2/2016 4:29	Only through the Blood of the Lord Jesus can we have a clean heart and hands. With Jesus, we will grow to be the men and women God wants us to be.
3/2/2016 14:51	I had many trials while on my Missionary

travels. The time came when my mother was dying. I did all I could to get the money I needed to see her, but she died before I could. The death of my mother while I was in Argentina was extremely hard, but as I said earlier in this book, God sent a messenger through a child and a bird to let me know she was in heaven. I found out later that she was hurt so badly that I did not see her while she was dying; she took me out of her will. I caught hepatitis after eating in a restaurant in Peru. I had to be separated from the home Church for six weeks (actually, that was a blessing, as I was able to get deep into the book of Acts and Revelations). I got so into the mission that I did not give enough time to my wife. She got homesick after being away from her family for ten years. We never had the funds to visit the USA, and our families did not have the funds to visit us. My wife left to see them and didn't come back. When I was able to get back to the States, she wanted to marry a man she'd met. I was broken. Many other difficulties have passed through my path, and the Lord has given me the Grace to pass through all, even still allowing me to have His joy, peace, and love and continue in His work of reaching the world with His Good News. Jesus did not say it would be easy to follow Him; in fact, He told us to take up our cross and follow Him. That the world hated Him, and it would hate us. He also said great peace have they that love His law, and nothing shall offend them. I can say with all truth this is true. I now have a great mission, a wonderful wife and brothers and sisters in the Lord with whom I know I will spend eternity.

3/3/2016 3:58   I can be stubborn, but I keep an eye out and fight against it when it sticks its ugly head up.

3/3/2016 13:11   Some of my family and friends have hardened their hearts and have not received Jesus for who He is. This is extremely hard for me because I know their lives without the Lord in it will lead to destruction and eternal shame, even possibly. Hell, if they never received Jesus as their Lord, master, and Savior.

3/4/2016 12:49   I believe this is something we grow in day by day as we stay faithful in the Lord. Believing vs. Seeing

3/4/2016 13:49   By sharing with others about God's saving Grace. Daily prayer and study of His wonderful Word, we can have extravagant Love.

3/5/2016 1:53   We can always give more of our lives to God.

3/8/2016 14:33   Our Lord, through the Holy Spirit, is faithful to lead and correct us through others and personal guidance. We may need to take a U-turn.

3/9/2016 3:20   Stay close to the Lord and each other.

3/9/2016 4:36   Oh Lord, please give me the grace to do Your will. The strength to follow Your leading and the wisdom to know the way You want me to go and not my own way.

3/10/2016 3:20   Lord help us to hear the Holy Spirit's voice clearly and obey it. Thank you, Lord, for coming to earth and giving us Your mercy. I know I need Your mercy and Grace.

3/10/2016 3:25   Training as many as He gives me to Share Their Faith in The Gospel of Jesus and training others to do the same is my vision and goal.

3/10/2016 16:40   Heaven is a free gift. We do not work for it; we do not deserve it. All humans are sinners and cannot save themselves. God loves us, but he is just and will judge all sins. He sent Jesus to take our sins. We receive the forgiveness of our sins by believing and trusting in Him to do what He said He would do. Save us from our sins.

3/11/2016 4:57   Many times in my life, I did not know what to do, so I ask God to give me a sign. Sometimes He did, and sometimes He did not, but He always worked things out for me.

3/11/2016 13:50   I am so thankful. Without God, His Son Jesus, and The Holy Spirit in my life, I would be an empty vessel living a vain life with nothing to look forward to except death and decade. But instead, I will live in eternity with my Lord in His world, which we call Heaven.

3/13/2016 13:08	I praise God for His merciful way in my life. He has allowed me to be a vessel of the Holy Spirit and has used His Words though me to bring many to know Jesus as Savior. He is allowing me to train others on how to share their faith. Therefore, raising up more laborers for His great harvest.
3/13/2016 13:11	Many people today plan and strive to find ways to gain money and power for all the wrong reasons. Not to serve others, but to rule over others. Jesus said we are to serve one another.
3/13/2016 13:24	Daniel 12:3 says, and they that be wise shall shine as the brightness of the firmament, and they that turn many to righteousness as the stars forever and ever.
3/13/2016 13:25	Teach your children, Daniel 12:3 And they that be wise shall shine as the brightness of the firmament; and they that turn many to righteousness as the stars forever and ever. Sharing and Warning
3/20/2016 0:30	I love using the wonderful evangelism training that I received throughout my life. How Can They Hear?
3/20/2016 0:33	By His grace, I will live as Jesus wants me to, so I will be the sample to the world that He wants me to be.
3/20/2016 0:34	By reading the Bible, His Word, and prayer, we get to know God!

3/21/2016 4:22	If they are not lifting up Jesus and what He did on the Cross, they are false.
3/21/2016 4:23	Let's give up our life as a Living Sacrifice for our King and God Jesus.
3/21/2016 14:18	We can serve in the Lobby of our Church by seeking newcomers and making sure they understand what true saving faith is— trusting in what Jesus did on the cross.
3/23/2016 12:12	I believe that every human being lives in a way that they think is right. We all deceive ourselves. The test, do we desire to be more like Jesus, are we striving to let Jesus live through us, and are we making sure we are telling others about Jesus and how He's leading us to do what we do?
3/23/2016 12:13	John Chapter 15
3/23/2016 12:15	Trusting in Jesus alone for our eternal life in heaven. Then living a life that reflects that.
3/24/2016 18:18	Grief withheld will cause problems until it is dealt with. Concealing Hurt
3/25/2016 12:27	Greed can be defined in many ways; it can be financial or spiritual. Almost every middle-class citizen in America and worldwide could give more, not just speak of the wealthy giving more. If this happened, the world would change. Spiritual greediness is anyone who knows about Jesus and is not sharing the eternal gift that He gave them. This will bring eternal shame. Mar. 8:38

3/26/2016 13:49	Pray as you go.
3/28/2016 12:57	I am not a lazy person, but I could use my time better.
3/28/2016 13:02	Oh my Lord and King, thank you so much for Your loving kindness. This life is truly nothing without You. I Praise Your Name, Jesus. My Father, who is in heaven, thank you for sending Jesus Your Son. Your plan is so righteous, so wonderful, so true. You have shown us we cannot abide by Your righteous Laws, but then You had mercy on us. We need your mercy; we need Your love.
3/28/2016 13:03	There have been times that I have been trapped by my words, and the only way out was by asking for forgiveness.
3/28/2016 13:04	Oh, yes. What a joy it is to see anyone going strong for Jesus and the Kingdom of God.
3/30/2016 4:53	Eating anything with love with those around you is better than anything eating where there is hate.
3/30/2016 4:54	Trust in the Lord with all your heart, and He will guide your path. Pro. 3:5
3/30/2016 4:55	The Word of God has led me into eternal stability
3/30/2016 12:57	There are times when I do well. I realize it is because I am praying that the Lord helps with mercy in my weakness.
3/31/2016 12:33	He that wins souls is wise.

3/31/2016 12:34	When I fail, I have missed God's Will but not His Salvation.
4/4/2016 12:52	We should be trusting Him to supply all our needs as He said He would. Both Spiritually and Physically in Everything
4/4/2016 12:57	So much going on, I am setting priorities and going step by step in prayer.
4/4/2016 13:29	To reap the harvest of God takes getting your hands dirty at times.
4/4/2016 13:30	Eternal life began when we received Jesus.
4/4/2016 13:31	Wisdom comes from the Word of God; Jesus is the Word. John Chapter 1
4/5/2016 13:07	It is all about my Lord Jesus whom we preach.
4/5/2016 13:08	Jesus said not to call Him good. He said only God is good. Hold On.
4/5/2016 13:09	Many people need to hear the Gospel. Faithful Preaching
4/5/2016 13:09	Idle Christianity is dead Christianity.
4/5/2016 13:24	Paul made it clear that God told us to work. You Shall Not Eat 2 Th. 3:10
4/5/2016 13:32	When I gave my life to Jesus 46 years ago, my father and mother forsook me. My mother took me out of her will and only wrote or called me once or twice in the 17 or so years that I was in Argentina, Brazil, Bolivia, Peru, and Spain. I wrote to them frequently. I praise

the Lord that my father now has bonded with me and that he knows he is going to heaven. I found out that my mother received the Lord before her death. I am so thankful.

4/6/2016 12:11	Thy Word have I hid in my heart that I might not sin against thee. Psa. 119:11 Trust in the Lord with all your heart, and He shall direct thy path. Prov. 3:5
4/6/2016 12:14	Pray always. Lord, you know that I truly want to be led by you, because when I'm led of You, I will be more like You.
4/8/2016 2:30	I love it when God sends His Holy Spirit, who leads me and shows me what He wants to be done and what He wants me to do. Then He does it. I just float along for the ride and watch Him do miracles in others' lives.
4/8/2016 2:31	Blessed is the man who walks not in the counsel of the wicked. Pas. 1 Oh, the Joys!
4/8/2016 2:32	We are not our own, so we must obey our Master and Lord. The High Cost
4/8/2016 2:33	1 Cor. 13 To the Pure...
4/13/2016 4:39	Follow the Leader, Jesus
4/13/2016 4:40	I only wish Jesus was coming back for us today. Looking forward to the coming of the Lord in the heavens.
4/13/2016 4:40	Don't Scoff
4/13/2016 4:41	Thank our Lord for His Holy Spirit, who guides us into all truth.

4/13/2016 4:42	, I want to become more like Christ. We need to witness. John 4
4/13/2016 4:44	The wicked crave the world righteousness, which is always fading. We seek first the Kingdom of God, which is eternal.
4/14/2016 2:20	We live in a world where we always have to be aware as it will push us into saying those little lies, which are even worse as they can be hidden.
4/18/2016 3:50	By not working the work of God, they have destroyed the world.
4/18/2016 3:51	Many wealthy have fallen, and their wealth could not save them. Security of Money?
4/23/2016 0:07	Keep Listening to the small still voice of the Holy Spirit, and you will see Him do incredible things.
4/23/2016 0:09	Most of the time, I Think through things. Sometimes I slip, but God is very gracious towards me.
4/27/2016 11:40	There is no escape for liars. It always catches up to them and even us.
4/27/2016 13:15	I love sharing the Gospel Join, the Family of God.
4/28/2016 13:41	We all like to receive comforting words, so let us give them.

5/4/2016 4:29	I know I have been called to call out to all Christians, telling them we must find the lost. Praying they do not reject the Saving grace of God through Jesus. God First
5/4/2016 4:33	The wisdom of our Lord is both a gift and something to seek after. Each day that goes by, I come to understand how much I need God. Ask for It!
5/6/2016 13:51	We need to share the Gospel with as many as possible, then the Holy Spirit does the winning. Growing Populations
5/6/2016 13:54	Our Hearts Never Left You Lord, but our words to others have. Jesus gives us the boldness to tell everyone about You.
5/6/2016 13:56	We need to awaken the Church and tell them to reach the world with the Gospel of our Lord Jesus. Your God-Given Job
5/6/2016 13:56	By yielding to the Precious Holy Spirit, He will give us words of love.
5/6/2016 13:57	It is impossible to be two-faced and be walking with Jesus.
5/7/2016 18:49	, I desire to see Jesus. Not that I am worthy, I yearn as all creation for the coming of our maker and Lord. Thief in the Night
5/7/2016 18:52	In this world, I want to be closer to Jesus, but the needs and cares of this life and my weakness hold me back. When I am with Him, all will change.

5/12/2016 1:12	I am excited, Lord come soon.
5/12/2016 11:30	Jesus is the Light of the world.
5/12/2016 11:33	Anything we put before the Lord is an idol. Therefore all humankind has an idol or idols. By His grace, we are saved.
5/24/2016 12:02	Jesus lived a sinless life then took all the sins of the world.
5/24/2016 12:07	God is above our understanding. He is all-consuming, all-powerful, and wonderful.
5/24/2016 12:12	We all want deep Love, so we all want God. 1 John 4:8
5/24/2016 12:13	If I were judged by my sin, I would not get into heaven, but because I receive the gift of God through Jesus, I will. Free Gift
5/24/2016 12:14	All that I see in this world's natural creation is evidence enough for a Creator.
5/24/2016 12:15	All of His Bible amazes me even after 46 years of studying. It still amazes me.
5/24/2016 12:17	Heaven is free. I share this with as many people as the Holy Spirit tells me to.
5/24/2016 12:18	Get Up and Go for God daily.
5/24/2016 12:19	Jesus is the Key to Freedom
5/24/2016 12:21	If I stay in God's Word, the Bible and keep clean from sins, then I know our Lord's Holy Spirit will guide me. Avoid the Immoral
5/24/2016 12:22	The Bible is the building Blocks for Wisdom

5/24/2016 12:37	Life after death is real.
5/24/2016 12:40	Testing the Spirits is important. If they do not speak of Jesus, they are of the Devil.
5/24/2016 12:43	By His grace, I try to stay close to Jesus, but being a man, I still miss the mark sometimes.
5/24/2016 12:46	It is wise to pray always.
5/24/2016 12:48	My only comfort is that Jesus paid the price of my sins.
5/24/2016 12:50	When someone dies, it gives us comfort knowing we would see them again if they knew Jesus. It will make us sad as if someone we love is going on a long journey. We will be seeing other believers in heaven.
5/24/2016 12:51	Thank you, Jesus You are our Rock.
5/24/2016 12:52	We trust in Jesus alone for our entrance to heaven.
5/24/2016 12:53	The beautiful sky is the all mighty God showing Himself.
5/24/2016 12:54	We came alive so that we could live in Him.
5/24/2016 12:55	By His Grace and for His Glory He will give us Wisdom and Righteousness.
5/24/2016 12:56	It is not easy understanding God in the hard times, at least until He reveals His wisdom.
5/24/2016 12:57	When we believe in His death for our sins, we believe in our eternal life with Him.
5/24/2016 13:00	Many are called, but few are chosen, by His

grace I am. Called to Salvation

5/24/2016 13:01	Most people are running after the things of the world and leaving God behind. Do not Be a World-Lover
5/24/2016 13:02	We are commanded to love one another if we are Jesus's disciples. So, let's Love
5/25/2016 12:54	Our Almighty God and our Lord Jesus and Holy Spirit deserve Glory Forever
5/25/2016 12:56	Seeking wisdom is when I seek the leading of the Holy Spirit. If He is leading me, then I am wise.
5/30/2016 3:18	We as Christians must be led by the Holy Spirit if we want to accomplish anything
5/30/2016 3:19	I want more communication through constant moment by moment prayer.
5/30/2016 3:20	The still small voice of the Holy Spirit will guide us if we listen
5/30/2016 3:22	The witness of God's Power is all around us
5/30/2016 3:26	Human love without God is passing. Only love connected to God and others through Jesus gets into His kingdom. John 14:6
5/30/2016 3:28	It is a horrible thing to not be right with God
5/30/2016 3:28	Through His Word, the Bible, and Prayer, we hear the voice of God.
5/30/2016 12:33	Lord, I need Your wisdom, Your guidance. As without You, I am nothing. Without You, I am

but a worm, flesh, and blood that comes to nothing but death. With You, I can do all things. I need You the Wise Conqueror

5/31/2016 0:06	By Your grace Jesus, I will be a sample, not a sermon.
6/2/2016 4:44	We need to work hard and be competent workers showing that we are children of our Father in heaven.
6/2/2016 4:44	By His Grace the king's heart is moved
6/2/2016 4:45	Without a vision, the people perish
6/2/2016 4:47	If I'm being led by our Lord precious Holy Spirit, then all will be as planned
6/2/2016 12:06	His Word have I hid in my heart, so I don't sin against Him.
6/3/2016 12:04	We are in a war to win the world for Jesus. I need to keep a clear vision of that goal.
6/3/2016 12:05	Jesus King from ages past and present
6/4/2016 3:17	Sharing the Gospel with everyone to Feed the hungry souls
6/13/2016 12:09	, I claim and stand on the truth of the Bible.
6/14/2016 12:10	Well done, my faithful servant, enter into the joy of the Lord.
6/14/2016 12:12	Every day, it is a battle between self and unselfishness, between my will and God's will. By His grace, I will do His will.
6/14/2016 12:14	Our God and Lord is the maker of the

universe, and He deserves all honor and Glory; anything less is robbing Him of what is His.

6/15/2016 14:39   , I am humbled and truly grateful for how our Lord is allowing me to serve Him. Thanks & Praise

6/15/2016 14:41   Only Jesus knows my heart, and only Jesus has the mercy and grace to love me anyway.

6/16/2016 3:42   If a person really knows Jesus, they will grow towards Him. Not lip service

6/16/2016 13:05   Do What's Just

6/17/2016 11:51   I like to help as it is showing God's love.

6/17/2016 12:34   We will be continuing to be transformed till the day we go back to be with Jesus. To be transformed into the likeness of Jesus is a never-ending task.

6/20/2016 12:13   By His Grace, with His Mercy He will guide us through. Listen and Do.

6/20/2016 12:14   Understanding our own soul, we see our weaknesses and sins. This allows us to be in the right position to Worship God.

6/20/2016 12:17   In our group prayers, we pray for each other, with personal prayer. I need to reach into the center of my being, something I am still working on.

6/20/2016 12:25   We are to teach and lead others, though the Word. Win those to whom God leads us, and do His will, which is the go into the streets and compel them to come into His wedding feast.

6/20/2016 12:27   By His grace, I see Him daily, in His Word, and in my continual communications with our Lord throughout the day.

6/20/2016 12:28   I strive to finish the work He has given me to do. Finding Life's Purpose.

6/23/2016 12:32   Giving praise to Jesus for everything.

6/23/2016 12:33   Jesus is the only good thing I have; without Him, I am nothing.

6/23/2016 12:33   God's Word and prayer are my strength

6/23/2016 12:35   , I want to walk closer and closer in my relationship with Jesus.

6/23/2016 12:37   I can give more, more money, more time, more of myself. By His grace, I will become more of Him and less of me. Wisdom   with Wealth

6/23/2016 12:40   Training Pastors, Church leadership, and laypeople how to share their faith is my goal and desire. The harvest of God is around us daily, and there are so few laborers. My calling is to seek and find them, then train laborers for our Lord's waiting harvest. It's a Big Job

6/23/2016 12:42   Man's ways are not God's ways. As the heavens are higher than the earth, so is

God's ways higher than man's ways.

6/25/2016 1:40	Jesus knew that the Jewish leaders wanted to trap Him, but He still told it as it was. We are to give unto Cesar what is his and unto God what is Gods.
6/25/2016 1:46	There are many parts to the Church. We need the Church, but one thing I've found is that the majority of all denominational Churches have left their first love. They have left Jesus' first love, "the lost." The majority are not training disciples as Jesus did, and these days Church members have no desire to reach God's lost sheep.
6/25/2016 1:47	Grace is an ever-growing area of my life.
6/25/2016 12:10	When a person has a relationship with Jesus, their lives change, sometimes fast, sometimes slowly but always growing even if it is very little. When God's seed is sown, it will grow in God's timing.
6/27/2016 13:56	I am starting to assist the Evangelism Trainings in Spanish in Churches. Using the gift of the Spanish language.
6/27/2016 13:57	I have a list of people I pray for. This doesn't limit me to pray for others.
6/27/2016 13:59	What is my ambition, to be useful to God for eternity.
6/28/2016 11:51	He is my Creator, My God, and my Father. I am a son who has much to learn. By His grace alone, I am saved.

6/28/2016 12:38	A faithful follower is a person who follows by faith. A person who seeks our Lord's perfect will, and as they follow, they obey His last command, which is to go and make disciples of all nations. This means here in the USA also. We must be prepared to share the Gospel with all whom our Lord leads us
6/29/2016 12:18	Jesus showed me His Love by taking my sins, and I must share this truth with others.
6/29/2016 12:19	A fool does not understand that drinking poison will kill them, and unless they take the antidote, they will die. Also, if their sins aren't forgiven, they will face eternal death.
6/30/2016 12:55	I received Jesus when I was 22 and served God full time until I was 43. 4 years in the States and Canada and 17 years as a Missionary in South America and Spain. I ran a business for 17 years. During that time, I went to Church but did little for our Lord. Now for the last six years, I have been serving God full time again. I want to serve Jesus until my last breath, then for eternity in heaven.
6/30/2016 12:56	And they that be wise will win many to our Lord and will shine as the stars above.
7/2/2016 13:02	Lean not on your own understanding, but in all my ways, trust in Jesus.
7/2/2016 13:06	Almost every day, I give tracts out, and by the grace of Jesus, I am sometimes able to lead

people to know Him.

7/2/2016 13:11	I do reproof people in love when I believe our Lord leads me to do so.
7/4/2016 13:32	Share the Gospel and then share how one must study to show themselves approved unto God.
7/6/2016 12:08	Tell the truth with humility and love.
7/6/2016 12:10	As I get older and this old body gets weaker, I look forward, even more, to being in heaven, in God's timing, of course.
7/6/2016 12:13	Love God with all your heart and your neighbors as yourself. I'm working towards living these commands more every day.
7/6/2016 12:14	God loves you no matter who you are, where you live, what your language is, what sex you are or what you look like
7/7/2016 12:05	I try Teaching the Wise, those who want to know about God
7/10/2016 18:58	The Law is for the lawbreaker
7/12/2016 3:44	We realize how weak; we are when we look at Jesus.
7/12/2016 3:45	All Praise and Glory to God
7/12/2016 12:08	The older I get, the more I understand that our Lord and God is to be respected, loved, feared. I desire to do His will to reach His lost sheep. Fear = Respect

7/13/2016 13:37	I am so grateful for Jesus. I know I am not worthy of being called God's child, but I am His child because of Jesus.
7/13/2016 13:42	By His grace, my pride, will stay out of the way. Strength in Submission
7/14/2016 12:52	Lay not up for yourself treasures on earth as they do not last, layup treasures in heaven because they are eternal.
7/14/2016 12:52	I love sharing the Gospel everywhere I go.
7/15/2016 14:28	We are one body. All true believers, regardless of doctrine, they are my brothers in Christ. We must live this way so we can show the world the love of God through Jesus. One Body
7/15/2016 14:30	I always need the grace of God in the moment of the trial
7/20/2016 12:08	I fight with both thinking I know more and thinking I am not as smart. This, in no way, is something that stays with me as long as I know I am who God made me to be. I try not to allow this thought to overwhelm me.
7/20/2016 12:10	I enjoy prayer in the morning and seeking to communicate with Him during the day. Studying the Word and giving out Christian tracts, sharing my faith as often as possible during my daily activities.
7/20/2016 12:11	Have peace with God and man.
7/20/2016 12:13	Wisdom guides with the guidelines of God.

He that wins souls is wise. Strength is good when used for the Lord.

7/20/2016 12:16	Trusting in Christ alone for our Salvation and living acquitted of sins
7/20/2016 12:49	I think we will be seeking for wisdom for the rest of our lives and for eternity.
7/20/2016 12:52	I am blessed to go to Church's and give trainings on how to share our faith as a way of life. Equipping God's People
7/20/2016 12:52	Falling to Your Knees Daily is a good thing to do. We will fall on our knees when we see His incredible glory.
7/22/2016 12:12	Prayer is how we have open communication with Jesus. Studying the Bible, God's Word is how we get to know Him. Worshiping our Creator, God opens Fellowship with Him. Sharing Him from our heart brings others to know Him. Becoming a witness to others is obeying Him.
7/22/2016 12:13	Training others on how to share their faith is the highest calling of God in this world.
7/22/2016 12:15	God is love. If we lift Him up, all men will come unto Him. Love can be shown in many ways, and there are many atheists who are kind and even loving, but they are doing it for their own glory, not Jesus', so it's temporary glory of men. We have to lift up Jesus. As His love is the only eternal love, all other love is fleeting.

7/23/2016	12:38	My brothers and sisters in the Lord and those who support His mission are following the path that Jesus led. Pastors and churches, jobs are to help get dedicated brothers and sisters to win the lost for the Lord.
7/23/2016	12:39	I am so thankful, incredibly thankful, for the people that pray for me. It just breaks my heart and humbles me and encourages me all the same time.
7/26/2016	12:31	Love always gives.
7/26/2016	12:39	We are what we eat both physically and Spiritually. No one has obtained perfection; therefore, no one can always be right all the time.
7/29/2016	4:20	They see boldness and conviction when we talk about our Lord and King Jesus, all this comes through the Holy Spirit. Acts 1:8
7/29/2016	12:39	I have been told that I'm too happy. I've learned to live in the joy of the Lord
7/29/2016	12:43	So true, I know Jesus loves me as the Bible says. My heart's desire is to walk with Him daily.
7/29/2016	12:44	Sharing the Gospel is sharing wisdom.
7/29/2016	12:46	I do my best to understand others and then try to lead them to the answers that are in the Bible.
7/31/2016	3:30	His strength is a Safe Fortress
7/31/2016	3:44	Seeking His will.

7/31/2016 3:46	By Jesus's blood and His blood alone, can we get into heaven.
7/31/2016 12:08	If it is according to what the Word of God says, it's True
8/1/2016 14:16	Our Lord's ways are higher than our ways, and He is always right.
8/2/2016 2:32	I know He has made me for His use, and I marvel when He uses me in ways I just didn't know were possible.
8/3/2016 2:13	How pleasant it is for brothers to live together in unity.
8/3/2016 2:14	When my old ways of life come back, I don't like it.
8/4/2016 1:27	Faith in the power of God's Word changes lives.
8/4/2016 1:29	By His grace, I will stand on God's ground daily.
8/5/2016 13:04	, I seek Jesus, and I am trying to walk being led by Him. I am trying to speak the things He wants me to speak. When I do these things, I am strong in God's power.
8/6/2016 12:05	Pray for Your Pastors.
8/6/2016 12:06	My mother passed away at 63. She was sending me strong religious materials so by His grace she is saved, my father and I talked about the gift of salvation, by our Lord's grace, he was saved.

8/7/2016 12:42   If I were fighting this spiritual war alone, I would be afraid, but I know Jesus has won the battle, and as long as I stay close to Him, I'm covered.

8/10/2016 14:04   Lord, please help me to reach others and help others to reach others too.

8/10/2016 14:06   It humbles me daily to know I did nothing to deserve my relationship with God, but I desire a communication with God daily.

8/10/2016 14:09   We are God's family, and we need to act like it.

8/10/2016 14:11   I really know that God has called me to reach out to others and by his grace and inspire them to reach out to others with His Gospel.

8/10/2016 14:16   God is my Father in heaven. He loves me more than anyone on earth. He knows me better than I know myself. He guides me and leads me when I listen to His Holy Spirits' small, quiet voice. It's meek but incredible and magnificently strong. It brings me to tears sometimes.

8/11/2016 12:00   Psalms 100   The Place to Start

8/11/2016 12:21   God is true to His promises in both the old and new testament because God is a True and faithful God who has told us He loves us so much that He came and showed us. He personally died on the cross in the person of Jesus for all the sins of the world. Thank you,

Jesus.

8/12/2016 12:24	Psalms 133 Christ's Body

8/13/2016 14:24   Every day, I pray to walk closer and hear more from the Holy Spirit

8/13/2016 14:26   I know God loves us and wants what is best for us.

8/16/2016 12:12   God is present in many ways, but I feel His Holy Spirit most of all when I am sharing with others about His love and Salvation.

8/16/2016 12:14   Our Lord is already pouring out His Spirit onto the earth. By His grace, we will receive it.

8/16/2016 12:17   Our Lord's voice and His wisdom comes through the Holy Spirits' small still voice. If we listen and obey, He will keep us.

8/16/2016 12:25   Jesus said to go to the highways and byways that His house would be full. That He loves the world so much that He sent His Son to die for us.

8/17/2016 12:33   God, the Son Jesus, and the Holy Spirit are all one. They all were there in the creation of the world because they are one.

8/18/2016 12:53   Many Pastors are feeding the flock, but not training them to share the full Gospel with the waiting world. By God's grace, He will use my life to train disciples. People who are willing to lift their voices for Jesus.

8/18/2016 12:57   We were created to love and adore God, and

His love is always waiting for us. Since the beginning of time till today and into eternity.

8/22/2016 3:06	It always comforts my heart to know Jesus loves me no matter what. It is up to me to allow His love in. The Grace of Jesus
8/22/2016 3:14	I know the Lord has His plans in each life, and He knows what is best. Even when we are sick, and He does not heal us. He knows what we need to go through to mold us into the eternal persons He is creating us to be. He knows best. He loves us and has a perfect plan for every moment of each life.
8/22/2016 3:16	Prayer is a great way to start the day.
8/22/2016 3:18	Through prayer and faithful study of God's Word, we can resist the enemy.
8/22/2016 3:30	God is love, so without love, we are lost and walking in the darkness.
8/22/2016 3:32	True love always wants to lift up others.
8/22/2016 14:15	To bring praise and glory to God daily is a moment by moment decision. By His grace, I will do this as much as possible and more and more each day in Jesus' name.
8/23/2016 3:54	My goal is to daily seek the knowledge of God, the Creator of Earth, heaven, and everything. I'm seeking to grow in understanding of the reasoning of why He sent his Son to give mercy, grace, and peace. God is there at any time of the day or night when we reach out to Him. This is

better than riches and glory.

8/24/2016 13:17	Understanding that God is real and loves us is of eternal importance. He is our creator, and we need to seek Him to find His will for our lives. Sad to say, most people live all their lives without finding God, then die being separated from Him for eternity.
8/24/2016 13:22	Loving God leads us to the true meaning of life and helps us to love others. Jesus taught us how to do this. We just need to study His word and make it part of us then live it.
8/25/2016 12:53	I must truly humbly say, I am led of the Holy Spirit often. He allows me to find God's lost sheep continually. It is truly humbling to know a sinner like me can be used by God Almighty. Praise His Name forever. Thank Him for coming to earth to give us this connection as it was in the Garden of Eden. Even when we are weak in sin, His love never fails. Understanding the Bible
8/26/2016 11:48	Growing in God's everlasting Love is the goal of every Christ-follower. This is an incredible challenge and impossible to accomplish alone. We need the Holy Spirit to assist us in walking towards this goal. All things are possible for God. It takes God through Jesus and His precious Holy Spirit to make us the persons He desires us to be. Active Love
8/27/2016 13:07	We can trust in Jesus. He Does NOT Change
8/27/2016 13:11	Jesus is our Creator because He created all

things with God, our Father. The Gospel of John Chapter 1 says, In the Beginning, the Word and the Word was Jesus.

8/27/2016 13:14	Reading and meditating on His Word; the Bible allows His Precious Holy Spirit to flow through me on to others while I share the Gospel with them. When we pour out, He pours in, and we can never outpour Him. Thank you, Jesus. Unskilled Speaker.
8/28/2016 12:55	Every Christian needs to share about their first love Jesus, not just those who have the gift of Evangelism. You know for a Reason
8/28/2016 13:29	God our Creator, the Creator of all things, has His reason for everything that happens, although we do not understand, He has the eternal vision we don't. We must put all things in His hands.
8/31/2016 11:43	When someone corrects you, it is in the hope that you will go straight. God has corrected me so many times it would take a small book to write them down. Accepting Discipline
8/31/2016 11:46	Jesus is happy when we love Him and do His will. He is our Beloved.
8/31/2016 13:26	I have so much to improve. I am far from the finished product of God's will for my life. His grace will get me there.
9/2/2016 16:31	My heart's desire is to bring Joy and Hope to as many as I can.
9/3/2016 13:32	Jesus is the head over the Church (us), and

He wants to fill us up with His Spirit.

9/3/2016 13:34	We are His disciples, and when people look at us, they judge Jesus.
9/5/2016 12:20	Let us seek the lost and help others to do the same. When we pour out, He pours in, and we will never outpour Him. To keep God's people fresh, they Have to pour out to others, first with His Gospel and then with their works.
9/5/2016 12:22	Division is one of Satan's first methods in his goal of winning in the spiritual war. His motto is dividing and conquering. We cannot allow it to take place in our ranks.
9/5/2016 12:26	I do my best to live the love of God, with my siblings who live in other States.
9/5/2016 12:28	Greater Love has no man than this, that he (or she) lay down their life (or pride when they share the Gospel) for their friends.
9/9/2016 2:34	God's love was shown through Jesus
9/9/2016 2:37	I strive to be more sensitive to the Holy Spirit day by day.
9/9/2016 2:40	When I allow the Holy Spirit to use me, by first listening, then doing what He says, then I know He's with me... John 15
9/9/2016 2:41	By His grace, we are learning how to treat others as we would be treated.
9/9/2016 2:41	Trying to get in a closer communication with God every day.

9/12/2016 17:32	I do my best to show my wife God's love every day. We tell each other most days, "did I say I love you today? "
9/12/2016 17:34	On my business Web site I tell all clients, the jobs not done until you say I Love it. I live up to this saying.
9/12/2016 17:35	I know God's hands are guiding all things, but at times it is a challenge to work through some issues
9/12/2016 17:40	I seek to Live Together in love, and by the Grace of our Lord Jesus, I will live His love more and more till the day I go back to be with Him.
9/12/2016 17:41	Trouble will find you in this life, but by staying in the Word and seeking to stay close to the Holy Spirit, we will overcome it.
9/12/2016 17:46	Being corrected can be challenging, but it is definitely more manageable when it is given with love and compassion. It is much harder when the correction is given in a harsh, unloving spirit. Let us try to follow this rule with our children
9/12/2016 17:59	I have asked for our Lord's Grace to be on my Dad as he goes through the process of finding a bleed in his intestines.
9/13/2016 12:31	Another gift of children, they can carry on for the Lord when you are gone and take care of you when you are old.
9/14/2016 13:00	Christ Cares incredibly

9/15/2016 13:03	We are the house of God; each one of us is part of the Church. We need to abide in the Love of God.
9/16/2016 12:23	Accepting advice from the leadership and my wife is to my benefit.
9/16/2016 12:24	Jesus said, let not your heart be troubled, you believe in God believe also in Me. He came to earth to save you and to open a channel of communication with God.
9/17/2016 1:15	God has made us, and He loves us as His children.
9/18/2016 11:58	We are to be humble and have mutual submission while serving everyone.
9/18/2016 12:14	I have constant prayers for Susie, my wife.
9/19/2016 2:54	Good Godly counsel is better than listening to your friends.
9/19/2016 13:59	We as the body of Christ need to be one. I am an Evangelist, and by God's grace, He will use my life to raise up many others to cry out to Him.
9/20/2016 13:02	I praise God that He has called me to share my faith daily. Sowing seeds of His Word, which waters, prunes, plants, and sometimes reaps in His harvest.
9/20/2016 13:04	I give thanks for my mentors.
9/21/2016 12:06	I genuinely enjoy bringing joy to others and bringing the King of Joy to them.

9/21/2016 12:20	I feel that God loves me and knows me better than I know myself. I feel unworthy to be called a child of God, but I know He loves me anyway. I know the best way I can show my gratitude is to seek His will and help others to do the same.
9/22/2016 12:18	My mom died when I was serving Jesus as a Missionary in Argentina. I tried to raise the funds to see her before she died, but could not, so she died thinking I did not care. She prayed with me, but not much change took place in her life. She said she submitted to Jesus a few years later. I thank the Lord I will see her again. My father died at 89. I stayed in the USA after a visit home from the mission field, when finding he was having open-heart surgery. I chose to stay in the USA to take care of him. I went to his house a minimum of three times a week to help care for him from 1993 until March 28, 2018, when he died. He would tell everyone how much he loved me—giving Your Parents Joy.
9/23/2016 12:45	On That Day that amazing day when we see Jesus coming in the clouds, oh yeah, looking so forward to that day.
9/23/2016 12:46	When I see young men and women get excited about sharing their faith with happy faces, it gives me such Joy.
9/30/2016 15:13	I am so unworthy and incredibly thankful at the same time.

9/30/2016 15:14	My greatest Joy currently is seeing young Christian students at the University of Maryland sharing the Gospel by my side.
10/1/2016 13:28	I believe Churches are giving, but most do not really share the Gospel when they give. I mean the full understanding of what Jesus did.
10/1/2016 13:29	The cause for Joy comes from living a Christ-like life.
10/1/2016 13:31	As life goes by, day by day, I see what a sinful person I am compared to Jesus and our great God. It seems the closer we get, the more we see His perfection. I see so clearly that without the mercy of Jesus, I will in no wise get into heaven. Joy = J for Jesus than O for Others then Y for You. I am filled with thankfulness for the Holy Spirit, and the Joy He Gives me.
10/1/2016 13:37	When I realize that everything is God's and I live that way, I am filled with JOY
10/1/2016 13:39	Oh yeah... When God's Holy Spirit pours through me, it is Incredible. It amazes me that He can use a man like me at times. Experiencing the Love of Christ
10/1/2016 13:41	We can renew our thoughts and attitudes only by His abounding grace.
10/1/2016 13:43	Living a righteous life is more caught than taught. Training the Younger followers.
10/1/2016 13:45	God knew what Moses was called to do. I

believe everyone that believes has a calling. The question is, do we choose to do it?

10/1/2016 13:46	Every knee will bow, and every tongue confesses that Jesus is Lord when He returns to earth. This is a fact. All people of the world need to believe Jesus as King and Lord before Jesus returns. It will be too late then.
10/1/2016 13:50	As I step into each day, I love seeing the Holy Spirit guide me, and if I listen to His leading, I see God move in lives as I talk to them about Jesus. This is a gift, a wonderful gift that all God's children have. The question is, will we use it.
10/3/2016 0:05	Since Jesus came to give the world a way back to God. God made it the only way to get to Him. God opened a door for all to get in. There are no other doors. Should we continue to strive to live the ten commandments, of course, but no one could live all the law. God always would show His mercy in the old testament too. It was always through His forgiveness. Now that our Creator put Himself in the physical body of a man and died for all, it changed the way to mercy. It is now through Jesus and Jesus alone that God pours His mercy to us. It is a free gift to all who believe and receive it.
10/3/2016 0:06	God looks at the heart, not the language or color or financial position. God Has No Favorites.

10/4/2016 12:57	All bearers have been broken that separated us from God's Holy Spirit when Jesus came.
10/4/2016 12:58	Evangelism is also training Christians to be disciples so they can do what we were commanded to do. To fulfill the Great Commission by sharing with the world about Jesus.
10/7/2016 12:11 are.	, Jesus knows what true Justice and mercy
10/7/2016 12:15	Without Jesus's sacrifice, we would be lost and far from the Father. Truly it is by grace.
10/7/2016 12:17	When I allow myself to be led by the Holy Spirit, my actions show a story of discipleship. When I am not, It is not. We are known by our actions.
10/7/2016 12:29	According to the questions in the Standout book test, I'm a stimulator first and a connector second. I focus on people. I'm an emotional person. I get my strength from other people. I'm a good host, and I make my presence felt and build energize the room, I have a magnetic quality, I have an acute awareness that that other people are looking at me, I pay attention to my appearance. This is what the standout test says. It is humbling to think of some of the actual talents it says I have as gifts. I am seeking to use them for the Glory of God.
10/7/2016 12:30	I am so happy I trust in Jesus; it gives me such joy, so much Joy.

10/9/2016 12:47	We, as humans, must fight pride daily.
10/10/2016 13:12	Stand for Justice by His Grace and with His mercy.
10/10/2016 13:13	Lord help us to be sensitive to others.
10/10/2016 13:15	Lord, please help me to always seek Your guidance through the leading of Your Holy Spirit.
10/10/2016 13:16	Marital advice, take time to listen to your spouse.
10/12/2016 12:30	Every day, we commit some disobedience towards God, we all do. I have a state of mind to keep my mind and heart on Jesus, and a desire to hear and be led of the Holy Spirit, on a moment by moment bases, but I still fail. By His grace, I will grow in this area.
10/12/2016 12:32	Whether I eat or drink or whatever I do, I try to do it all to the Glory of God.
10/13/2016 17:38	By His Grace, I want to always be an Encourager for my sponsors and trainees and others.
10/14/2016 12:30	He wants us to serve the Church. Jesus says, "I Want You!"
10/14/2016 12:34	The only truly reliable person anywhere is Jesus, but I praise God for my wife Susie, the many friends, and supporters that the Lord has sent my way. I am humbled and incredibly grateful for them as without them. I could not do what Jesus is leading me to

do. Train disciples, who are Truly Reliable.

10/15/2016 15:17	One thing I know, I need God's everlasting love and mercy. God Never Changes!
10/15/2016 15:18	Love Never Fails. A King's Protection
10/18/2016 13:16	My parents divorced when I was eight. My father married a woman who had no idea how to love children. I rebelled, and for the next seven years, I had a very difficult childhood. Now I have come to understand how hard it was for them to have four children.
10/18/2016 13:18	I try to do things the right way, but there have been times that I have taken a shortcut to get prosperity. Thankful the Lord has had mercy on me.
10/18/2016 13:20	Serve others in all things. I believe this is the best way to end any conflict. I know this to be true; I cannot say I always live it out.
10/18/2016 13:26	I am so thankful for the Word of God. It feeds me and comforts me.
10/18/2016 13:28	By talking to God using the magnificent Name of Jesus, seeking Him, seeking to be led by Him, studying His Word, and telling others about what Jesus did for them. I am pleasing God
10/18/2016 13:32	, I reach out to people I meet daily with the Gospel. This is the best we can offer anyone. Praise our Lord Jesus that I am able to financially give to the Church and other

organizations with my tithe.

10/19/2016 12:43   I remember as if it was yesterday the joy I had for every letter that came from home. During the three years in the Navy, the 17 years living overseas as a Missionary, and now receiving letters, text, and emails.

10/20/2016 3:13   The Holy Spirit gives us the desire to share about God's saving grace of salvation through Jesus Christ with others.

10/21/2016 14:29   I know submitting to each other is something I must continually work on.

10/21/2016 14:33   Some Churches have great outreaches helping the needy and planting Churches and feeding their congregations with the Word of God. There is something I am concerned with, though. 1. I would like to see a better method of training their members as a method of sharing the Gospel as they give.

10/22/2016 15:45   I have a mindset to be loyal, I believe I am but knowing that we all fall short at times, I repent when I think I have fallen short.

10/23/2016 12:48   We need to expose darkness by His grace.

10/24/2016 1:20   I encourage the timid to share the Gospel, as they will reach people who I cannot.

10/25/2016 14:00   We must seek those who will hear while we can. Our time is short.

10/26/2016 2:02   I know what is right, but I still fight some of my old ways "the old man" I know I am right when I'm sharing the Gospel with another person.

10/27/2016 2:46 Preaching, teaching, fellowship, inspiration, and vision are great, but two things I would like to see more of. 1. In this election, we need to help the Congregation see that God's Word does not promote abortions or Marriage equality or same-sex marriage. These are sins like spouse abuse, alcoholics', hate-mongers, and thieves and adulterers, to name a few other sins. God loves all humanity. Therefore, we His creation will be happier if we follow His commands. We know God has used some interesting men before in the history of the world, so if the person stands with the Bible, even if he doesn't live it as well as we would like to see, we need to vote for that person. 2. I would really like to see more Evangelism taught, but not only taught, modeled in the Church.

10/27/2016 2:46 A healthy, growing Godly Church does Evangelism.

10/27/2016 13:05 Having wholehearted Love is the goal for a Christian.

10/30/2016 1:32 Jesus told us not to lay up treasures on earth, but to lay up treasures in Heaven.

10/30/2016 1:35 I am learning how to be led by God's Holy Spirit, so by His grace, I can do His work. The work that He has for me to do on earth.

10/30/2016 1:39	I know that no greater love has any man than this, that he lay down his life for his friends. Sharing the Gospel is laying it down daily too.
10/30/2016 1:41	Gods Word leads us, feeds us, protects us, and gives us comfort.
10/30/2016 12:51	I know that all things work for the good to those who love the Lord, sad to say in the midst of some things, I must remind myself after that fact.
11/1/2016 3:43	Stay Alert and continue growing in the areas you need to grow in every day.
11/1/2016 3:45	Vengeance is Mine, says the Lord. I ask for mercy for those who need to repent.
11/1/2016 3:46	Our bodies will be raised. Revelations 21 and 22 says they will. Amazing.
11/2/2016 0:26	Anytime I see something good come out of me, I just must Praise the Lord.
11/2/2016 12:17	Love Equals Time. Beautiful, Lord, please put this truth in the heart of men and women. In Jesus Name
11/3/2016 14:27	I try to stop and look for God's hand everywhere.
11/3/2016 14:30	We are the Church. We are commanded to love one another so that the world can see God, and He can be Glorified.

11/3/2016 14:31	When I am weak, He is strong.
11/4/2016 13:23	We all go through different sufferings, some physical, some spiritual, and some mentally. Suffering for Christ is when we stand for God's Kingdom, no matter what is thrown at us.
11/4/2016 14:40	I am so thankful for His constant Love and Mercy. The One Who Never Changes
11/5/2016 15:10	A Gentle Answer turns away wrath. Something I am working on.
11/6/2016 13:17	Eagerly giving is the only giving God blesses.
11/8/2016 4:37	I lived by faith as a Missionary in South America for 17 years. Jesus always filled the needs of the Mission. I have been living in the US for 23 years, and I have come to where my needs are different. Wealth Disappears
11/8/2016 4:38	Others see us, as the disciples of Christ, as an end sample of Jesus.
11/8/2016 15:55	Lord help us to know where and who to give to so that our gifts lift up Your Kingdom and Glory. The Balance of Giving
11/10/2016 5:29	Maturity in the Lord comes when we see that the only thing truly important is to fulfill His will for our lives. If what you think is His will is not in some good percentage building His Kingdom on earth by reaching the lost, you need to pray. Things of this earth pass away.

11/14/2016 1:30	There's so much going on around us every day. If we don't stop and get silent, we will not hear the small still voice of the Holy Spirit.
11/14/2016 1:35	, I am still seeking to communicate with God right away when things get tough. After reflecting on the incident, I come to see His wisdom, but in the very tough times, I sometimes have a tendency to react in the flesh then pray.
11/14/2016 1:37	My father took pride in being honest. I have learned to do the same.
11/14/2016 14:04	God's Word is God's Word; all other guidance is vain and evil. It is the Source of Truth.
11/14/2016 14:08	The Purpose of Pain, we comfort others with the comfort which we have been comforted.
11/14/2016 14:09	Salvation, a gift received. We could not obtain the needed perfection without Jesus.
11/14/2016 14:10	Vengeance is Mine, says the Lord.
11/14/2016 14:11	Making the most of life by scheduling more time to witness
11/14/2016 14:13	Lay not up treasures on earth, but lay up treasures in heaven.
11/16/2016 13:05	The Holy Spirit cannot be shaken
11/16/2016 13:08	When we abide in the Vine (Jesus), we bear much fruit.
11/16/2016 13:11	We all have so many things to do during the

day, every minute, every thought, every desire, but the most important is to share your faith.

11/18/2016 15:51	Whom the Lord loves He chastises. Lord, have Your mercy on us when You send Your loving chastisements. We know it is given in love and patience. Please give us the grace we need to receive it. Heb. 12:8
11/18/2016 15:55	Our Lord knows our weakness, and He loves us as a Father.
11/18/2016 15:58	I don't believe that I envy anyone. I'm just so grateful and humbled to see our eternal Father in Heaven, allowing His Holy Spirit to flow through me some time.
11/21/2016 13:39	The Most Important Commandment is love because Love is God.
11/21/2016 13:40	By God's grace, I will continue learning.
11/27/2016 14:12	God's love is the broadest Love of all.
11/27/2016 14:13	Love Holiness.
11/27/2016 14:14	By reading and absorbing the Word of God, we will find His will. Committed to Instruction
11/27/2016 15:17	Abortions, homosexuality, lying, stealing, cheating, etc. We are to hate the Sin But love the sinner.
11/29/2016 1:11	Thank you, Jesus, for Your mercy.
11/30/2016 14:12	God's glorious, unlimited resources are obtained by prayer.

11/30/2016 14:42	It is Wise to remember what God does daily, moment by moment. This is the key to faithfulness.
11/30/2016 14:59	Knowing God is with me, His Holy Spirit guides me when I'm sharing the Gospel with others or training others to share the Gospel. Without Him, I truly am nothing.
11/30/2016 15:09	I've been through many tests, and His Grace got me through them. I trust He will have His way in my life, by His Grace He will say to me, well done, My good and faithful servant.
11/30/2016 15:10	When I fall, He is faithful to lift me up.
11/30/2016 15:11	Eph. 2:8-9 Declares Us Righteous
11/30/2016 15:22	I see it in my mind's eye, desire it in my heart, I am excited and waiting with open arms for Jesus to come.
11/30/2016 15:24	My sponsors encourage me to reach out and train disciples, who will reach the world around them. I love it when others see the true meaning of life. To love God and reach others with His love.
11/30/2016 15:26	I know God loves us and His desire is that we choose to give our lives to follow Jesus.
11/30/2016 15:34	, I have been terrified at times, and my reactions varied, but I have always come back to trusting that God knows what He's doing.
11/30/2016 15:34	Daily prayers of the upright.

11/30/2016 15:35	I really love David's heart.
11/30/2016 15:36	Mat. 6:21 Your Heart
11/30/2016 15:40	Jesus has helped me through many hard times in the 46 years that I have been His. He has allowed me to tell what happened in these hard times with others, and I have seen how it has comforted them.
11/30/2016 15:43	I know wicked will get their just reward for being wicked, so I am working on remembering this when I see the wicked act.
11/30/2016 15:44	Hearing His small; still, voice, moment by moment, and allowing Him to use me is joy.
12/2/2016 13:13	Jesus told us to go to the highways and byways to get them into His wedding feast. He also told us to make disciples who will do that work.
12/2/2016 13:21	We do not deserve Jesus's Holy Spirit, but He has poured His Spirit upon all flesh. We just must seek Him.
12/2/2016 13:22	As Jesus rose from the grave, we will also.
12/4/2016 15:03	We can be free from condemnation and the Devils' accusations. To know that we cannot save ourselves, that only through Jesus, we have hope. When we know this and believe it, then we are free. Free from ourselves, free to become like Jesus.
12/4/2016 15:04	Jesus created the world and us with God, His

father. Therefore Jesus is God. We can trust Him for our lives both now and for eternity.

12/4/2016 15:07   Gods Word is eternal, the only eternal truth, and we need to get to know it.

12/6/2016 13:04   A Father who loves His children has mercy on them wants the best for them. A Father cares for His children all the days of His life and their lives. A Father knows that the child is a child and that being a child, they will make mistakes. A Father never stops loving his child no matter what childish things they do, but his desire is that they turn from their foolish ways. He knows if they do not turn from those foolish ways that those ways will lead them into death. He warns them to turn back to Him. He will not force them because they will rebel even more. This is how God sees the peoples of the world.

12/6/2016 13:13   Father of all, our Creator, without You, we would not exist. Without You, we are nothing. You are my Father in heaven, my Creator. I lift up Your Name, the Name above all Names, my Savior, Jesus. There is no Equal.

12/6/2016 13:19   Jesus will return in the Father's perfect time. I wait as a bride waits for her beloved, and I am giving out invitations to everyone so that the wedding will be full of people.

12/11/2016 1:27   I love the Bible; I've been studying it for 46 years, and I never stop learning new things from. It is truly the living Word of God.

12/11/2016 1:27	I have been sharing the Gospel since I received Jesus in 1972. I also have found I have a few more gifts like Helps, discernment, and Mercy. The Holy Spirit Gifts.
12/13/2016 13:11	My faith has been tested many times. Every time I go out to share the Gospel. And the 13 times I was in jail in Argentina. Even when many sicknesses hit me, but God has always been faithful to give me the grace for the battle and has seen me through. I have learned precious lessons from every trial.
12/13/2016 13:14	Use a Bible study guide. Great advice.
12/13/2016 13:17	Every day, I try to pray about everything, seeking to hear God's guidance about everything, even the direction I drive and who to speak to as my witness. The Holy Spirit guides us if we listen. Listen as you go.
12/13/2016 13:32	John 3:36, When I was a child, I was beaten weekly, confined to my room weeks at a time, and in no way felt the love of God, but after receiving Jesus, I haven't only felt love, but I knew how to love others. Thank You, Jesus. In Christ, I am Accepted.
12/13/2016 13:33	My desire is to be led by the Holy Spirit; therefore, I will be in God's plan.
12/13/2016 13:37	Jesus is the Resurrection and the Life.
12/18/2016 4:28	With God's vision, the people, do not perish.

12/18/2016 4:35	I trust Jesus has prepared a place for me in heaven. Death, where is your sting.
12/18/2016 4:36	Each day brings the change He has designed. By His grace, we will flow with it.
12/18/2016 4:40	I have many Pains, truly too many to write about, from times in the Argentina jail to extreme back pain in Salta Argentina, to pains of loved ones. God sees me through all my pains and helps me grow closer to Him through them.
12/18/2016 4:41	We are told to listen to the Holy Spirit's small still voice. Waiting on God. 1 Kings 19:12
12/18/2016 13:13	Through pain and sorrow, my eyes have been set on heaven. There will be no more pain or sorrow in heaven.
12/19/2016 1:26	46 years ago, Jesus removed all my sins. I have been growing ever since.
12/19/2016 13:16	God has sent a Love Letter to Everyone. If anyone is reading this, please pray family and loved ones understand that the Bible is the Word of God, and if we do not study it then, we are, in reality, showing that we do not believe it. Without the Bible, people create a god of choice, not God, the Creator.
12/22/2016 14:31	Praying for Your Peace.
12/22/2016 14:33	There are times in everyone's life when we feel like a disgrace. Jesus has given His life that our sins, yes, even the times of disgrace, are washed clean. Never hold on to

disgraced give it to Jesus

12/23/2016 13:57	God is in control of the now and eternity,
12/26/2016 17:56	Oh my Lord, my King, my God, thank You for Your everlasting mercy.
12/26/2016 18:00	Our Lord lives in our hearts. We can know Him even more. He made a way for us to communicate with Him making us His children. God's design and desire are that we seek Him.
12/27/2016 6:33	Jesus was wrapped in a Manger after being in heaven. Amazing
12/27/2016 6:45	When we trust, we need not fear. The key is to trust. Joy Beyond Fear.
12/27/2016 13:22	God dictated to His prophets. The Word of God is just like a president dictating to his secretary, they just write what He says, or they will be fired.
12/27/2016 13:28	To find God's will, try running through these tests; 1. Does it coincide with the Bible? 2. Does Godly consul agree with you. 3. Does it lead others and you towards the love of Christ? It must bear the fruits of the Spirit that we see in Galatians 5:22-23
12/27/2016 13:33	The Father, Son, and Holy Spirit does not live in time as we do. They have never been bound by time or space. Everything, even the breath I breathe, and any good thing makes me sing. You are worthy, Lord, thank You.

12/27/2016 13:38	How can anyone who knows Jesus and is led of Jesus not confess that He is our King, Lord, and Savior. He gives eternal life to all who believe. It is like I believe in my heart that I must eat, drink, and breathe to live.
12/27/2016 13:43	Lord have mercy on me and talk to me. Please use my life today. Lord, please show me what You want me to do today. Please lead and guide me today.
12/27/2016 13:44	I have missed the mark at times in my life, mainly because I was too busy, and I did not stop, look, and listen. We must be alone at times and abide by the reality that where there are two or more gathered in His Name, He is there with them. Listen.
12/28/2016 5:28	The Precious Holy Spirit wants to always guide us and lead every move every day, the problem is we are so busy, and we miss His leading. Jesus, thank you so much for Your never-ending love and mercy. Without You, I am nothing, and my existence is for nothing, but with You, I can please our Father who art in heaven.
12/30/2016 5:08	Hell is also calling everyone. Ask Jesus to save you.
12/30/2016 5:09	God seeks those who will worship Him in Spirit and in Truth.
12/30/2016 5:11	God wants to give us ultimate rewards for our service to Him.

12/30/2016 5:11	When you absolutely love someone, you believe what they say. Do you believe Jesus?
12/30/2016 13:53	I have seen His overflowing grace, and I am so thankful for it.
12/31/2016 16:07	Have patience as He leads us to reap His harvest.
12/31/2016 16:08	I so want the Lord to say to me, well done, My good and faithful servant.
12/31/2016 16:10	God is always many steps ahead of me; in fact, He knows the future. I am just trying to keep up with Jesus. Surprise! Surprise!
1/1/2017 1:08	I am with patience waiting with desire for Jesus to come in the clouds. It would be wonderful if He came today, but only God knows when Jesus will return.
1/4/2017 5:04	The best way to reach the world is to open our mouths and tell the lost about eternal life that Jesus has given us. If we give all to the poor and do not tell them about Jesus, it is for nothing, as they will praise us and not Jesus.
1/4/2017 5:08	God loves us period. He always has our eternal best in mind, no matter what. Our duty is to trust Him, no matter what.
1/4/2017 5:09	Blessed are those who suffer for His Name's sake—suffering for Christ.
1/4/2017 5:11	Only by the grace of God can we follow

Matthew 5. This is something I need to grow in every day, but I know Jesus will help me through each day.

1/4/2017 5:16   No one is an island; we are always influencing someone.

1/4/2017 15:18   I know this to be true. I have not been to a Seminary, nor have I been to college. I feel as though I am not capable of going to Pastors and leaders and teach them how to share the Gospel one on one. I praise and thank the Lord that He has called me to this mission. The Mission of the Great Commission, training others to train others to harvest the souls of men, to become fishers of men. It has to be God, as I'm nobody.

1/5/2017 5:28   Jer. 3:33. Says call unto me, and I will show you great and mighty things. The Holy Spirit opens our eyes. The Holy Spirit teaches us.

1/9/2017 5:34   To joyfully share the Gospel may be tough, but it shows genuine faith

1/9/2017 5:35   God's Word is all the proof we need.

1/9/2017 5:37   Believers are receivers of the freedom from the fear of death and hell, and freedom to love God and others.

1/9/2017 5:38   Jesus is God, and our Creator read John chapter 1. Who is God?

1/9/2017 5:39   Jesus wept because of the lack of faith in the world.

1/9/2017 5:41	It is impossible for God to lie. He is the all-powerful Creator. Who are we to even try to understand Him?
1/9/2017 5:42	God's Holy Spirit overwhelms me and fills me when I stop, look, and listen for His small, still voice.
1/12/2017 1:22	Our Lord has been patient with humankind since the beginning of time. He knows everything. We just need to try to keep up. God does what He has to do in order to bring His creation to His final plan. Things that God' does may seem to be anger, but He knows best.
1/12/2017 3:36	I still need His forgiveness, even more now as I see clearly how my fleshly righteousness can never be able to come up to the righteousness of God's. The Holy Spirit convicts us.
1/12/2017 3:38	Because no matter how good we are, we are far from the righteousness of Jesus.
1/12/2017 3:40	, I am so far from true humility; it is one of my desired goals. I fear Him, the Lord, and that is the beginning of wisdom. I want to do His will, but my flesh is weak. As for riches, I just want to be rich in His Spirit as that is what truly satisfies.
1/12/2017 3:47	One thing I know, that is, I want to share Jesus with as many as I can while I am on this earth. I want to tell them that God so loved the world that He came in the flesh to

give us a way to come to Him. Salvation Is a Gift given by Jesus.

1/12/2017 3:48   All of His promises are written in the Bible.

1/12/2017 14:02 Lord help me to be the man you want me to be, that I might please You.

1/14/2017 1:40   I know it is only by the grace of Jesus that God can look at me or use me and communicate with me. If God did not have His Grace on me. No one could say anything because He is God. I am so thankful that He is true to His Word.

1/14/2017 1:42   I know that Jesus beat the devil when He was here on earth, so I just call on Jesus and rebuke the evil one, the devil, and his demons in the Name of Jesus, and they have to leave.

1/14/2017 1:43   When Peter walked on water, as long as he kept his eyes on Jesus, he had nothing to fear, but when he took his eyes off Jesus, he sank. Keep your eyes on Jesus.

1/14/2017 15:54 Jesus came to show the world that God's ways are higher than man's ways, as the heavens are above the earth.

1/17/2017 4:19   Yes sir being a Christian is a call to action, a call to take the world for Jesus. Love Is Not a Noun; it is a verb.

1/17/2017 4:23   I met a man in Akron, Ohio, in 1972. I do not remember his name, but I know how God used him to lead me to Jesus. I have been calling others ever since. We are Fishers of men.

1/17/2017 4:24 Sharing the Gospel is serving the Lord. If you want to know what God's calling is for you, it is telling others about the saving grace that Jesus gives. Earn eternal rewards. 1 Cor. 3

1/17/2017 4:27 Jesus told them about His death so His disciples would know that He had to fulfill His calling when He died. When it came to pass, they knew. I would have had an extremely hard time knowing that Jesus was going to die. My heart would be broken.

1/17/2017 4:29 Jesus being God, knew He was going to die on the cross, but I believe He was sad when His disciples forsook Him. Jesus also knew the disciples would fulfill what He called them to do after seeing He rose from the dead.

1/17/2017 13:12 Where the Spirit of the Lord is, there is joy and peace. Peace be with you.

1/19/2017 13:50 In most cases of deep grief, we are to just be there, saying nothing. In other cases, speaking, uplifting, and comforting words and assisting where possible.

1/19/2017 13:55 In the USA, there are people at stoplights that beg to buy alcohol and many who are making it their job. There are others who truly are in need. I pray for discernment and give with a Christian tract.

1/19/2017 14:00 They that be wise shall shine as the

brightness of the firmament; they that turn many to righteousness as the stars forever and ever.

1/20/2017 20:35   We must be willing to do the going in order to be used by God.

1/21/2017 16:51   To see a son suffer would be terrible. God knew His Son would come back to Him, but the moment Jesus was suffering and dying, God brought on darkness and an earthquake. This showed God's displeasure very clearly.

1/22/2017 6:20   Others know that I love God through Jesus because I tell them. I see God's love pretty much everywhere, in His people, in His creation, and most definitely in His Word.

1/23/2017 3:44   We followers of Jesus will stand in front of Him one day. He will show us how much we believed. MANY will hang their heads in shame. By His grace, I want to yield to His Holy Spirit. I desire to SHARE THE GOOD NEWS, THE GREAT NEWS, THE ONLY ETERNAL NEWS, that Jesus came to earth. Our Creator came to earth and lived here for 33 years, fulfilling His Prophecies. His Word said the Messiah would come and die on the cross to take our sins. It tells us that IF we believe, then we would follow Rom. 10:8-10. If we believe in our hearts, we will confess with our mouth. Also, whosoever believes in Jesus will not be ashamed. Oh Lord, my heart goes out to those who practice religion but have not come to have a relationship with you, oh Lord, I cannot say that I in any way deserve to have a relationship with you, but by your Grace, You have given me this eternal relationship. Lord, do what You must to bring the many who come to the buildings called Churches to a relationship with You. Lord, show Yourself that they may know You.

1/24/2017 13:18	I am as positive as possible while around others. Lifting up Jesus.
1/25/2017 3:44	Integrity, being honest in the things we say and do, holding high morals, both of these qualities are how I want to be and what I want others to see in me.
1/26/2017 14:06	Do evangelism, encourage others, help your leaders. Use Your Gifts
1/26/2017 14:07	Training fishers of men.
1/26/2017 14:09	All love shows patience. Love Is Patient.
1/30/2017 5:25	Giving is much more than just giving dollars. It's doing all you can do here on earth to lead others to the Saving Grace of Jesus—using your time, voice, heart, and money.
1/30/2017 5:27	We were sinners and are sinners, the difference is we are saints, sinners saved by Grace.
1/30/2017 5:31	Joseph's brothers hated him, but they had to in order to do God's will, which was to sell him so God would lead him to Egypt. Does that mean we are to hate our brothers, God

forbid? We are to love them. It means we are to trust God no matter what comes our way.

1/30/2017 5:45	Understand that this life is a vapor; we are here for a short time, then we return to the Lord for the judgment.
1/30/2017 14:22	Teaching and training them to reap the waiting harvest of the Lord.
1/30/2017 14:24	The best we can do is to teach others to follow Jesus by doing the work He sent us to do daily
2/1/2017 16:24	When we rest in Him and trust Him, we can live in His peace.
2/1/2017 16:53	We always are thankful to those who love us.
2/1/2017 16:56	I am giving to the persecuted Church.
2/4/2017 0:31	God's arms are always waiting for us to come to Him. It has been this way from the beginning of creation.
2/4/2017 0:32	Giving is God's love coming through us.
2/13/2017 13:20	I sow seed daily.
2/13/2017 13:26	All those who do evil will reap evil.
2/13/2017 13:27	The closer we get to Love, the more the Lord is shining through.
2/13/2017 13:29	We develop a loving household by being God-fearing, by reading the Word of God daily, by praying with your family.
2/13/2017 13:29	We are to be giving both physically and

Spiritually to each other.

2/13/2017 13:31	We are to give to the poor both physically and spiritually. Jesus said we would always have the poor with us.
2/13/2017 13:36	Riches and silver I have little, but what I have is the Gospel, which is more valuable than all the riches in this world. I give it freely and to as many as I can.
2/13/2017 13:36	This is my desire to be filled with Gods' Love.
2/13/2017 13:39	My wife and I have friends over, and we pray for our meals always.
2/13/2017 13:41	I love lifting up others. When I do, I feel the Holy Spirit flow through.
2/13/2017 13:41	Because God lives in us, we can see the future of heaven.
2/13/2017 13:5	God gives to us, so we will have to give to others.
2/13/2017 13:53	I love, loving others; I am growing in loving my enemies
2/13/2017 13:54	I desire to give the gift of Evangelism to as many as I can.
2/14/2017 14:54	I believe the Word of God changes lives, so I share it with others.
2/16/2017 1:38	Being led by the Holy Spirit is the key to having a fruitful life.
2/16/2017 1:39	Sharing the Gospel will be Remembered

Forever.

2/17/2017 6:02	Be honest with others and do your best to lift them up to Jesus.
2/17/2017 6:03	When I'm walking in the Spirit, He leads me to be gentle and kind.
2/26/2017 13:08	Listen and pray.
2/26/2017 13:09	Stay positive, lifting everyone to Jesus.
2/26/2017 13:10	I pray so to have overflowing Love.
2/26/2017 13:12	A living Church is not just going on Sunday.
2/26/2017 13:17	The Bible is the Word of God, and it leads us, fills us, instructs us, and feeds us. It is the eternal guide. It is God's love for us put into Words.
2/26/2017 13:18	God is love, and He never fails.
2/26/2017 13:20	There are people who are poor in spirit and people who are poor financially. The people who lack the knowledge of Jesus is the neediest.
2/26/2017 13:24	I am always humbled and thankful for kindness. It brings me to tears.
2/26/2017 13:27	Doing good works without the Gospel is a lost opportunity. We need to give the best gift, an eternal gift that will be with them forever.
2/26/2017 13:28	Have you been hungry, thirsty, sick, and lonely, I have, and yes, God was with me

there too.

2/26/2017 13:31   As we show the world patience, kindness, and love, they will take notice that we have been with Jesus if we tell them about Him.

2/26/2017 13:34   Every person has an eternal soul. God has allowed them to be where they are for His reason. We have to reach every eternal soul and lift them up to Jesus.

2/26/2017 13:37   The Eternal soul is most important. If you are filling their physical needs to reach their Eternal soul, you have done well, but unless you care for them spiritually, their temporal lives will end, and they would be lost for Eternity.

2/26/2017 13:38   His desire is that we are one as He is one with His Father.

2/28/2017 4:44   May I have God's radical faith in love, which is a beautiful thing.

3/4/2017 13:45   Whether we live or die, we are God's.

3/4/2017 13:54   Earnest Prayer with passion will be heard, but only God truly knows what is best.

3/4/2017 14:00   We will be full of light by sharing Jesus as He is the light of the world.

3/4/2017 14:05   God told us not to have other gods before Him. Two Masters.

3/5/2017 18:01   By staying in the Word and prayer, we become Wise and Innocent.

3/6/2017 13:51	The majority of the world's population work towards the goal of retirement, not realizing that they are leaving the most important behind. This is to love God and others as ourselves. This means reaching out to others with the Gospel daily. Foolish Wisdom
3/6/2017 13:52	By seeking His guidance in every moment. Having knowledge without Jesus leads to nothing.
3/6/2017 13:54 It's Our Job	Preaching the Gospel to every creature. Hey,
3/7/2017 14:13	Lord, please have mercy on me. Please help me walk in a path of obedience to You, Your Word, and Your Holy Spirit.
3/9/2017 3:38	Being in the center of God's will is succeeding.
3/9/2017 13:52	Daily guidance of the Holy Spirit.
3/9/2017 13:59	God is calling all humanity to come to Him. I'm called to let them know that there is no other place where we can find perfect fulfillment than when we are lifting up Jesus to all those around us. To raise disciples who will go to others and teach them the will of God is to believe that Jesus is Lord, so they too will go and tell others. Life Worthy.
3/11/2017 15:52	The end result of living in this world is Heaven or Hell. By His Grace, He will use my life to reach others with this truth.
3/11/2017 15:59	Jesus said we will rule with Him. A Jew is an

inward reality, not a bloodline. Romans 2:28-29. The only true Jew is a Jew who has received Jesus as Lord as Savior. All the non-believing Jews are as lost and wicked as everyone else who have rejected God by rejecting Jesus.

3/11/2017 16:00	Pray in humility.
3/13/2017 13:02	We can always grow in our trust, and when we trust, we have peace.
3/13/2017 13:05	Be faithful to God, put Him first. This is my goal, and I, by His grace, will grow to be more faithful each day. Live by Faith.
3/13/2017 13:06	As in Romans 13 says, God has allowed the powers to be in this world for His reason. Respect ALL Authority.
3/22/2017 0:32	I need Jesus more and more each passing day.
3/22/2017 0:49	I seek the Holy Spirit, so when I move and walk, He can lead me.
3/23/2017 13:12	Jesus is my Lord, my King, and my Savior.
3/24/2017 2:40	Sometimes, I receive His grace right away, and sometimes it takes longer, but His grace carries me through.
3/24/2017 3:15	All God wants is for us to grow in Him.
3/24/2017 3:18	We all fall short of many of His laws. He just wants us to know, to see, and trust Him, and He will give us the victory. Without Him, we are nothing and can do nothing.

3/24/2017 3:24	By His grace, I have been seeking this crown for 47 years. I am amazed that God is allowing me to train others to seek this crown too. I know only God's Holy Spirit can reap His harvest, and it needs to be reaped. God's Kingdom is in the hearts of humans. James 1:12 and Revelation 2:10
3/24/2017 3:26	Jesus wants our all. He said Love the Lord with all your heart, mind, and soul. This is the goal.
3/24/2017 3:29	We call God our Father in heaven, and we live in His Glory now and forever.
3/24/2017 3:32	Head knowledge is not God-dependent.
3/24/2017 3:33	We must always remember, we are not our own. We are Gods. It truly humbles me to see my Christian brothers and sisters support my Ministry.
3/24/2017 3:38	We have to trust in the Lord and lean not to our own understanding.
3/24/2017 3:40	God, our Creator, He can do anything. He has told us we can stand on His Word.
3/25/2017 1:17	Keeping a clear conscience is a blessing. When we seek to keep ourselves clear of sin. Seeking forgiveness is how we keep a clear conscience.
3/28/2017 12:19	God, our Father in heaven, corrects us for our good and heals us in His time.
3/28/2017 12:21	God is the Almighty, and at the same time,

He is my friend.

3/28/2017 12:22	I obey the laws of man as far as I can until the law holds me back from serving my Father in heaven.
3/28/2017 12:26	Jesus told us to love God with all our heart, mind, and soul, and that is the direction we have to be headed for in our life.
3/28/2017 12:34	Our God loves us.
3/28/2017 12:36	We need to rest in God. The Reason for the Sabbath.
3/28/2017 12:38	His Word, the Bible reveals who Jesus is. To know Him, we need to read the Bible and then seek to be Led daily by His Holy Spirit.
3/28/2017 12:42	Praying in His Spirit, knowing that God lives in us and hears our every thought. He wants us to grow to be like Jesus
3/28/2017 12:43	Our Lord takes care of us even when we do not see it.
3/28/2017 12:45	Everything Jesus said is true. Truth is honesty. We need to be honest and true with God and others. This pleases God.
3/28/2017 12:48	I plead with God to use me. I feel as though I cannot do things that He is sending me to do, so I plead for Him to give me the strength to do His will.
3/28/2017 12:51	I think we all have at times forgotten God. God has made us to seek Him. If we are not doing this moment by moment, then we have

a way to go.

3/30/2017 12:18   Yes, without Jesus, we can do nothing. Jn. 15. The biggest problem in the Church today is most Christians have never brought anyone to Jesus the Christ by sharing the Gospel with them. It seems they always feel the people around them are not ready. The sad truth is the Church as a whole has not equipped them by showing a sample of personal witnessing. The Church in Jesus' day did because they saw Peter, Paul, Steven, and all the others sharing the Gospel.

3/30/2017 12:22   Prayer and reading the Word in the morning is imperative. Start the day seeking God's grace and Spirit. Then as we walk, seek His guidance moment by moment during the day. God wants to walk with us as He did in the garden with Adam and Eve.

3/30/2017 12:29   Jesus was both totally man and totally God. He knew His flesh would suffer, but most of all, He knew He was going to take the sins of the world. On the cross, He said, Father, why have You forsaken Me. It seems that while Jesus was taking the sins of the world, it caused a temporary separation between Him and His Father God. This was, without any doubt, the most terrible thing that could happen. Jesus had made the world with His Father as the Bible says, and had never been separate from Him in Their eternal heaven. It was terrifying. I guess the closest thing that we as humans can feel is when we are separated from the ones we genuinely love.

4/1/2017 0:15   I am waiting with desire to see my Lord and King Jesus. WOW, it is going to be incredible. I am bringing with me as many as the Lord allows.

4/2/2017 12:26   Face it, as in Genesis, the devil told Eve then Adam, "if you eat this forbidden fruit of the tree of knowledge, the knowledge of good and evil you will be as God." Humanity is still eating from that same tree and still trying to be more than they are, God's creation, created to love and adore Him for eternity. This life passes; eternity does not.

4/2/2017 12:28   Our eternal life is what life is all about.

4/2/2017 12:28   Reading the Word of God feeds my soul. I lose true vision without it. It revives the soul.

4/2/2017 12:31   If common sense means following the trend of man or following Gods' Word, then I will follow God's Word.

4/2/2017 12:37   He who believes will understand that Jesus is our Creator. When we believe, we submit to Jesus as King and Lord. If not, do we genuinely believe? Or truly understand?

4/2/2017 12:40   Abraham believed so deeply that when he was told to kill his son, he was going to obey God and kill his son, but God knowing Abraham's heart, stopped him.

4/2/2017 12:42   Living with a relationship with Jesus leads to being a friend with God.

4/2/2017 12:44	God's greatness is just that. He is the Creator of all things, and He has a reason He does all things. The end result is His eternal purpose. We live in the present. God lives in the eternal. His greatness is based on that truth.
4/4/2017 12:40	This life and all things in it are but a vapor in time, that appears a short time then vanishes.
4/4/2017 12:43	When a person walks the narrow road, they are considered a fanatic, even crazy. I chose to be a fanatic for love, the love that Jesus taught. Will you join us—the Narrow Gate.
4/4/2017 12:46	I could grow in Faith. Jesus said if you had faith the size of a muster seed, you could move a mountain. Don't Lie to Yourself we all need to grow
4/4/2017 12:50	We know Jesus took our sins away when He died on the cross, but Sin is a daily battle. It's a battle we will fight till the day we die. The day we stop fighting Sin is the day we lose the battle. The battle to become the beings that God wants us to become.
4/5/2017 12:29	I know I have been created by my Creator. He knows best, this I know, but when things get tough, I don't always think of that right away. Sometimes it has to sink in, then I see His wisdom in the thing He did, and I give Him the Glory.

4/5/2017 12:34	God sees who we are and how He will use us for eternity. Therefore, He does what He must to mold us to fill His eternal purpose.
4/7/2017 18:08	My first time in Argentina. I was in jail many times for sharing the Gospel, so I fled the Country thinking it was a mistake to go there, but six years later, the Lord had me return back to Argentina, and He gave us a very fruitful Mission there for nine years. God's detours.
4/8/2017 0:10	Our earnest prayers are needed more and more every year.
4/8/2017 0:25	The more I give myself to the Lord, the more I sense His presence, and the more my prayers match His will and are answered.
4/8/2017 0:26	God's Holy Spirits small still voice that guides me. God's Presence.
4/8/2017 0:37	God's love is unfailing. Without His mercy, we would all be lost.
4/8/2017 0:42	There are many times in our lives that we just do not know how to pray, for issues and trials that we have, but God's Holy Spirit knows our needs, and He intercedes for us. The Holy Spirit Prays for You.
4/10/2017 5:10	To lean not to my own understanding is a constant effort. I love it when my spiritual ears are open, and I know His leading.
4/10/2017 5:12	Jesus being totally God and totally man, prayed this prayer once. I follow Him in His

prayer. Lord, not my will but Your will be done.

4/10/2017 5:14	God will give you more than enough. When in Argentina, Jesus supplied a 5-bedroom house for free for three years. I know it had to be Him, as I also know I did not deserve it.
4/10/2017 5:17	The fear of the Lord is the beginning of wisdom.
4/10/2017 5:18	All Christians are called to build up His Kingdom on earth.
4/13/2017 6:06	When I step out to serve Jesus, I see Him do miracles. God is faithful to those who are faithful. We see His mighty hand move when we trust Him and do His will.
4/13/2017 6:07	I claim a Blessing for Susie, my wife, and her mother.
4/13/2017 6:10	We will take into eternity the works God leads us to do on earth. Tis One life will soon be past, Only what is done for Jesus will last.
4/13/2017 12:30	Sincerely seeking Jesus.
4/14/2017 12:23	Becoming one with God through Jesus. As Jesus was one with the Father, so are we to become one with the Father with Jesus.
4/14/2017 12:30	I'm so grateful for God's grace. His true plan for humankind was demonstrated by His Son Jesus. Jesus was perfect and without Sin. We are without Sin if we allow Jesus to

remove all our Sins.

4/14/2017 13:52 The trying of our Faith strengthens our Faith. It's like muscles; the more we exercise them, the stronger they get.

4/15/2017 18:45 Once saved by grace, always saved by grace. We have been sealed. The Holy Spirit Seals You. If you are saved, you love Jesus.

4/15/2017 18:50 Praise the Lord, so thankful for being His child.   God is eternal

4/17/2017 12:36 Our Father's plan amazes me. His vision for what He will make us into, His grace and unfailing love. Looking at Him makes me smile. It's like the butterfly's I get when I look at the one I love.

4/17/2017 12:40 Jesus is ruling heaven and earth as He said He would. Of course, there are times I'm concerned about my human weaknesses; many times, I'm delighted as His Holy Spirit is flowing through me.

4/17/2017 12:42 When the going gets rough, the best thing we can do is seek the Lord.

4/17/2017 12:43 Jesus not only cares, He is patiently molding us into children of God.

4/20/2017 14:13 Jesus is coming back. So, pray, read the Word, and share the Gospel

4/20/2017 14:15 Jesus has given me a job to partner with Him to reap His harvest, and train others to do the same. Praise the Name of Jesus forever.

4/20/2017 14:17	We are all loved by God. Jesus has no favorites, but He will be giving rewards to those who are serving Him here on earth.
4/20/2017 14:18	In the times we feel lost and when we feel God is far from us. He wants to see if we will seek Him as one would seek a lost love.
4/20/2017 14:23	Those who win souls are wise. Even the simple-minded are wise when they follow Daniel 12:3. Those who are wise will shine like the bright expanse of the Heavens, and those who lead many to righteousness, like the stars forever and ever.
4/20/2017 14:24	Yearning for my Glorious Body, being with Jesus, and learning from Him.
4/21/2017 12:32	When we are unsure of something, we seek help and guidance. The same goes for the things we do for God.
4/21/2017 12:34	As Paul said, we die daily to the flesh in order to live in Christ. As for healing my body, I know Jesus keeps me strong. I need to grow in my faith for healing. I have seen God heal me and others, but I still am weak in this area.
4/21/2017 12:42	I know for myself that if Jesus had not come into my life, I would have gone the way of all flesh and would be lost in a sinful life with no reason to live but for sex, drugs, and rock and roll. My life would have been a disaster. Thank You, Jesus, for saving my life, please use my life for Your Glory. In Jesus Name.

4/26/2017 12:11	When I do the right thing, I pray, listen, and follow. God gives understanding.
4/26/2017 12:12	Thank You, Jesus, for winning the Victory over my Sin and death. I Praise and Thank You.
4/26/2017 12:13	Jesus and His Holy Spirit guides us and cares for us.
4/26/2017 12:15	Jesus has won the battle, any and all battles if we allow Him to take the battle on for us.
4/26/2017 12:16	Train up children in the way of the Lord and hold not the rod (with care and prayer) from them while there is Hope.
4/26/2017 12:22	All things are lawful for us, but not all things are profitable.
4/26/2017 12:24	God's will is for all men to know Him and to walk with Him as Adam and Eve did in the garden.
4/26/2017 12:26	Our Lord can and does heal us, in His time and in His way. We live in a fallen world. Therefore the Sin that is all around us will have an effect on us, but Jesus has given us the victory over sin and sin's effects.
4/27/2017 14:10	We are in a spiritual war. Our Lord and God want to win us back to Him. So, His love will never fail us—sin/Grace.
4/27/2017 14:31	This is the reason for life. God has created us with the need to know and love Him. It's not just a desire to know Him, it's a human

need, and until our connection with our Creator is made, we will never be fully fulfilled.

4/27/2017 14:46	I'm so thankful that someone trained me to Share the eternal saving grace of the Gospel. God has given me His vision for the lost, His harvest.
5/1/2017 2:30	By His mercy, Jesus is still with me. I know I have many weaknesses and areas where I can improve in my walk with Him. He still guides me and uses me to bring others to Him. His Grace amazes me
5/1/2017 2:35	God has appointed and gifted many people in many ways. We do the work in this life that we choose, but regardless of our profession, the only work God wants us to do is share what He has done through Jesus.
5/1/2017 2:37	When the burden gets too tough, we have forgotten to give it to Jesus.
5/3/2017 5:24	Matt. 6:33 Purpose of Salvation.
5/3/2017 5:27	These times are hard, but if we stay faithful, Jesus will never leave us. Only we can leave Him.
5/3/2017 5:29	Some people who are close to me, even Christians who do not understand God's calling in my life, try to stop me from doing God's will for my life. Others are being used by the enemy, trying to stop me from being used by the Lord.

5/3/2017 5:30	God has His plan for all of His children; our job is to find it and be faithful to it.
5/8/2017 4:46	All of creation, all humankind is in God's hand to do with them what He knows best. God has a plan, and it is working as He knows best. He will continue to bear the fruit of Sons and daughters, which is this world's full reason for existence, to bring forth children of God who choose Him over all else. God has borne this fruit since the beginning of creation, and He will continue bringing children of light into His Kingdom till the end. Since the coming of Jesus, who was God in the flesh, God has poured His Holy Spirit over all the world. It is all around us like the air we breathe. This has brought in the last days of His magnificent plan. When this time has ended, there will be a new heaven and a new earth. (NIV) God, and Patience.
5/9/2017 12:14	By His grace, I will invest in His Kingdom with both my time and money. Giving from the Heart.
5/9/2017 12:16	God's mercy is renewed every morning.
5/9/2017 12:18	His ways are higher than our ways. God's not a liar.
5/9/2017 12:20	Psalms 1 says we are Blessed if we walk in God's way.
5/9/2017 12:28	He has brought me to a place in my life where I am compelled to preach the Gospel. When someone is convinced of anything,

they will, by nature, tell others. Believing is more than a word; it's an action.

5/9/2017 12:53   We will all, every human who has ever existed, will all fall on our faces when we see the Lord Jesus. Remember Paul, when he was on the way to persecute Christians. He fell on his knees, and his eyes were blinded and burnt when he saw Jesus. At the same time, Jesus said, great peace I give to you. When we truly know God, we have a balance of praise, comfort, and fear. We are full of joy and desire to do His will. We realize that only what's done for Jesus will last.

5/11/2017 4:30   Jesus knew God's Holy Spirit is the key to this generation and all the generations after Jesus's death on the cross. He told the disciples that God would send a comforter, one that would guide us and lead us to do God's will. He said that God's Holy Spirit was poured out onto the world and that it was crucial that we receive Him. Jesus said without Him; we can do nothing. The same is true of the Holy Spirit as He is with Jesus. We just have to sincerely ask for Jesus to come in our life, and He will fill us with His Holy Spirit. We must believe that Jesus is patiently waiting for us to submit to Him. The same with the Holy Spirit. We just have to ask Him into our lives and then know He is with us.

5/11/2017 4:38   It's an insult to God when we doubt Him. He is merciful because He knows who we are and that we are human, but He hates it when we fall back.

5/11/2017 4:41   God loves the humble and resists the proud. He said He came to heal the sick and give sight to the blind. He told the Pharisees they were clean on the outside but filthy on the inside.

5/11/2017 4:42   God protects us.

5/11/2017 19:25   Repentance, yes, because the worst thing that can happen to us is going to Hell for eternity.

5/11/2017 19:27   We must trust God in all things. This is the goal. I don't know about you, but I have a ways to go before I can say I always trust our merciful God in all things right away. Sometimes it takes a few days.

5/11/2017 19:32   God has no favorites in persons, but He also said He will reward some 30 others, 60 and others 100 percent for their services here on earth.

5/11/2017 19:40   God put Himself in a virgin, and the man was called Jesus. Jesus lived in this world for 33 years. Then we see Him in Revelations chapter 21-22. This is what it says; Then I saw "a new heaven and a new earth," for the first heaven and the first earth had passed away, and there was no longer any sea. I saw the Holy City, the new Jerusalem, coming down out of heaven from God, prepared as a bride beautifully dressed for her husband. And I heard a loud voice from the throne saying, "Look! God's dwelling place is now among the people, and he will dwell with them. They will be his people, and God himself will be with them and be their God. 'He will wipe every tear from their eyes. There will be no more death' or mourning or crying or pain, for the old order of things has passed away." He who was seated on the throne said, "I am making everything new!" Then he said, "Write this down, for these words are trustworthy and true." He said to me: "It is done. I am the Alpha and the Omega, the Beginning, and the End. To the thirsty, I will give water without cost from the spring of the water of life. Those who are victorious will inherit all this, and I will be their God, and they will be my children. But the cowardly, the unbelieving, the vile, the murderers, the sexually immoral, those who practice magic arts, the idolaters, and all liars—they will be consigned to the fiery lake of burning sulfur. This is the second death." One of the seven angels who had the seven bowls full of the seven last plagues came and said to me, "Come, I will show you the bride, the wife of the Lamb." And he carried me away in the Spirit to a mountain great and high, and showed me the Holy City, Jerusalem, coming down out of heaven from God. It shone with the glory of God, and its brilliance was like that of a very precious jewel, like a jasper, clear as crystal. It had a great, high wall with twelve gates, and with twelve angels at the gates. On the gates were written the names of the twelve tribes of Israel. There were three gates on the east, three on the north, three on the south, and three on the west. The wall of the city had twelve foundations, and on them were the names of the twelve apostles of the Lamb. The angel who talked with me had a measuring rod of gold to measure the city, its gates, and its walls. The city was laid out like a square, as long as it was wide. He measured the city with the rod and found it to be 12,000 stadia in length, and as wide and high as it is long. The angel measured the wall using human measurement, and it was 144 cubits thick. The wall was made of jasper, and the city of pure gold, as pure as glass. The foundations of the city walls were decorated with every kind of precious stone. The first foundation was jasper, the second sapphire, the third agate, the fourth emerald, the fifth onyx, the sixth ruby, the seventh chrysolite, the eighth beryl, the ninth topaz, the tenth turquoise, the eleventh jacinth, and the twelfth amethyst. The twelve gates were twelve pearls, each gate made of a single pearl. The great street of the city was of gold, as pure as transparent glass. I did not see a temple in the city because the Lord God

Almighty and the Lamb are its temple. The city does not need the sun or the moon to shine on it, for the glory of God gives it light, and the Lamb is its lamp. The nations will walk by its light, and the kings of the earth will bring their splendor into it. On no day will its gates ever be shut, for there will be no night there. The glory and honor of the nations will be brought into it. Nothing impure will ever enter it, nor will anyone who does what is shameful or deceitful, but only those whose names are written in the Lamb's book of life. Then the angel showed me the river of the water of life, as clear as crystal, flowing from the throne of God and of the Lamb down the middle of the great street of the city. On each side of the river stood the tree of life, bearing twelve crops of fruit, yielding its fruit every month. And the leaves of the tree are for the healing of the nations. No longer will there be any curse. The throne of God and of the Lamb will be in the city, and his servants will serve him. They will see his face, and his name will be on their foreheads. There will be no more night. They will not need the light of a lamp or the light of the sun, for the Lord God will give them light. And they will reign forever and ever.

The angel said to me, "These words are trustworthy and true. The Lord, the God who inspires the prophets, sent his angel to show his servants the things that must soon take place."

"Look, I am coming soon! Blessed is the one who keeps the words of the prophecy written in this scroll."

I, John, am the one who heard and saw these things. And when I had heard and seen them, I fell down to worship at the feet of the angel who had been showing them to me. But he said to me, "Don't do that! I am a fellow servant with you and with your fellow prophets and with all who keep the words of this scroll. Worship God!" Then he told me, "Do not seal up the words of the prophecy of this scroll, because the time is near. Let the one who does wrong continue to do wrong; let the vile person continue to be vile; let the one who does right continue to do right and let the holy person continue to be holy." "Look, I am coming soon! My reward is with me, and I will give to each person according to what they have done. I am the Alpha and the Omega, the First and the Last, the Beginning and the

End. "Blessed are those who wash their robes, that they may have the right to the tree of life and may go through the gates into the city. Outside are the dogs, those who practice magic arts, the sexually immoral, the murderers, the idolaters, and everyone who loves and practices falsehood. "I, Jesus, have sent my angel to give you this testimony for the churches. I am the Root and the Offspring of David and the bright Morning Star." The Spirit and the bride say, "Come!" And let the one who hears say, "Come!" Let the one who is thirsty come, and let the one who wishes take the free gift of the water of life. I warn everyone who hears the words of the prophecy of this scroll: If anyone adds anything to them, God will add to that person the plagues described in this scroll. And if anyone takes words away from this scroll of prophecy, God will take away from that person any share in the tree of life and in the Holy City, which are described in this scroll. He who testifies to these things says, "Yes, I am coming soon."
Amen. Come, Lord Jesus. The grace of the Lord Jesus be with God's people.

Now let's make this very simple. The true reason for this life is before the earth was created by God. He reined in the heavens. Satan also called lucifer, and the devil rebelled against God, His Holy Spirit, and His Son Jesus. God being the Great Creator that he is used Satan's rebellion to create a better heaven. Earth is the location that He is using to allow total freedom of choices, thereby creating beings that are choosing Him and His Son over Satan.

You see, Lucifer wanted to be God, and he rebelled with 1/3 of the angels. God created human beings, and we have a choice to join Satan's rebellion or join his Son, Jesus. It's that simple. By not joining Jesus, you are making a choice. When you say to yourself and others, I just don't believe in God, or I don't believe in Jesus, you are being blinded by Satan & his rebellion. There's no in-between you are either on God's side under His Son and commander Jesus or Satan's. Whose army will you be in?

If you say you are following the commander & chief Jesus, then are you reading His commandments? You can't truly follow the commander in chief unless you are reading what he told you to do. Jesus told us to do much more than just hear about him. Hearing about Him does not in any way make you a Christian. Do you believe in him? What do you do to show it? Believing takes much more than hearing and having knowledge of something. When you believe, you take action. I heard someone say, "Don't tell me what you believe, I will see what you say and things you do, and I will tell you what you believe.

Christ said: Luke 10:18, And he said unto them, I beheld Satan as lightning fall from heaven. In Ezekiel 28:12-19; You were the model of perfection, full of wisdom and perfect in beauty. You were in Eden, the garden of God; every precious stone adorned you: ruby, topaz, and emerald, chrysolite, onyx and jasper, sapphire, turquoise, and beryl. Your settings and mountings were made of gold; on the day you were created; they were prepared. You were anointed as a guardian cherub, for so I ordained you. You were on the holy mount of God; you walked among the fiery stones. You were blameless in your ways from the day you were created till wickedness was found in you. Through your widespread trade, you were filled with violence, and you sinned. So, I drove you in disgrace from the mount of God, and I expelled you, O guardian cherub, from among the fiery stones. Your heart became proud on account of your beauty, and you corrupted your wisdom because of your splendor. So, I threw you to the earth; I made a spectacle of you before kings.

We learn in Isaiah 14:12 How you have fallen from heaven, O morning star, son of the dawn! You have been cast down to the earth, you who once laid low the nations! You said in your heart, "I will ascend to heaven; I will raise my throne above the stars of God; I will sit enthroned on the mount of assembly, on the utmost heights of the sacred mountain. I will ascend above the tops of the clouds; I will make myself like the Most High."

And in Revelations 12:3-5; And there appeared another wonder in heaven and behold a great red dragon, having seven heads and ten horns, and seven crowns upon his heads. And his tail drew the third part of the stars of heaven, and did cast them to the earth: and the dragon stood before the woman which was ready to be delivered, for to devour her child as soon as it was born. And she brought forth a man child, who was to rule all nations with a rod of iron: and her child was caught up unto God, and to his throne.

Who will you join Satan's rebellion or join Gods' Son Jesus Christ? It is your choice. Please remember by not choosing; it is a choice to be on Satan's side. Even if you say, I do not believe this. John 3:36

2 Corinthians 4:4 In whom the god of this world hath blinded the minds of them which believe not, lest the light of the glorious gospel of Jesus Christ, who is the image of God, should shine unto them.

To be a follower of Christ

Psalm 1:1-6
Blessed is the man who walks not in the counsel of the wicked, nor stands in the way of sinners, nor sits in the seat of scoffers, but his delight is in the law of the Lord, and on his law, he meditates day and night. He is like a tree planted by streams of water that yields its fruit in its season, and its leaf does not wither. In all that he does, he prospers. The wicked are not so but are like chaff that the wind drives away. Therefore, the wicked will not stand in the judgment, nor sinners in the congregation of the righteous; ...
Revelation 20:1-15
Then I saw an angel coming down from heaven, holding in his hand the key to the bottomless pit and a great chain. And he seized the dragon, that ancient serpent, who is the devil and Satan, and bound him for a thousand years, and threw him into the pit, and shut it and sealed it over him so that he might not deceive the nations any

longer until the thousand years were ended. After that, he must be released for a little while. Then I saw thrones and seated on them were those to whom the authority to judge was committed. Also, I saw the souls of those who had been beheaded for the testimony of Jesus and for the word of God, and those who had not worshiped the beast or its image and had not received its mark on their foreheads or their hands. They came to life and reigned with Christ for a thousand years. The rest of the dead did not come to life until the thousand years were ended. This is the first resurrection. ...

John 13:34 A new commandment I give to you that you love one another: just as I have loved you, you also are to love one another.

How to join Jesus Christ and His army against Satan

Ephesians 2:8-9
For by grace, you have been saved through faith. And this is not your own doing; it is the gift of God, not a result of works, so that no one may boast.

John 3:1-21 Now there was a Pharisee, a man named Nicodemus who was a member of the Jewish ruling council. He came to Jesus at night and said, "Rabbi, we know that you are a teacher who has come from God. For no one could perform the signs you are doing if God were not with him." Jesus replied, "Very truly, I tell you, no one can see the kingdom of God unless they are born again." "How can someone be born when they are old?" Nicodemus asked. "Surely they cannot enter a second time into their mother's womb to be born!" Jesus answered, "Very truly I tell you, no one can enter the kingdom of God unless they are born of water and the Spirit.

Flesh gives birth to flesh, but the Spirit gives birth to spirit. You should not be surprised at my saying, 'You must be born again.' The wind blows wherever it pleases. You hear its sound, but you cannot tell where it comes from or where it is going. So it is with everyone born of the Spirit." "How can this be?" Nicodemus asked. "You are Israel's teacher," said Jesus, "and do you not understand these things? Very truly, I tell you, we speak of what we know, and we testify to what we have seen, but still you people do not accept our testimony. I have spoken to you of earthly things, and you do not believe; how then will you believe if I speak of heavenly things? No one has ever gone into heaven except the one who came from heaven—the Son of Man. Just as Moses lifted up the snake in the wilderness, so the Son of Man must be lifted up, that everyone who believes may have eternal life in him."

When you ask Jesus to come into your life, He performs what your doctor did for you when you were born in this life. Jesus smacks your spiritual behind, and your spirit is born. Jesus is waiting with His arms open, all you have to do is ask Him to come into your life and then be willing to submit to His leading in your life, and by studying His words of life in the New Testament, you will see things you will have to change in order to be the person He wants you to become.

Jesus is waiting for you to open the door of your mind, heart, and soul. He is telling you, Revelation 3:20 Behold, I stand at the door and knock. If anyone hears my voice and opens the door, I will come into him and eat with him, and he with me.

5/17/2017 0:35	Without the Holy Spirit, I would be as a sheep without a Shepard. With the Holy Spirit leading me, I know I'm joining God in His harvest. He is my guide. He leads me, warns me, comforts me, and uses my life for the Glory of God. It's so important for me to deal with my sin when I fall short, so I keep my connection open to the Holy Spirit.
5/19/2017 4:03	Jesus said, I Will Give you God's Holy Spirit
5/19/2017 4:04	Some people are criminals because they believed in Jesus.

5/19/2017 4:06	Praise the Lord for His mercy, for those who repent.
5/25/2017 13:17	Without the Lord, there is no reason for existence. No moral standard.
5/25/2017 13:18	God's Great Power.
5/25/2017 13:20	Even the birds sing to the Glory of the Lord. We sing when we are happy. We sing for joy.
5/25/2017 13:22	Being a Christian is being CHRIST bride. What do you think it means to be a Christian?
5/25/2017 13:25	If our prayers bring Glory to God, they will be answered.
5/25/2017 13:30	The Holy Spirit has been sent to all the world. He gives us wisdom, guidance, and boldness. When we listen, He accomplished God's will through us. Our job is to seek to be guided by Him in all we do. Spirit of Truth
5/25/2017 13:56	Without the resurrection of Jesus, the Christian faith is for nothing. If Jesus did not rise three days after being crucified and buried, then the Christian faith is for nothing. I guess you can say being Christian leads us to be good people, but anyone can strive to be good in the eyes of the world. You don't have to be a Christian to be good in the eyes of the world. A Christian is someone who knows that there is life after death and that there will be a judgment. We will have to account for what we have lived. There's not one person who has not done something

bad; in fact, there's not one person who has not done many things bad in the course of life. We have been born into a sinful world. When we as humans understand that God, knowing humans had fallen from His grace, fallen from a Spiritual life with Him, He came to earth in the form of a baby, so we could see and hear Him, then He lived a perfect life and died on the cross. When we realize who Jesus is and how He sent His Spirit into the entire world, desiring that we receive Him. When we ask Him to come and be with us, and in us, He does, as He said in Revelations 3 verse 20. This is when we become Christians, born not only in this flesh but also in the second birth of the Spirit. As said in the Gospel of John, chapter 3.

5/25/2017 14:12	Mark 16:15. God's Love
5/25/2017 14:14	Amen, it's an everyday trust till the day we die. Do Not Worry.
5/25/2017 14:16	There is life everlasting with the only God of the Living.
5/25/2017 14:17	I am asking God for health. By His grace, He will bring fishers of men to help me with this Great Harvest.Knock, Knock. He's There.
5/25/2017 14:19	I'm so grateful for the Road to the Cross
5/25/2017 14:21	I want my Jesus to Lead me. The Suffering Servant.
5/25/2017 14:23	Amen, He reigns now and forever. The

Cross Then Kingdom.

5/25/2017 14:25	I am God's child not because I deserve it, but because He chose me by His grace, He called me and now is using my life for His Glory.
5/25/2017 14:27	Thank You, Lord, for Your continued presence. Where Can I Hide?
5/25/2017 14:28	When I take the time to seek Grace and Peace, I find it.
5/25/2017 14:29	I run to Him most of the time as He is my Strong Fortress.
5/25/2017 14:30	Amen and Amen, everything is a Gift.
5/26/2017 4:11	Worshipping while fasting. More than anything, I believe the Church needs to share the Gospel in the highways and byways.
5/27/2017 3:59	It's the Lord that

opens the eyes of the spiritually blind. But we have to do our part to share the Gospel. Unexpected Belief.

5/27/2017 4:00	All creation Praises God. Humans have a choice,
5/27/2017 15:51	We too should be reaping His valuable Harvest, but His Church is too busy feeding themselves while the world goes to hell. I'm praying that all our Church members wake up and to see that they will be so ashamed for not sharing His eternal gift with others. It takes getting out of your comfort zone and

opening our mouths to proclaim Jesus to everyone. People cannot read your mind, even when you are doing things for them and giving them things. Most of the time, they are thinking how nice you are or how nice the religion you believe in is, but they still do not understand what Jesus did unless you open your mouth and tell them. The Holy Spirit will give you the words to speak. I can guarantee when we stand in front of God in the great white judgment, Jesus will show us who He Led us to when He led us to them and the result that could have been eternal. We are Farmers in His harvest field.

5/28/2017 17:38 Water baptism is an out showing of the inward change. It's our declaration of a new devotion to our King and Lord Jesus. Jesus baptized with the power of the Holy Spirit, and without Him, we can do nothing

5/28/2017 17:40 Oh Lord, You are my Provider. Thank You so much for caring for me. Jehovah Jireh

5/29/2017 23:59 Have you ever neglected to seek God's direction before doing something? Sad to say I have, but His Word tells us He will never leave us. Lord, please give us grace and faith in the hard times.

5/30/2017 0:10 Think on this, God loves us so much that He came to earth to show us His love and care.

5/30/2017 13:18 I share Jesus with people openly all the time, but with family and friends who know me and my faults, they know I love Jesus and His Word, sharing Jesus with them becomes harder. I have tried to share the Gospel with them, but it seems to fall on deaf ears. I'm praying for open doors to get deeper into the truths of God's Kingdom with them.

6/1/2017 4:31   He that believes will be saved. Let me add if someone truly believes that they received eternal life through faith, how can they stop themselves from telling others about the world to come, heaven?

6/1/2017 4:32   Jesus is the light of the world, and He shines through us IF we allow Him to.

6/1/2017 4:35   When the Lord allows me to train a Leader on how to share the Gospel, my goal is that those Leaders will train others, and the Kingdom of God will be established here on earth. All Glory to God, Training Disciples.

6/1/2017 13:34   , I love it when the Holy Spirit leads me to His divine appointments. I see how God has been working in lives even before He led me to them. Then I share the Gospel with them, and I am blessed to see them ask Jesus to take their sins away. When Jesus comes into their lives to guide them into all truth, it is the best thing I have experienced. I know I will see them in eternity. We will be with Jesus forever in His Kingdom as He promised. This is the greatest and most important thing in all life. This life passes quickly, and then we go into the real-life, life eternal. Each person has a divine choice; they can choose to believe Jesus or choose to reject Him. Jesus said anyone who believes in me has everlasting life. He also said God so loved the world that He gave His only begotten Son, and whosoever believes in Him has everlasting life. We just have to trust in what Jesus said, trust in Him and Him alone for eternal life.

6/2/2017 3:54	Repent means turn around, leave the old way you have been living and take on the new person, the person who seeks after God as a deer seeks water.
6/7/2017 12:17	Jesus is the Word. Reading the Bible and being lead by His Holy Spirit has changed my life
6/7/2017 12:19	We need to trust God's Word and believe it when we read it. We can trust His Word more than any other person or thing.
6/7/2017 12:39	God speaks to our hearts if we listen. His Holy Spirit speaks to us through His Word and in a small still voice. God's leading affirms He is with us and in us. When Jesus said, not everyone that says to me, Lord, Lord, shall enter into the kingdom of heaven; but he that does the will of my Father which is in heaven. Many will say to Jesus in that day, Lord, Lord, have we not prophesied in thy name? And in thy name have cast out devils? And in thy name done many wonderful works? And then will I (Jesus) profess unto them, I never knew you: depart

from me, ye that work iniquity. This moves me to seek God's leading. One thing I've found to be true is we find God when we 1. We take time to pray daily. 2. We take time reading the Bible daily, so we can know Who He is by seeing what He has said and did throughout history. 3. We find a Church to worship God in 4. We Fellowship with other Christians. 5. We have to share the wonderful things He has done for us and the Gospel with others. We know we are going to heaven because Jesus died to remove all Sin; therefore, we are going to His Kingdom when we believe that He took all our Sin off of us. When we come to know this to be true, we are saved from eternal separation from God, known as Hell. If we are blessed to know this, we are forced to share Jesus with others; otherwise, we do not honestly believe. The Gospel is summed up in these verses. John 3:16-19. For God so loved the world, that he gave his only begotten Son, that whosoever believeth in him should not perish, but have everlasting life. For God sent not his Son into the world to condemn the world; but that the world through him might be saved. He that believes on him is not condemned: but he that believes not is condemned already, because he has not believed in the name of the only begotten Son of God. And this is the condemnation, that light is come into the world, and men and women loved darkness rather than light because their deeds were evil. We just have to share this truth, and we will be doing God's will for our lives.

6/7/2017 13:03   Praise God. His mercy is forever and ever. There have been countless times when I came to the point that I knew how unworthy I am to be called a child of God, and there have been countless times when Jesus has taken me in His arms and said, "I love you with an unfailing love" We must share this love with our family, friends, and people we meet daily.

6/7/2017 13:07   God has adopted me, this I know, and it brings me to tears knowing it to be true. Surprise...You're ADOPTED!

6/7/2017 13:17   I know Jesus has come to win the hearts of men and women. When He does, it divides many families as it did mine. We that know God's will, know that we are not to love the things of the world. This divides us from those who love the things of the world, whether it be family or friends. We must choose this day whom we will serve. As for me, I will serve Jesus. Jesus says in the Gospel of John, chapter 15 If the world hates you, ye know that it hated me before it hated you. If you were of the world, the world would love its own: but because you are not of the world, but I have chosen you out of the world; therefore, the world hates you. Remember the Word that I said unto you, the servant is not greater than his Lord. If they have persecuted Me, they will also persecute you; if they have kept My saying, they will keep yours also. But all these things will they do unto you for My Name's sake because they know not Him that sent me.

6/7/2017 13:22   Jesus will never force His way with you. He patiently waits and calls at your door.

6/7/2017 18:01   Wisdom is a gift of God, as in the case of Solomon. Also, if we are diligent to study the Bible, it will give us Wisdom.

6/7/2017 18:08   Adam and Eve walked with God (I believe it could have been Jesus) and talked with Him face to face. This is where we are going to end up again. I love it when God's Holy Spirit leads me to do something or to speak to someone as I see Him working.

6/7/2017 18:13   Some of our Presidents have led our country to believe that many immortals acts of man are right, like homosexuality and abortion. They have allowed the education system to remove God's Word from our schools. These atrocities have happened over our time as a nation, pushing us farther and farther from God.

6/9/2017 12:16   If we take the time to show leaders how to share the Gospel with the lost, their followers will do it too.

6/9/2017 12:19   Jesus is the Word. Therefore, when we hide His Word in our hearts, we are hiding Jesus in our hearts.

6/9/2017 12:23	Without Jesus, we are nothing, we have nothing, all is vanity.
6/9/2017 12:34	I'm so pleased to humbly say yes. I've come to the place in my life that all I want to do is to share Jesus with others. I'm continually giving out tracts about Jesus. I'm always trying to be led by the Holy Spirit. Listening to His small still voice, so I can be led to those He wants me to share the wonderful news of the Free Gift of eternal life that Jesus is offering.
6/12/2017 12:31	Jesus is my God, my Savior, my Idol, my Helper, my Friend, my Hero, I adore Him, I want to be like Him, I need Him, and love being around Him. Without Jesus, this life is nothing. With Jesus leading us, we live in eternity now.
6/12/2017 12:34	Jesus is offering a reason for life, I took it, and am living it.
6/12/2017 12:38	Yes, it's radical for Jesus to ask us to give up everything, but without putting Jesus first, the things of this world will pull us down. If families are not following Jesus, they will do all they can to pull you away from Jesus.
6/12/2017 12:41	To believe in God is to obey Him. Jesus said the will of God is to believe in Him. Whom God sent. When we truly believe, we share Jesus with others because we know Jesus gives eternal life.
6/12/2017 12:45	God is willing to forgive all humanity; that is

why He made the greatest sacrifice that anyone can make. He died to save us. God and Forgiveness

6/14/2017 14:24	Just the fact that I received the gift of eternal life through Jesus makes me Very Wise.
6/14/2017 14:27	The Holy Spirit, being God's Spirit, knows what He wants to accomplish. He knows how to lead us to pray.
6/16/2017 1:52	Mat. 6. Remember Your Master
6/16/2017 1:55	God's precious Holy Spirit will lead, guide, instruct, and by God's grace, use my life for His Glory. My job is to seek to listen and then to obey.
6/16/2017 1:57	God's mercy has been shown in Jesus.
6/16/2017 20:42	After 47 years of walking with Jesus, I've found myself in many situations where I needed to wait on the Lord, and God has always come through for me. There are times I've fallen short, so God has opened my eyes to what He was doing, and He gave me comfort. I love the times when I was looking to see what He was doing, and then He totally surprised me. I'm praying that I learn to look to Jesus always! Even when life events are difficult.
6/22/2017 16:28	My Lord Jesus knows what His Will is for my life. It's up to me to stay on the straight and narrow so that I can be as effective in His plan as possible.

6/22/2017 16:30	Thank You Lord for discipline, at times it's awfully hard to receive, but if God didn't discipline us, it would mean He doesn't care. God's Discipline
6/22/2017 16:35	The moment we take our eyes off of Jesus, we start to sink. Just as Peter did when walking on water.
6/22/2017 16:35	By His grace, I seek Him daily.
6/22/2017 16:36	God is Always Watching. This is why I'm praying for grace.
6/22/2017 16:38	Thank You, Jesus. For Carrying the Cross
6/22/2017 16:40	God's justice is righteous and always for the best. We are short sited don't understand.
6/22/2017 16:41	The devil always tries to accuse me, but Jesus always gives me comfort.
6/22/2017 16:42	Our Father in heaven has always had His plan, and it cannot fail.
6/22/2017 16:43	Pray, believe, then leave it in our Father's hands.
6/22/2017 16:43	True Faith is patient Patiently Waiting
6/22/2017 16:47	God is all-knowing and always present. He sees all and knows all. He's is like the air. He is love. He even knows all our thoughts. This is why we all need forgiveness.
6/22/2017 16:48	Seeking to do God's will. As Jesus said, the Will of God is that we believe in Him. Believing is more than a thought; it's an

action.

6/29/2017 13:54	Jesus leads me, guides me, and takes care of me. Without Him, I'm lost
6/29/2017 13:56	Evangelism, compassion, discernment, Vision. Are Gifts from the Spirit
6/29/2017 14:00	David knew God's will would be done, and he trusted in Him. My main enemy is the devil, and he uses his people to slow me down and hinder me, but God is watching over me.
6/29/2017 14:03	I seek to be Led by Him moment by moment. When I'm in tune with the Holy Spirit, He does miracles.
6/29/2017 14:07	Only by His grace, He is with me & with You.
6/29/2017 14:12	Suffering is never easy. In the many times I have suffered, God has seen me through it. There is a perfect reason for everything we go through.
6/29/2017 14:48	God's grace through Jesus is so overwhelming and passes all understanding.
7/4/2017 0:09	I resist many fleeting thoughts that the enemy sends. By God's grace, I do not entertain them. Deepest Darkest Secrets.
7/9/2017 18:51	I want to always remember what God has done for me; if I do, I will always be at peace of mind. Why Should I Be Afraid?
7/11/2017 20:03	All that have received has been a gift of God. God is calling everyone to receive the gift.

7/14/2017 13:49	A rock is a solid foundation. God is a solid foundation for all those who seek Him through Jesus. The Only Eternal Rock
7/14/2017 18:53	Jesus's Power is only limited by my Faith.
7/14/2017 18:55	God is allowing me to assist others with Evangelism training. I'm so dependent on His Holy Spirit. The Unbelievable Work of God.
7/14/2017 18:56	The only way to have peace in our soul is by accepting God's grace and trusting Him in all He allows to happen in our lives.
7/14/2017 19:42	Thankful Jesus Died for me.
7/14/2017 19:44	When I'm in God's peace, I'm content. There are times when it takes time to receive His peace.
7/14/2017 22:45	JOHN 15 clarifies this; Only the Spirit of God can bring someone to the knowledge of the truth. This truth is that Jesus will cleanse anyone of all Sin if they would but ask. This is why it's urgent that all those who know this truth must understand that we are God's mouth; the Spirit desires that we use our words to allow others to hear and know that without the cleansing blood of Jesus, none will see the Kingdom of God.
7/14/2017 22:47	We must believe like a Child that Jesus is who He said He is.
7/14/2017 22:48	Loving Jesus comes first, then obeying by telling others of His love.

7/14/2017 22:58	, God is our Creator. We are just to learn from Him, adore Him, Praise Him, and become who He made us to be.
7/14/2017 23:11	Wait on Him, Wait.
7/14/2017 23:20	We live in a fallen world. A world that has rejected God, even after He came to the world in the form of a man, CHRIST Jesus. Jesus told us in the Gospel of John Chapter 15 If the world hates you, know that it hated me before it hated you. If they persecuted me, they would persecute you. If we are living like Jesus, there are those who will hate us.
7/14/2017 23:20	God Will Provide the rest.
7/14/2017 23:23	Lord give me Your grace and strength to live for You.
7/14/2017 23:24	We will live with Jesus, The Word forever.
7/24/2017 2:47	Resting in God is great.
7/24/2017 2:48	Obeying vs. Living for Jesus, is there a difference?
7/24/2017 2:49	We need to give Him the Glory He deserves.
7/24/2017 2:50	We are forgiven daily. We fall short of His perfection daily—the Mercy of Love.
7/24/2017 13:52	I'm lost without the loving mercy of God. During the course of a day, my mind is not yet totally on God. His Holy Spirit is with us 24 hours a day, seven days a week, but I'm in and out of connection with Him off and on

throughout the days. Oh, what a blessing it will be to have my mind on Him 24/7 when I'm with Him in heaven.

7/24/2017 14:00	I review the Gospel many times.
7/24/2017 14:06	His mercy is incredible.
7/24/2017 14:10	I know I need to invite Other to join the Evangelistic Mission the Lord has called me to.
7/24/2017 14:11	I am graced to say yes, my Lord has blessed me with His presence. God is Good. All the Time
7/24/2017 14:13	God is all-powerful. He allows us to seek Him, and when we do, we are filled with His Power.
7/24/2017 14:16	When I'm in God's presence, I have peace, Joy, vision for the future, and grace for every situation.
7/24/2017 14:21	, Trusting in the Lord, is a deepening relationship with Him every day. Something that is more precise than Gold. Finer than the finest Silver and is everlasting.
7/25/2017 12:14	I need Jesus all the time, but in times of stress, I need to seek Him right away.
7/27/2017 13:35	JOHN 3:16 Adopted and Accepted.
7/27/2017 13:36	Underserved grace.
7/27/2017 13:37	Eternal life, Jesus's covenant.

God's slow to anger, because He knows we are but dust. God is eternal, all-knowing, and the Father in heaven to those who choose to receive His forgiveness. He has always loved His creation but has never forced us to love and follow Him. This is Who He is, a loving Creator Who wants us to choose Him. Without freedom of choice, we would be no more than robots. God and Jesus, through Their Holy Spirit, created this world and us to allow all eternity to see how His love is given freely but has to be chosen. Separation from Him (which is called Hell) is the other option we as humans can take. God never sends anyone to Hell; they choose to reject God, and there's no other place to go. Jesus came to earth to demonstrate how we as humans should try to live, and then died to take away all the mistakes (or sins) we make. Finally, when we make mistakes like lying, stealing, saying hurtful things, getting angry, even thinking bad thoughts, all God wants us to do is ask for forgiveness (repent) both to Him and to the ones we hurt. Becoming like Jesus is the Someone we aspire to be, and this takes a lifetime. There is really only one day in the life of anybody that counts. Days of births, baptism, graduation, career, marriage, and retirement are all important, of course. But the critical day, the only truly acceptable day, is the day of salvation, which is the day when we are saved by the grace of God by accepting the forgiveness that only

Jesus Christ can give. Ask Him for it now. My desire is to help prepare members of Church congregations to share about the grace of God through Christ. We show them how to lovingly, relationally, and intentionally bring others to know Jesus. My goal is to assist congregations to know how to articulate the Gospel and articulate it with joy, so then, they can be Jesus' witnesses to others.

8/3/2017 16:21	I'm so humbled and thankful for God's grace on me. Justification
8/3/2017 16:23	Jesus fulfilled so many prophecies, and His life was lived as God wants us to live. Dying to our old life daily.
8/3/2017 16:30	I claimed these promises about 47 years ago, Romans 8:37-39 it says, yet in all these things we are more than conquerors through Him who loved us. For I am persuaded that neither death, nor life, nor angels nor principalities nor powers, nor things present, nor things to come, nor height nor depth, nor any other created thing, shall be able to separate us from the love of God which is in Christ Jesus our Lord.
8/22/2017 13:19	My God has supplied all my needs in CHRIST Jesus. God's Got My Back.
8/22/2017 13:21	The Lord is my rock and my salvation.
8/22/2017 13:29	He walks with me, and His Holy Spirit guides me when I seek to be guided by Him.

8/22/2017 14:32   When God created man and woman, they were living in the Garden of God, walking with God, and eating from the tree of life. In Genesis 2:22, God took them out of the Garden so they would not live forever in a life of rebellion against Him. They introduced death into this world when they rebelled against God by eating from the tree of knowledge of good and evil. This means they were choosing what they thought was good and evil, over what God knows is good and evil. This world is in that same state of being now. The majority of the world is choosing what they think is good and evil instead of reading God's Word, the Bible. This is evident by all we see happening in the world today. Jesus Christ, Who was God living in the body of a man, came to earth to live a perfect life, and He showed us how to come back to God. We need to turn around, repent, and come back to God, receive the forgiveness of all our rebellious ways, by asking Jesus to remove them, read His Word, and come back to God. Then we will be back where we started at creation in Genesis.

9/24/2017 12:56   , I do my best to pray every morning, and as I go throughout the day, so the Holy Spirit can lead me and use me to share the Gospel everywhere I go.

11/10/2017 15:22   When I look at Jesus and His way of living while on earth. It keeps me humble.

266

11/19/2017 0:48	I pray for His continual mercy every day.
11/19/2017 0:48	His grace is sufficient.
11/19/2017 3:45	The whole reason for God's creation is to change us to be like Jesus. This (at least for me) will take much cleansing from the Holy Spirit. I do pray for mercy during these times.
11/19/2017 3:45	It may take a few minutes before I seek God in some situations, but by His Grace, my desire is to seek Him always.
11/19/2017 3:46	I can truly say, I'm growing in understanding in the ways of our Lord.
11/19/2017 14:45	Yes, I've said to the Lord on more than one occasion, Lord, I'm ready, just take me, but He got me through, and I now see His wisdom.
11/19/2017 14:46	God sees what we don't, and He knows best.
11/19/2017 22:47	Our God has offered to remove all our sins so we can communicate with Him.
11/19/2017 22:51	Our God is good and perfect.
11/22/2017 18:50	When the early Christians were fleeing persecution. They were also sharing the Gospel.
11/24/2017 5:20	I seek the Lord, and He relieves any fears.
11/24/2017 5:22	We have a Good God Who knows what is best for us even when we don't understand.
11/24/2017 22:01	It amazes me how fast life goes by. I gave

my life to Jesus in full-time service at 22. Went all over the USA and some places in Canada then a good part of South America and Spain. Opened a business and ran it for about seventeen years. Now I'm back to full-time service for Jesus. Looking forward to hearing Him say Well Done.

11/25/2017 14:26	To be truthful, after the initial shock and reaction, I seek the Lord. I'm praying that God gives me the grace to go straight to Him.
11/25/2017 14:43	I'm so pleased the Lord gives me the grace and strength to stand firm.
11/27/2017 21:54	Our God is always ready to help and comfort. I always rely on Him, but at times it takes me a minute or two.
12/1/2017 20:58	The closer I get to God, the smaller I am.
12/1/2017 21:00	I've have found when I run to Jesus, He shelters me and carries me through all my problems.
12/1/2017 21:04	I know Jesus is over all things, but my battle now is to seek Him right at the signs of any physical or spiritual battle.
12/5/2017 4:38	Many times. Like Peter, I have had to call out to the Lord to save me. Walking on Water.
12/5/2017 4:43	I love it when He comes to me. God is waiting with open arms to revive and receive all that seek Him. Jesus says, Come Home to Me.
12/7/2017 21:25	God can do all and anything. He is only

limited by our Faith.

12/11/2017 16:30 We all make mistakes, so when we do, we need to look for forgiveness, both from those we have offended and the Lord.

12/11/2017 22:26 God knows all and uses all things for His Glory, even when we do not understand.

12/16/2017 15:14 God is my Creator, King, Lord. I know He loves me so much that He died for me. My desire is to please Him.

12/16/2017 15:22 All we need to do is trust Jesus. Trust Him in the good times, which is harder as we get tripped off, and bad times, which we do as we need Him.

12/16/2017 15:33 When you genuinely love someone, you want to please them, my desire is to obey God. To submit my flesh, mind, and soul to my God and Father. More Than Lip Service.

12/16/2017 15:36 God knows what will be good for our eternal life. This life will have trials, but we are to be of good cheer, looking unto God, our Heavenly Father.

12/16/2017 15:39 Jesus is the lamb of God and our Shepherd. His Word is the streams of flowing water; if we abide in them, we will never be thirsty or hungry.

12/18/2017 1:28 The desire of My heart is to see many come to the realization that we must reach those around us with the Gospel.

12/21/2017 20:06	Living in joy, in times of trouble only by the grace of God.
12/21/2017 20:07	When our treasures are in heaven, we have a heavenly vision. Set Your Sights.
12/26/2017 14:55	God's peace is a gift. Jesus can give it, and we can also choose to reject peace.
12/26/2017 14:57	We will need to trust and obey God for the rest of Eternity.
12/26/2017 15:00	We know when We have His peace.
12/28/2017 1:09	Without the guidance of the Holy Spirit, we are blind, but with the Holy Spirit, His Wisdom comes through us.
12/29/2017 20:27	God created the world and everyone in it. He gives us the option to know Him. He hates it when we turn away from Him—the Father's Desire.
1/2/2018 17:20	Jesus has full authority over all things and people. He knows what we are going through. May He continue to show His love and mercy when I forget it. Short-sighted.
1/9/2018 5:41	Those who stand on God's promise of eternal. Life through, Jesus will stand forever.
1/9/2018 5:42	Pray to be humble and gentle in heart as we lay our burdens on Him.
1/9/2018 5:57	It's been a tough month—lost water for two days, Air Conditioning for one day when it was 100 degrees. My wife had shoulder

surgery, my backbone started resting on nerves causing real bad pain, my father is in-home hospice, and the emergency light came on in my vehicle. BUT two different people who took Evangelism training with me brought two people to the knowledge of Who Jesus is. This is such an encouragement for me.

1/9/2018 6:02	I know my Salvation is by Grace alone. There are times where I think I am missing the mark. In my mind, I feel I have fallen short, and the temptation of condemning myself comes in, but by God's wonderful Grace, I remember it's Jesus and Jesus alone Who saves me—falling Short.
1/9/2018 6:05	Hope is the inspirational understanding that we will be in Heaven with Him when we leave this world. Be Joyful!
1/10/2018 13:12	, Enduring the hardships in life, builds character. The trailing of Faith works patience Rejoice in Trials?
1/14/2018 5:52	We are clay in the hands of our Maker—both Rich and poor. When we seek a relationship with Jesus, we are fulfilling our purpose for being here on earth. God knows what's best for us, so He leads us to it and through it. We are to stay close to Jesus.
1/14/2018 5:54	His love will lead us into eternity
1/14/2018 5:57	I thank Jesus for His love daily.

1/19/2018 15:22	I know God's plan will be carried out no matter what. By His mercy and grace, I am supporting it.
1/19/2018 15:24	His love and grace are forever.
1/19/2018 15:25	I want to stay close to Jesus in whatever He has in store for me. You are God; I Am Not.
1/19/2018 15:25	Pray without ceasing, Be Still!
1/19/2018 15:27	Jesus is always with us; it's us who leaves Him.
1/23/2018 22:27	God's Holy Spirit speaks in a still small voice. Be Still.
1/23/2018 22:33	I try to always give Him praise.
1/24/2018 19:12	Why do Communion, because that is what Jesus told us to do in remembrance of Him and what He Has done for us.
11/27/2018 16:30	Praising Jesus all day long.
1/27/2018 16:32	Every day, God is Good, Loving, and continuously raising His children in the way is best for us, even when we do not understand what's going on.
1/31/2018 13:56	To fear God is to know Who He is. He is the Creator of everything, including us. Therefore, we are to understand that He is, above all, and everyone. All the so-called mighty men can stand firm against God. He is stronger than the strongest wind, and He can be as gentle as a hummingbird. Our God rules the universe; how can man be so blind

to think we can live without Him. Jesus is Lord and God. Jesus created all things with His Father, as it says in the Gospel of John, chapter 1. When we submit to Him, He makes things right; He comforts us when our flesh is weak and failing us, and when we are strong. Jesus is the door to love, life, and eternity. Ask Him to come into your life. Read and seek to follow His Word. He will give you life, true life, both now and for eternity. Treasuring Wisdom.

2/1/2018 23:08	Only in Jesus is life, true life; otherwise, there is only eternal death. This is why I share the Gospel as much as I can with others. Listen to Wisdom
2/2/2018 5:13	We are the bride, and we are waiting on Jesus. We must be filled with the oil of His Love, His Holy Spirit, now and when He comes.
2/2/2018 5:16	Oh my Lord lead me and help me to submit to the leading of Your Holy Spirit, that I might be used of You to reach Your lost.
2/2/2018 5:17	Jesus, our Lord, and love, will take back His creation in His time. I get very excited when I think that I will be with Him forever.
2/2/2018 13:45	Very grateful. So grateful that I tell other people about what He did for me.
2/4/2018 14:03	Rev. 20 and 21. Is amazing, eternal, and wonderful. Caught Up to Paradise.

2/4/2018 14:04	I am excited, and I want to invite as many as I can to the Kingdom of God.
2/4/2018 14:09	God's Holy Spirit gives us vision, love, comfort, and truth. When He pours through me, I am filled and experiencing heaven. This happens when I'm sharing Jesus with others and my brothers and sisters in Christ.
2/7/2018 5:40	I would say the closer I get to Jesus, the more I see the shortcomings of my flesh. Whether it be laziness, selfishness, lack of self-control, and many more areas where I'm not Jesus, but when I yield to His Holy Spirit, I see Him in me. When He allows me to share His gift of Salvation, I see Him work through me. This is my joy. I want to be more and more like Jesus.
2/12/2018 15:05	The All-Powerful and all-Knowing God has created this world for His purpose and His Glory. Nothing can stop God, for He is the Great I AM.
2/12/2018 15:11	My Greatest desire is that My Lord and God is with me daily moment by moment till the day I leave this world to be with Him for eternity.
2/12/2018 15:13	I praise God that in these times of testing, by His Grace, I seek Him more. By His grace, I place it in His hands as I know He loves me.
2/12/2018 15:15	We mere men are so shallow to think anything made with man's hands can be idolized, cars, houses, jewelry, etc. Jesus

made the world with His Father; They are the only ones we are to worship.

2/12/2018 15:21 He's giving me the blessing of learning to put all things in His Hands. I'm learning to trust in Him in all things. Take note, I said, learning what a Blessing to know that God cares for me and has my best interest in mind during all things and events that come my way.

2/13/2018 17:00 If we love God, He loves us forever and eternally as we live with Him in eternity.

2/17/2018 12:55 The coming of Jesus, the Savior, had been prophesied for thousands of years. He came to save His people and the world. Joy = Jesus, Others then You.

2/17/2018 12:58 Our Lord has rescued me so many times it would take many pages to share them all. Suffice to say He never has left me or forsaken me; in good times and bad times, He's always there for me. God knows how to rescue us.

2/17/2018 13:02 I have desired to follow Jesus, there's no going back. My prayer is that I am sensitive to His Holy Spirit so He can use this old body to reach those He wills and lift my brothers and sisters as they lift me closer to Jesus.

2/17/2018 13:08 There are two eternal locations, heaven and Hell. Everyone who believes, repents, and receives Jesus with a repentant heart will be in Heaven. All heaven rejoices when anyone submits to God.

2/18/2018 13:45   Our God and Creator has invited us to talk and walk with Him. All we have to do is realize that our part is to humble ourselves and become as children so we can learn from our Father in Heaven.

2/19/2018 14:22   Jesus's joy that was set before Him was He knew He was going back to His Father in Heaven. Remember when he was with his disciples, they could not cast out a demon, and He said, how long must I be with this unbelieving nation. Mat. 17:17. The greatest joy for me is when I have the privilege of sensing the spirit of God on me. When I'm able to be used by God to bring someone to understand who Jesus really is and how much they need His love. When they come to Jesus, surrendering to Him asking Him to guide their life, giving them eternal life with Him in heaven. This gives me great joy.

2/20/2018 13:46   Jesus has a plan and purpose for each of us. He will lead us to His purpose if we allow him.

2/21/2018 20:28   Jesus gives us the right to decide to open the door of our life to Him or not. God wants to be around us all the time.

2/23/2018 5:22   I am so thankful God is using my life to reach others who, by His Grace, will turn around and reach the ones around them. I am also humbled and thankful for sponsors who have been generous and are supporting me.

2/26/2018 5:54 There are times I really need to seek His face to feel His presence, but I know He will never leave me or forsake me.

2/26/2018 5:54 So looking forward to being in His Heaven.

2/26/2018 5:58 Jesus is the Word. He gives us a clear vision of what God wants us to do and who He wants us to be. His Love passes our understanding.

2/26/2018 20:41 Our God is an all-Knowing God. Our job is to remember that in good and bad times.

2/28/2018 5:18 Only the God of Abraham, Isaac, Jacob is worthy of praise. Jesus was for the fulfillment of all prophecy. Anybody or any religion anywhere in the world, including the USA, who lifts anything, but Jesus is against Christ. Please do not be deceived, we should aim to win them, but we need to be wise as serpents and harmless as doves. The goal of all other religions is to win Christians to their faith, Muslims being one of the strongest religions that are doing this. Beware.

2/28/2018 16:26 I eagerly wait to go to the wedding feast.

3/3/2018 4:47 Only thing that shows honor to God is when we honor His Son, Jesus. Everything else falls by way of all flesh.

3/3/2018 4:50 Our God loves peace, but if it takes His heavy hand to bring it, He brings His heavy hand, as seen in the old testament. Jesus brought God's love, peace, and forgiveness. If the peace of Jesus is rejected, there is nothing left but destruction in Hell.

3/4/2018 12:22 Most of the time. When I believe something is unjust, I get upset, whether it be unjustly done against me or someone else. I am praying to become more like Jesus in this area of my life.

3/4/2018 13:26 God knows the thoughts of all of us. This is why I pray for Mercy and Guidance. Ps 119. How shall a young person clean their way by keeping their lives according to God's Word? Heart Examiner

3/5/2018 14:25 Three scripture leading me to seek peace. Proverbs 6:2-3, Matthew 5:23. Seeing all my brothers and sisters in Christ gives my heart joy.

3/7/2018 6:06 I am so grateful for the many that pray for me, and I pray for many. God has given me a mission, and that mission is to train as many disciples and laborers as I possibly can. By His grace, I will do so till I go back to be with Him in the wedding feast of the Lamb.

3/7/2018 14:10 Mat. 12:36 says every word we speak throughout our lifetime will be judged. This brings the fear of God into all who know this. I thank Jesus for taking my punishment. The

Foundation of Wisdom.

3/8/2018 13:20   I praise and thank the Lord that He is allowing me to reach college students with the Gospel.   Every Generation.

3/9/2018 13:36   I am so grateful that 1. I have learned to seek Him every morning and throughout the day. I know that when I do, He allows me to join Him in His plans of reaching His lost sheep. 2. He is allowing me to grow in Him as I read His Word. What scares me most is losing my connection with God's Holy Spirit. I truly desire to have Him with me.

3/12/2018 4:59   God's Holy Spirit calls us to His will, sometimes it's hard to leave behind things and even people and relationships we have and go to where He's led us, but it's needful for us to leave behind the things that hold us back from serving Jesus. Mat. 10:36-38.

3/12/2018 15:03   We are enemies of God if we continue in the rebellion of Adam and Eve. We continued to be enemies until we changed from doing what He tells us not to do, to do what He tells us to do. This is learned by reading what Jesus said. This is when we change sides by accepting God's Son Jesus and accepted Him as our Lord, guide, friend, Savior, King, and Master of our lives. Be Restored.

3/12/2018 19:06   Walking with Jesus and being used of God for eternity should be the goal of all Christians.

3/12/2018 19:11	I worship because I know God is my Creator. He is now and will be forever.
3/13/2018 18:58	I love talking to and walking with Jesus. One is the Loneliest Number.
3/16/2018 3:24	The trails and sorrow I am going through with my dad in hospice and my own daily illnesses are driving me closer to Jesus. I am confident that God knows and sees what we are going through, and I am confident that these trails are for our eternal good. I need and am thankful for His comfort.
3/16/2018 19:58	When speaking to friends and family who have heard the Gospel time and again and have not submitted to Jesus, this is the hardest burden for me. I want them to know the forgiveness of God through Jesus. I know it must be God Who reaches them, so I'm putting their salvation in His hands.
3/17/2018 14:49	Being 68 yr. Old, 46 of them walking with the Lord. Seventeen of them on the Mission field. I have been blessed to see my Lord move many times in my life. This has helped my roots to grow deep in God. By God's grace, He will allow me to serve Him for the rest of my life. I know what Jesus did for all humankind, and I desire to reach out to the world to let them know.
3/22/2018 4:39	Humbling our self before God, Who made us is the best state of mind to be in. When we are honest, we can see the areas in our lives

where we need to improve. Stop Hiding.

3/22/2018 4:43	God's love for His creation, me, and you are much more than the love of parents for their children. It's a love where He was willing to sacrifice His own perfect Son to reach His imperfect children.
3/22/2018 4:45	, God is perfect. His thoughts lift us out of this world's thoughts and takes us to Heavenly thoughts. Focus Your Thoughts.
3/22/2018 4:48	The ways of the world lead to death; this is separation from God. God hates death. That's why He sent Jesus to Conquer it.
3/22/2018 12:44	My challenge is to slow down enough to hear and obey. When heavy issues come my way, I go into "fix-it mode" and jump rather than stop, look, and listen to His Holy Spirit, so He can guide me. When I do stop, look, and listen, I am led, and I see God do what only He can do.
3/23/2018 12:43	God's free gift is freedom from sin and the entrance into the heavenly gates. Our Creator and God has opened His arms; in fact, His arms have been opened ever since creation, but man has ignored Him and went their own way. So, Jesus came to show us the way and to give us forgiveness for sins. He just asks us to come back to Him, Love Him, and therefore love others because, as the Bible also says, God is love.
3/23/2018 12:50	We are free indeed. I know I am loved by my

Father in Heaven. He has turned on the light, and I see Him clear as day. Love has made a way to reach my heart. Jesus, my Lord, and God is my light, and He has taken me by the hand, and He is leading me home. While I am on the way, I am taking others by the hand as we walk together towards the promised land called Heaven.

3/24/2018 12:49   I'm praying that dad is allowed in His presents soon. So thankful that he is sleeping now. It's been a long night.
(I wrote this just before dad died). My heart is broken. I will miss him until I see him again in heaven.

3/26/2018 15:46   When you're trusting in the Lord, He has your best interest at heart, therefore, know that we have peace in the midst of a storm. We can know there is an eternal purpose for everything He does.

3/27/2018 18:01   , Jesus knows our weakness. He was on the earth and saw the lack of Faith. Oh, how much more has this generation fallen from faith, how long will it be before the Lord comes. God created us, so He knows each one of us. In the Gospels, we are referred to as little Children. I realize who I am, and compared to Him; I am a child. I know how much I need Jesus, So I pray All the time.

3/28/2018 12:41   The secret Is to walk with God through Jesus. I am doing the best I can, and He, by His Grace and mercy helping me grow.

3/28/2018 12:45	I think we have to have total mercy with everyone. As Jesus said, loving my neighbor as myself is the key.
3/28/2018 17:03	I love praising my Lord and the God of my Salvation.
3/29/2018 16:41	I received this message today. God has his plans for our loved ones and us and everyone in this world. He is over everything that happens, but the decisions to put my father and hospice at the Casey house was to change his medications. It was with the Council of doctors, nurses, and social workers. All of which were fabulous and gave fabulous care for my father over the last five months. They counseled me to take him to the Casey house, and I accept it. Nine days later, my father died. I know God has His plan in all this, and I am doing all I can to accept that it was His plan and not anyone else's, not even my own. My heart is broken, but I know dad is with the Lord now. God and His Will be done
3/29/2018 16:43	I know there is no condemnation to those who trust in Jesus. This day my heart is heavy because of the passing of my father. I will see him again by God's grace in His kingdom. Lord, give me grace, vision, peace, and even Joy, that he is with you today. In Jesus' name, amen.
3/30/2018 19:23	We die when it's God's time for us to die. My father's death has been tough for me. I've

shared with others about the reality that dad is in heaven with Jesus.

3/30/2018 19:24 Jesus overcame the Devil when He died and overcame death by rising from the grave. God sent Him to overcome sin so that we will be in the next World with Him. Yes, it is an encouragement to know that we will be with Jesus in the kingdom of God. In Heaven for Eternity because of what Jesus did.

3/30/2018 19:25 I definitely need Grace and peace at this time in my life. I know that your hand is over us, Lord. This time with my father passing, watching him slowly decline and end up going home to be with You. I pray he is at peace while he is sleeping. There were many tough times before, seeing him decline, but I know he's with You now. Thank you so much for that, amen

3/31/2018 23:35 We had some problems with family members wanting to leave before dad's passing, leaving me and my wife Susie alone in his final hours. My older sister and her husband said they would be leaving in the morning. She stayed, and by chance, dad's final breath was taken when she was on watch with him. Now it's time for me to let it go. And show the love of God. Rich in Mercy.

4/1/2018 6:36 When we are truly sorry, we do our best to repent of the things that seem to hold us back. It's a growing experience, an everyday experience in the grace of God.

4/1/2018 6:39	To be a light in this world, we have to seek God's holy spirit moment by moment every day. We learn how by reading God's word and prayer. It's something that you must seek to do. It's something that you have to desire to do. I've seen God do many things of late. My father's death has been a growing experience and a very difficult one. But I know, according to His word, my father is in heaven.
4/1/2018 6:42	We as His people need to understand the depth of the reality that God is in control. Waiting on Him in the many times that we do not understand what He is doing—trusting in Him even when we are confused. I cannot say that I've always trusted right away, but I do when I stop, look, and listen. That is when I get His Direction and light on the situation. Our goal is to stay close to Jesus, regardless. When we do, we see what he's doing at the end of the trail. Quiet Waiting.
4/3/2018 4:55	I went through a storm in my life when getting things out of my father's apartment and organizing the needed papers so we could bury him. Yes, but I found I just have to call out to Jesus in the storm, and when I did, He came to me, and the waves and storm were calmed.
4/3/2018 4:57	When we genuinely love the Lord no matter what we're doing, we are always working Him. We do everything as unto the Lord, working for Him and looking to please Him by

what we do in this world.

4/3/2018 5:02   I am so thankful that he's giving me the vision to reap His harvest of souls on this earth. I'm very thankful that I'm able to do it with joy.

4/3/2018 16:18   We are much more valuable than sparrows or any animals, Jesus created all things. I can say with confidence that He has supplied all my needs according to His riches and Glory all my life. He amazes me how He does what He does for us—even the Birds.

4/4/2018 3:26   I daresay without God's unfailing love, none of us would come into the presence of our Lord and King. I'm so grateful to know that He loves me, knows me, cares for me

4/5/2018 5:23   The only way to grow is to see where we are mistaken and then understand our mistakes. Mistakes will be made by all of us, so therefore if we learn by our mistakes, which sometimes takes going through them more than once or even many more, then we will grow by them.

4/5/2018 5:24   I have been going through an exceedingly difficult nine days with my father passing. I know God promises us Green Pastures in Psalms 23. I seek them now for myself and my father. Only God can give us perfect peace in the midst of storms.

4/5/2018 16:29   Humble yourself in the sight of the Lord. Oh, I'm in the midst of that now, and by His grace, I'll be able to submit to Him even more daily and every day as I get older and weaker living in more pain. We are his creation, and the only place where we can have true joy is by having Jesus in our hearts, minds, and souls; this is the reason for His creation. He is our God, our creator, our Lord, our life, and our light. Humble Yourself.

4/5/2018 16:33 Many Nations from the beginning of time have rebelled against God. Lord, help us to stay in contact with Your Holy Spirit daily, so we understand Who We Are and Why You have called us to do His will.

4/6/2018 1:42 As many before me, I feel I'm not big enough to take on the mission He's called me to, but I'm on my way to complete what He has called me to. God has always taken care of those who seek and listen to Him.

4/6/2018 12:52 To God alone be the glory for all He allows us to do for the Kingdom.

4/6/2018 18:10 Our God wants our love Above All Else. He wants to teach us how to have love for Him Above All Else. Love for Him and love for others. God will never forsake or leave us even when we leave Him. He will always be waiting with arms open as long as we repent and return, He will take us back.

4/7/2018 4:15 Faith is mysterious and incredibly powerful. Believing, without any doubt, knowing that God will do something. My body is breaking down, so I need faith at this point for my health. My back, my hemorrhoids, my stomach, acid reflux, high blood pressure, many issues of this age of 68, but I know our physical being can only live for a set time. I will, by His grace, trust him as it gives way to death. I can say that I have asked Jesus to forgive me for all my sins; therefore, I am clean and will be given a white robe as I come before God.

4/8/2018 4:37   I am so grateful that I know that Jesus paid the price for all sin. I can get into heaven because of what Jesus did for me, and also know I can help others to do the same. Heaven is so past our understanding so past, even the Apostle John's understanding he could not even describe it, but Jesus told us we will be in the wedding feast of the Lamb. What a glorious day that will be.

4/8/2018 4:39   When we understand how little we are, and know when anything good happens, it's because God has allowed it. God is molding each one of us by the things we go through in life. I know I'm still learning, and I will always be grateful for what He does.

4/8/2018 4:41   We know God feeds the birds daily and during every season. He will also Feed us if we put our faith and trust in Him. I've seen this in my life. I've been blown away by what He's done and how He did it. I'm astounded by His graciousness. He has fulfilled His own word. God promises us that we will be in His kingdom. Because of what Jesus has done.

Trusting the Shepherd.

4/9/2018 5:13	Peter saw the Glory of God in the face of Jesus. We just need to trust in the Word of God.
4/10/2018 4:41	, I feel like Peter walking on water each time I share the Gospel. I am amazed at how He is allowing me to be used to lift up His Glory on earth.
4/10/2018 13:00	God is love. I think God allowed all that happen to Solomon to teach us a lesson, showing us that all is folly.
4/11/2018 16:29	To honor the Lord with your wealth is just investing it into his kingdom. Lord, I'm praying that you show me the best way to invest in your Kingdom.
4/11/2018 16:32	When I talk about Jesus with other people, I know He's pouring through me. When I read His word and contemplate on it, it takes hold of me, then I know he's with me.
4/12/2018 2:51	We can have truth in a time of torment. I have found that I can find peace after the fact. I'm pleased to say I hold no grudge with anyone, but if I could only do it in the moment of the torment and trial at the moment yield to Jesus, in the moment not let anything push me over the hill. Lord, help me to yield to you always Lord and in every situation, immediately.
4/12/2018 13:42	Humbling oneself is a work of God. We can

try to be humble, even set our minds to be humble, but I believe true humility comes from God. Of course, when I think of God, I submit myself as I know who He is, my God and Creator. But true humility with God and others is a gift of God.

4/13/2018 18:55   We are God's workmanship, meaning that He has created us for a purpose. If we yield to Him, He will complete that purpose to the end until we're standing in front of Him.

4/15/2018 20:23   My God and Savior, I thank you so much that You have had grace on me. You are Whom I run to in times of trouble. This, too, is by grace. All is by Grace and Mercy, for I know who I am, a sinner saved by Grace.

4/15/2018 20:33   What an incredible blessing. We can be partners with God in the building of God's eternal Kingdom on earth and heaven. Every soul, we lead to Jesus. Everything we do here on earth to help others to understand God's love for them. Each time we share with others about the wedding feast of the Lamb, Jesus. By His grace, He is allowing us to build God's Kingdom here and for eternity. The Marriage Supper of the Lamb. The book of Revelation 19:6-9 says; Then I heard what seemed to be the voice of a great multitude, like the roar of many waters and like the sound of mighty peals of thunder, crying out, "Hallelujah! For the Lord, our God, the Almighty reigns. Let us rejoice and exult and give him the glory, for the marriage of the

Lamb has come, and his Bride has made herself ready; it was granted her to clothe herself with fine linen, bright and pure" for the fine linen is the righteous deeds of the saints. And the angel said to me, "Write this: Blessed are those who are invited to the marriage supper of the Lamb." And he said to me, "These are the true words of God."

4/16/2018 14:56   As when an extremely rich man marries an extremely indebted woman, the wealthy man pays off all the debt of his bride, so it is with the world. Jesus being the all-powerful when He marries anyone who is in extreme debt or debt of any degree, He pays off all our debt of sin when we give ourselves to Him. This is what is called being saved by grace. Ephesians 2:8-9

4/16/2018 14:57   When we really have a true understanding of God's love for us, we can rest assured, in his arms, no matter what we're going through in this life. He is there to guide and comfort us always.

4/16/2018 16:17   I am so truly undeserving of His grace, but I love seeing Him move through me.

4/16/2018 16:24   Oh, by His Grace, I will bring others to know His Saving Grace. No matter what we do or where we are, we can share the gift of God's Salvation with others. One of the verses in the Bible that drives me to share the Gospel with others is Mark 8:38. We cannot be ashamed of Jesus.

4/16/2018 16:28	I know for myself; I could spend more time with Jesus in my daily life. I am also seeking to give more, to teach more, and to disciple more. I fall short in many ways when I think about eternity. We can only bring what we have done for Jesus into Eternity.
4/16/2018 16:38	When I think about my thoughts alone, it makes me so grateful for His mercy.
4/17/2018 5:26	The more we stop and seek God's face and direction, the more He can use us. God speaks in a small still voice, in our hearts.
4/17/2018 16:27	I am pleased to say that I have no one whom I need to seek forgiveness. We are to be bearers of peace. Even when I slip, He gives me the grace to lower my pride and seek forgiveness.
4/17/2018 16:29	There is nothing that we can hide, physical, spiritual, or mental. God knows all; in all, there is no hiding.
4/18/2018 5:22	Because He created us. Without Jesus, we are just dead bones.
4/18/2018 14:59	God is both a loving Father and Creator. He lovingly leads and guides His children through revelation and corrections.
4/18/2018 16:29	I am so thankful that I know Jesus.
4/19/2018 4:15	As Paul said, be thankful in all things.
4/19/2018 12:55	It is a joy to stop and allow ourselves to hear from God's Holy Spirit. It's as if we are

drinking from freshwaters. Taking into eternity, filling up with His energy. Then we feel as David did in Psalms 100.

4/19/2018 16:24   We will be in Heaven with our Heavenly family for eternity. Our earthly family needs to know Jesus; if not, they will not be part of our eternal family. Lord, please help us to reach them with the Truth. Jesus is the Truth. No one is Worthy of Christ, but He wants to know us all.

4/20/2018 17:22   We think more of ourselves than we should. Lord, help us to always know that anything we do for You is You working through us.

4/20/2018 17:25   I claimed this verse 46 years ago. Matthew 6:19-21, Lay not up treasures on earth but lay them up in Heaven.

4/21/2018 16:57   The Lord has to wait on us because he gives us the option as humans to seek him or not. Those who do not are living in rebellion against Him. Those who do find His will and peace, vision, contentment, and love. Yes, I have seen God move in my life many times. I am so unworthy, but grateful, thank you, Jesus. Those Who Wait.

4/22/2018 14:35   Let's stay in constant prayer, stay humble, and let's judge everything according to God's Word.

4/23/2018 4:17   , I love the Gospel of John; it's so full of God's love shown through Jesus. John wrote Revelations also. When you believe in someone, you believe in what they said, you trust them. We, as God's chosen, his children, we have to believe "trust" in His Words.

4/23/2018 4:20   Jesus said many times, "your faith has made you whole" there's a mystery between our faith and God's power. It's not that God doesn't have the power, but we can't use the power unless we have the faith to turn it on. It's like a light switch; the power is on the switch, it's at the switch, but until we turn the switch on, the light does not come on, the power is there.

4/23/2018 4:34   Anything we do in this world should always be with Jesus, the Name, the precious Name of Jesus to give Him glory, and He always gives God glory because He holds the same Glory as God. So Good Deeds here on Earth always has to be salted with the Words Jesus, the Name of Jesus.

4/23/2018 16:58   There is nowhere else to go but to trust in God. He is God, All-Mighty, the creator of all things, and He knows what is best for us. When we ask God for something, if it is for His glory, it will be done. Sometimes he gives us things to learn from. Sometimes we asked for the wrong things, things that would be bad for us eternally.

4/23/2018 17:02   Jesus the Christ is coming again to take the world over. He will lead and guide it for a thousand years. And then we will all go to the great white throne judgment. A new Earth and new heavens will be created. I am so eager to see it come. I want to tell others about it before it.

4/24/2018 17:09   The scriptures says that the Holy Spirit is here to lead us and guide us, to bring all things to remember this whatsoever He's taught us. He is our connection to the Eternal God, Jesus. He leads us, guides us, and comforts us.

4/24/2018 17:11   My desires is to be with Jesus in His perfect time.

4/24/2018 17:14   Throughout the Bible, Wisdom has always been desired by true men of God. They were seeking to follow God. I definitely want to be led by Wisdom and learn Wisdom. Wisdom is nothing more than being led by the Holy Spirit because that's the wisest thing to do. The more Wisdom we have, the more we know what we don't know and how small we are in comparison.

4/25/2018 18:58   I look at myself, I look at God. I know I need His Mercy as a child that I am. I am so thankful for His Mercy on a daily basis.

4/25/2018 19:05   We all lack in different areas. We are human beings with character flaws Etc. We are to seek to grow in those areas and ask for mercy and forgiveness. Our Lord has asked nothing more, as He is our Father in Heaven.

4/26/2018 13:03   God can do anything; He did not have to put his hands on someone to heal them; I think that was just showing the crowd Who did it.

4/26/2018 21:03 Wisdom is not only good for this life, but the next life also because the wise will shine as the brightness of the filament, Daniel 12:3. Therefore God gives you more days when you're wise because you're not overstressed, you're not overworked, you know how to judge your time, your days, and you're just properly seeking the Lord for his peace on a daily basis, which gives you a longer life.

4/27/2018 16:25 I'm amazed at what Jesus is doing in my life. By His grace, I will serve him till the day I die.

4/27/2018 16:28 When I reach out to Pastors and Christians with an understanding that they need to reach out to the people around them with the Gospel, and they ignore the reality of the need to reach those around them, this breaks my heart.

4/28/2018 4:22 I take medications because I found that my faith has not worked to bring my sicknesses in check. Therefore, I find myself asking God to take care of me by using the medications that doctors and scientists have found. I understand that God gave them wisdom and understanding to find these medications. To be used by us who lack faith in this time of history. I only pray that He has Mercy and allows me to continue to serve Him. Even in my weakest and the lack of faith for my health.

4/28/2018 16:46   Our God is our Father in Heaven. He is Holy, righteous, loving, and just. He has our best in mind when he does anything he does. At this point, my health is failing. I have a lot of pain and a hard time sleeping at night. It's just driving me closer to Jesus; that's what it's designed to do.

4/28/2018 16:47   God knows everything. He goes before us in every situation. I know that I have been through many situations where I was fearful, I wasn't trusting, but when I slowed down enough, I stopped, looked, listened, and prayed. When I did, He solved the problem every time. He Will Not Abandon us.

4/29/2018 3:29   So thankful for the possibility of growing into our Fathers Love. Thank You, Jesus.

4/29/2018 13:07   I believe we as human beings need to seek to be cleansed of our sins every day to become as God wants us to be. We are expected to be loyal, loyal to God, and every moment in every aspect. He said if we are ashamed of Him in this adulterous generation, then He will be ashamed of us in His Heavenly Kingdom.

4/30/2018 13:09   Worry does us no good, whether it be a pastor, someone in front of a group of people, or even when out sharing the Gospel.

5/1/2018 4:48   We are called to be the light of God in this world, but I know I am not always a light to the world. There are times when my flesh gets in the way, and I must fight my way through, to do God's will. By His grace, I pray, and He gets me through. I don't understand it, but He does. I can say that I'm very grateful for the times that I've reached out to people one by one with the Gospel. Over my lifetime reaching thousands with the Gospel. I have worked with and trained others who have done the same.

5/1/2018 4:49

We are saved not because of what we have done; it's what God has done through Jesus. We are saved by the grace and for God's Glory alone.

5/1/2018 12:40

Lord, I pray that my thoughts, words, actions, everything I do bring glory to you.

5/2/2018 4:01

Just keep going on for Jesus, patiently stepping out daily to do His will, which is finding the Lost.

5/2/2018 18:22

King David knew about his sin with Bathsheba and confessed it. We all sin daily, and we have to see those sins, face those sins, then trust Jesus that He has taken those sins. It's very important that we don't allow our sins to stop us from serving God.

5/3/2018 14:59

Our faith is that Jesus can give eternal life to all that ask. When somebody is full of the Holy Spirit, they know this to be true. Of course, our physical bodies and Minds do not comply with that reality. When we share this good news with other people, we allow the Holy Spirit to pour through us.

5/3/2018 21:12   The work of every Christian is the harvest, God's harvest. We, as His children, should understand His Word enough to share it with other people. Then by His grace, while we use the Living Word of God, the Holy Spirit takes over and fills the person you're sharing with the love of God if they receive it. Work Hard

5/4/2018 4:13   God is my father, my Leader, my Comforter, my Guide, my merciful God. His kingdom is forever and ever. And we as human beings could never understand Him or His kingdom completely. But we can seek to know Him on a daily basis. He is reality. We are just seeking to know Him

5/4/2018 13:57   God is eternal, all-knowing. When we understand what He wants, Who He is, and where He wants us. We need to join with His forces of Eternity.

5/4/2018 16:15   God already knows what we need. He just wants us to voice it to Him.

5/5/2018 2:45   God is the only One that can give us wisdom because He is the only one that can see the future. He leads us in the path of righteousness for His name's sake. By His grace, we stop, look, and listen only by God's grace because we as humans fail all the time. But He continues to love us, care for us, and guide us. His love is from Everlasting to Everlasting and will never end. By God's grace, we are saved through faith and not of ourselves. It's just grace; everything is Grace, thank you, Lord, for Your grace, Your love, Your mercy, Your kindness, and your Everlasting Everlasting Joy.

5/7/2018 4:31   I could truly write a book on how many times He's brought me through tough times, the time that somebody was robbing the car of one of my sponsors and Argentina. With a gun to my face, but the robber didn't shoot. The time that I was in Cordoba, Argentina, the police broke into our house because we were sharing the Gospel with young rebels. I was only 22 at the time. Throughout my whole life, there were so many times Jesus kept me safe. Dark Valleys.

5/7/2018 4:38   I've seen the Lord's hand moved so many times in my life, as I shared earlier. I am so thankful God has sent sponsors so that I can do His will for my life. I know that I'm not worthy of serving Him and others. I have no idea why I'm where I am serving Him. Speaking to Pastors and helping them understand the need to equip their members so they can reach those around them with the understanding about the Precious Blood of the Lamb. Lord, help me in Jesus' name. Pastors need to be the example and the lead in sharing the Gospel in the highways and the byways compelling others to come to the wedding feast of the Lamb, then their members will follow.

5/7/2018 4:43   We must understand that God's will is not our will. He's leading everything. Therefore, we must stop, look, and listen and wait for His will as He is setting things up. As for me, my heart is to reach Pastors so that they will start training their clergy and their congregants to learn how to share the Gospel to reach the lost; I am having such a hard time at waking them to do that. Lord, it has to be You, please send Your Holy Spirit.

5/7/2018 17:38   It's easy to know we should always stop, look, and listen to the Lord first before we do anything, but sad to say I know this is something I am still learning to do. When I do, I see the wonderful fruits. I love seeing Him accomplish what He had planned.

5/8/2018 16:46   Using wise words is something that I'm trying to grow in. It's a gift of the Holy Spirit.

5/8/2018 16:48   I need God all the time to stand in front of me, to use me, guide me, and give me the strength. I need to be used by Him. God Is in Your Corner

5/8/2018 16:54   I know I have areas to grow; this keeps me humble. By his grace, I'll continue to grow in Jesus. I pray that you help me, Lord, to be an example of who You are. Most of all, help me not to stop sharing you as you are perfect.

5/9/2018 15:10	After being in South America for many years, I met many very wealthy people. Because I was American. I was able to get close to their families, and I saw the problems they had and what it cost to keep their finances. It would be extremely hard for someone that is trying to care for their money and power to give their lives to Jesus. Not impossible. God can do anything, but it seems to cost more. I just need enough money myself to be able to serve him in his calling for me. I'm laying my treasures up in heaven by His grace.
5/10/2018 16:35	I am amazed at God's gifts. I did not know how to pray. I am amazed as He takes over when I pray. I don't even know what I am going to say; the words just come out. In Our Weakness
5/10/2018 16:46	If it weren't for Grace, I would not be saved; it's all by Grace. When I think of God, He is amazing, Almighty, Creator of all things. I am but a small man who knows who God is. I praise God, who, through Jesus, showed me the way, the truth, and He has given me Life. Find His Lost Sheep.
5/10/2018 16:52	Every person who we help in any way to eventually come to saving grace through Jesus is someone who will live for eternity. All praise and glory to God, as we are only His mouthpieces on earth.
5/11/2018 4:45	I know one thing, everything we give to the kingdom of God is eternal, whether it be

finance, time, effort, heart, and sharing the Gospel.

5/11/2018 12:57   At 22, I realized that my call was to share the Gospel. We're All in This Together.

5/12/2018 2:37   I know as long as I stay close to Jesus regardless of my situation, whether I am poor, wealthy, or middle class. I know that as long as I stay close to Jesus in whatever status, He is with me, and that's the most important thing.

5/12/2018 2:39   My goal is to study, obey, and teach God's Word. I study every day but could study more. I'm teaching those who don't know how to share the Gospel, and in all these things, I am growing. I have my eyes set on the vision of growth.

5/13/2018 16:39   Like radio waves, the Holy Spirit is continually broadcasting. In order to listen and hear the Holy Spirit, you must tune into His channel through Jesus Christ. I have seen Him do many things in my lifetime; I pray it will never end by His Grace; he will allow me to continue to serve Him until the day I stand in front of Him. It seems as though He leads me most when I share the Gospel and pray for someone. The Holy Spirit is continuously Broadcasting; it's up to us to Tune In. Follow the Leader

5/13/2018 16:42   The Holy Spirit will guide us and keep us from going in the path of unrighteousness. I can't say that I've followed His righteousness my whole life, but by his grace, I'll do it from this time on.   Wisdom to the Rescue.

5/14/2018 17:32   Please remember, the only reason God sees us as perfect is that He sees Jesus in us.

5/14/2018 17:34   We are a family, the family of God, so we are overjoyed to see each other. I genuinely love seeing my Church family and all my Christian family.

5/16/2018 5:07   I'm utterly amazed to see how the Lord has been able to use me. I truly do not understand it because of my weakness. I see Him using me even when my knees are knocking, and I'm totally unsure of myself. I still walk up to the plate to try to hit the ball. Then I see him take over the bat and do what he needs to do for the moment. I'm amazed at God's grace.

5/16/2018 22:57   God's Word, the Bible is God, as it says in the first chapter of the Gospel of John. Therefore our words are who we are also. Think about the things you say so you can see yourself.

5/16/2018 22:58   We have to trust in God for all things. When we arrive at that point of this understanding, we know that He is caring for us, and we can have all joy because of it.

5/16/2018 23:00   I'm so thankful that God is giving me Vision, understanding, and drive to lift up heaven on Earth; that's what it's all about.

5/16/2018 23:01	It's man's choice not to follow God, which is wickedness. Wickedness comes from the heart of man because he's not following God. God hates that. He wants us to follow Him as He created us to do. To love Him and to allow Him to give us the joy and fulfillment in this life that He wants to give us.
5/17/2018 11:40	To fix your eyes on something is to be steadfast, going towards, devoted to the task. For us to accomplish what God has created us for, we need to read His Word daily.
5/17/2018 11:43	Wisdom will keep you out of trouble. Wisdom will give you Joy as you share His Wisdom with others. It is wise to read the Word of God and to seek Him. To listen to Jesus and His Holy Spirit is to live a life of love.
5/17/2018 11:51	Righteousness comes from Jesus because He is our righteousness. Keep your mind stayed on Him.
5/17/2018 13:09	If we follow the leading of the Holy Spirit, He will lead us to do what God wants us to do. Many times, in the course of a day, I have been blessed to be guided by His Spirit. He leads me to look to find whom He wants me to share His Gospel. He wants to lead us in our daily walk of life.
5/17/2018 17:42	I have been sowing seeds for 46 years, can't wait to see the crop in Heaven.
5/18/2018 2:14	Things in life will get in the way of serving

God at times. It is very possible that if the rich young ruler had forsaken all, he would have been trained by Jesus to lay up treasures in Heaven.

5/18/2018 13:05   When I forget to listen to God, so He is with me, things that I do, I do in my own flesh, my own knowledge, my own understanding, then I fall short. When I know that God is with me, that is, the Holy Spirit is pouring through me, using me, I sense His presents. The best way to put this is, I don't even think about anything; I just do it. Thank you, Jesus. Keep Going.

5/19/2018 3:51   If we hope for something, we need to pray for it, then have the patience to see how our Lord sees fit to fulfill it. I'm growing in this.

5/19/2018 3:53   When a person believes in something, they take steps towards what they believe. They also do what they believe. I praise and thank the Lord that He has given me the boldness to share His Gospel with whoever He sends my way. I absolutely love seeking His lost.

5/20/2018 20:51   We all have a place in our spirits where we feel empty. That place was put there when God created man and woman. At the fall of Adam and Eve, humankind lost that connection, therefore losing the relationship with God. Then they began seeking after knowledge. Knowledge without God is like a car without gas; it's not fulfilling why it was created. I am totally refreshed by the presence of God's Holy Spirit when I stop and look for Him.

5/21/2018 12:13   We live in a world of sin. That's why there are so many bad things happening. The sin comes because we are ignoring God. This is why we need Jesus so badly; He came to help us have a relationship with God and to cleanse us from all sin; otherwise, we could not get into heaven. God will not allow any sin into His heaven.

5/21/2018 12:19   We must realize and accept that God is our Creator. He can do with us as He pleases. We are as the grass of the field. The change takes place when He fills us with His Holy Spirit. We become the children of God.

5/21/2018 12:20   When I am weak, then I seek the Lord with more of my heart, and that makes me strong.

5/21/2018 12:24   All I can do is praise the Lord for all He has done. Jesus found me in Akron, Ohio. Led me to Canada, then Argentina, Brazil, Bolivia, Peru, Spain. He allowed me to serve Him here in the USA for years. By His grace, I will serve Jesus until He returns, or I go to meet Him in heaven.

5/21/2018 12:27   As the saying goes, money can't buy you, love. Things and power will never give anyone contentment or love. Only God can. He sustains you, comfort you, lead you, and pours His Spirit on you, giving you the only true contentment, love, peace, direction, vision, and eternal life.

5/21/2018 18:22   It does inspire me when reading about Paul or Peter or John, all the things they did, how the Lord use them. Jesus sent them His Holy Spirit. He came upon them and gave them boldness to share the Gospel. He frees us by His grace as the Holy Spirit falls on us to do the same. Witnesses.

5/25/2018 5:05   Jesus said He is the Truth. We know He frees us from all sins, this sets us free, free from sin, free knowing we will be with Him forever, so we are free from worrying about death and the afterlife. Set Free.

5/25/2018 5:10   Jesus is with us now, and He will never leave us. His Holy Spirit wants to lead us daily and use our lives to verbally share His Gospel with as many as He leads us to.

5/25/2018 5:15   I would be a liar if I was to say that I am in perfect harmony with God's Holy Spirit all the time, but one thing I know, I seek to be led by Him daily. No matter where I am, I seek to hear His small still voice.

5/25/2018 5:16   I have to stop and listen when things happen.

5/25/2018 5:19   So wonderful to know that no one can snatch us out of His hands.

5/25/2018 5:21   We are in the potter's hands, and He is making us what He has designed us to be. This can be hard to take at times, but God never gives us more than we can handle.

5/25/2018 18:13   Jesus took back what was God's by beating Satan while He was on earth. Now we can be saved by His Grace.

5/29/2018 3:52   How do I get when things don't go as I plan, truthfully at 1st, I usually get upset, then in God's time or my time, usually a few minutes, I have always been blessed to be able to forgive anybody, anything. Thank You, Jesus.

5/29/2018 3:56   Discipline can be very hard to take; it depends on the person giving the discipline. That should not be the case, but it is, if the person giving the discipline gives it in the spirit of wisdom, humility, love, passion, and compassion, then I take it well, very well. But if a person does it in harsh fashion, that's hard for me to take even if it's true, but after a period of time, I realize, or the Lord gives me the grace to understand, and I grow. Rebuke Better Than Lashes

5/29/2018 3:57   Respect is eternal wisdom and is eternal wealth. You learn much more by respecting others.

5/29/2018 3:59   I love sensing the Holy Spirit. When He tells me to do something, I know it is going to bear much fruit. Divine Compulsion.

5/29/2018 4:00   I guess all of us have some fear, discouragement, and distress. I can say with conviction that the Lord keeps me stable and without discouragement, stress, or fear. I give it totally to the glory and grace of God. The Lord's Comfort.

5/29/2018 4:01   Being 68 years old now, I do not know how much longer I have in this world. I'm driven to do all I can to seek His wisdom and to be used by Him in these last years.

5/29/2018 4:02   To be a leader takes a lot of work, little thanks, and much prayer.

5/29/2018 4:04   To run the race, you must be disciplined. The more disciplined you are running, the better you will run. I'm running, and I seek to follow the Holy Spirit so to be used of him daily; hopefully, I'm being used to my full extent.

5/29/2018 4:07   I wish Jesus returns every day. The day we will see him in the heavens. I just want to fly up to him. Looking forward to going to the Wedding Feast of the Lamb. These bodies of ours grow weak. Mine has gotten weary. I pray that He allows me to have health and strength to do all I can until He comes or until I'm laid at rest waiting for Him to come or going directly to Him. 1 Corinthians 15:51-52, Thessalonians 4:14-16, Luke 23:43. Our Lord and King knows.

5/29/2018 17:13   Thank You, Lord. I need You and Your comfort daily. Revive Me.

5/29/2018 17:14   As Bob Dylan put it, "You got to serve somebody. I want to serve God.

5/30/2018 17:21	There's nothing wrong with money as long as it's not your God. The problem is when you have a lot of money; you have to concentrate on it; therefore, it can easily take God's place.
5/30/2018 17:24	In many places of the world, giving gifts is very acceptable and normal. The best gift we as Christians can give is sharing Jesus.
5/30/2018 17:25	When somebody honestly believes something, they share it with others. So, therefore, if we genuinely believe that Jesus is the Son of God and that He can give us eternal life, how can we hold that back from others.
5/31/2018 1:39	Trying to get the riches of this world only is an effort of fools unless they invest it in God's Kingdom.
6/1/2018 4:32	Seeking to find Him and be led by Him. This is what God wants; He wants us to find where He is working and join Him in His work— working to win the world for Jesus.
6/1/2018 4:34	God's love is overwhelming. He is with us through every moment of our lives.
6/2/2018 17:32	Inter beauty is by far more lasting than physical beauty.
6/2/2018 17:42	God is truly the only true reality. He is the Creator of all things. He is, as He told us the I Am.
6/3/2018 12:52	I love the reality of our God's plan. It is to give

the ones who submit to His Eternal Kingdom.

6/3/2018 13:07	I pray that Jesus gives me the grace to follow Him no matter what. I could say, "I will never leave Him," but I know it's always by His Grace.
6/3/2018 13:09	Wealth is only bad when it takes the heart of those who have it away from Jesus. Sad to say it happens more often than not.
6/3/2018 13:12	I know our Lord always has our eternal best in mind, but at times it's not easy. I am going through a change in my health, which is not easy to take, but I am praying for His grace and healing.
6/4/2018 15:30	I am working on immediately seeking God the moment things go wrong. I do seek Him afterward, even only minutes afterward, usually, but that minute can hurt others. Lord, help me to grow. Captive to sins.
6/5/2018 5:53	I am resting in my Lord. I desire to have His humble and gentle heart.
6/5/2018 5:55	I ask for Him to lead me daily. My heart aches to be led by His Holy Spirit.
6/5/2018 16:01	We need to keep God's Word in our mind. By His Grace, He feeds me with His Word daily. Remembering the law kills, but the Spirit of the Word gives life.
6/6/2018 4:08	I am praying for my friends and family, that they will yield to God's Holy Spirit and come to the knowledge of His Saving Grace

through Jesus.

6/6/2018 14:21	We are pruned by His Word, hearing His Word, listening to His Word, living His Word. After 46 years of service, He's purged me so many times it's unbelievable, and I thank Him for it. Pruned and Purified
6/7/2018 13:50	Make disciples and teach them to obey.
6/7/2018 13:51	Trust in the Lord, and lean not to your own understanding for a Happy Heart
6/8/2018 1:31	We study the Word of God and teach others to do the same.
6/8/2018 1:35	We will inherit the Kingdom, only by the Grace of God. I am so thankful that in the times that I suffer, our Lord gives me the grace to get through it.
6/8/2018 13:24	Jesus has cleansed me from all sin. I want to share this with as many people that I can and train others to do the same.
6/11/2018 1:31	God's grace will give me the humility I need to get through anything. Suffering for Christ.
6/11/2018 1:33	There is one life to stand up for Jesus. Always be ready to share Jesus with others. Without Jesus, no one gets into Heaven. Lips of the Wise
6/11/2018 1:33	It gives me great joy to know that God reigns forever.
6/11/2018 1:37	Forgiveness is something I have learned through life. I share those lessons with others

often. Pass It On.

6/11/2018 1:39	One of the leaders in my Church has found it necessary to separate me because of my new job. I am praying for us to fulfill this verse. Harmony Builders.
6/11/2018 1:45	I claimed Matthew 6:19-20 at the age of 22. Sold everything I had and gave my life to Jesus. I had nothing after coming back from South America at 43 years of age. Jesus has given me homes and family, wife, and love, plus service for Him. Store Your Treasures.
6/13/2018 15:57	I seek to walk in the Spirit of the Lord. When I do, He does incredible things—reaching the unreachable. As I do, He gives me JOY.
6/13/2018 15:59	I seek to walk with Jesus, can't say I don't slip and miss sometimes, but when I do, I repent and seek Him again. He Loves You.
6/13/2018 16:02	Sin blocks our communication with the Lord. It's like a cloud blocking the Sunlight. Our Lord wants us to get rid of the Sin so we can see the way He wants to lead us.
6/13/2018 16:04	Jesus gave everything, His life, even leaving heaven for 33 years to live as a man for us.
6/13/2018 16:11	I have seen and have been touched by loves forgiveness. I, too, have been able to show His Love to others.
6/13/2018 16:26	At this time, I have a lot of pain in my spine as it is out of alignment. The L4 and L5 vertebra have slipped. Also, my hip has no

cartilage. All this to say, this earthly body is temporal. In God's time, I will have my new body. Refining Fires.

6/13/2018 16:31   It's perfect when we trust in the Lord with all our hearts; this gives peace in the midst of any storm.

6/13/2018 16:33   Flooding in my house and roof damage. Physical pains from a failing body, back, hip, and lungs. By God's grace, I will continue sharing His Gospel, no matter what. In Jesus Name. Continue in Faith.

6/13/2018 16:36   Can't say I have plenty, but I have enough to share.

6/13/2018 16:38   So grateful for His Saving Grace. Jesus Saves.

6/13/2018 16:42   Jesus knew His flesh was going to be tortured, and that He was going to be hung on a cross, but He did it for us anyway.

6/14/2018 12:05   We know we will die then, we will be reunited with our King. Everything else is temporal. Keeping my eyes on this gives me peace, joy, strength, and hope.

6/14/2018 12:07   If we stay in prayer and in the Word, we will keep our eyes on Jesus.

6/15/2018 14:53   I am in a time of life with much physical pain. Our Lord knew these times would come, and He has given me the grace to bear it. I am praying for healing, praying to be led to where I can find relief. By His grace, I will be able to serve Him till the day He takes me home. Grace and Weakness.

6/16/2018 12:13 God's love for us is eternal. He created us for the purpose of being His children. He is our Heavenly Father; He wants the best for us. God has shown me unfailing love so many times. I praise Him and thank Him daily for His love and for hanging on to me through all my tribulations.

6/16/2018 12:16 I am part of the bride of Christ. It sounds strange as I am a man in this flesh, so it means I have become one with Jesus.

6/16/2018 12:19 There are many ways that help us grow deeper in Christ. By reading His Word, Praying, showing His love to others, and sharing the Gospel as we do.

6/16/2018 12:25 There is no shame in sex in marriage. Our God made man and woman and told them to have sex. He wants the world to multiply. He also told us to enjoy sex with our wife/husband. If He didn't give sexual drive and desire to man, the human race would have died off long ago. They Felt No Shame: genesis chapter 3, Song of Solomon.

6/16/2018 12:27 We are God's Church because He lives in us. I feel most confident when I am obeying His leading.

6/19/2018 3:05 We are all one in Christ because He has made us one. We are one bride of Christ. Praying, we grow closer as the Church body.

I thank You, Jesus, for helping us to be one. All One, unity in Jesus.

6/19/2018 3:06   It's so good to know that God is faithful and just to forgive us of all our sins. I'm just so thankful for Jesus. Cleansed and Forgiven.

6/19/2018 3:08   The Word I have hidden in my heart that I may not sin against God. It's just amazing that we need to do more of that. His Word changes lives daily—his spirit guides when we listen. I know I need to listen even more by His grace, I'll take those new steps closer to You, God.

6/19/2018 3:09   Only God knows how He works in each person's life. I am amazed and very, very thankful that He has allowed me to know Him and see Him walk with me through my life. I have brothers and sisters who do not know Jesus. I am praying by God's grace, that I can encourage them, enlighten them, and love them into His kingdom of love.

6/19/2018 3:13   Jesus said many are the afflictions of the righteous, but the Lord delivers them from them all. He's got His reasons for us to have many afflictions and difficulties. I honestly believe that we are actually proving ourselves to God when we hold on to him, regardless. Never Give Up; it leads to eternal rewards.

6/19/2018 3:14   The reality that gets me the most is, God wants our loyally.

6/19/2018 3:16   It is a mystery, but at the same time, it's logical, our Lord will refine us by allowing us to go through the fires of trials. We become pure on the inside. Pure as gold refined in the fire. Without those trials and tribulations, we would not be able to show who we really are. I prayed many times, asking the Lord to give me the grace for the times that He sees me going through. I pray, asking Him to hold on to me and do not let me go in Jesus' name. Trials Lead to Faith 1 Peter 1:7.

6/19/2018 19:21   Our Father in Heaven has an eternal vision for our lives. He is molding us with everything that happens. Worldwide He knows why He has allowed everything. God, our Creator, will get Glory in all things. We do not see as He sees; our job is to hang on to Jesus through good times and bad times. As in any marriage, our marriage to Jesus is till death, the death of ourselves, our ego, and old ways. Then death gives us life, eternal life, with our eternal God. As Jesus says, we are to take up our cross daily and follow Him. Oh, to be like Jesus, the all-consuming love of God. By His grace, we are being sanctified daily. This is the reason we are here on earth. 1. To love God with all our hearts. 2. To love our neighbors as ourselves. The only everlasting love we can show is when we share Jesus with our neighbors. Who are our neighbors, everyone who passes our daily paths!

6/21/2018 17:25	The only reason we are here on this earth after receiving Jesus as our Lord and King is to be used of God to reach His lost. His light lights into the universe of eternal life. He shows us that we can lead others to his light, which is infinite—Jesus Our Guide.
6/21/2018 17:27	Little children listen to their parents if they're good little children. We need to be good little children to Our Father in heaven who wants to lead us with His holy spirit. He is guiding if we are listening. That's what He means by; we must be converted and become as Little Children to enter the Kingdom of God.
6/21/2018 17:30	All that we have, all that we own is God's. He's giving it to us to use for His Glory. By His grace, we will be smart with what He's given us so we can invest it and what He's leading us to do—all to the Glory of God.
6/21/2018 17:34	By God's grace, He's allowing me to train others to reach His Harvest. If there's anything that we can do in this life, anything we can do while we're here on earth, it's to reach others with the salvation of Jesus Christ. Better yet if we can train others to do the same. I praise and thank God for allowing me to do this.
6/21/2018 17:41	Jesus Who is God came in the Flesh. He knew all things. While He was in the desert, He confronted the devil and beat him. He has all the authority on Earth and in Heaven. Yes, I have been led by the Holy Spirit into difficult

situations during my 46 years of service. He's given me the grace to go through it. I can't say I've done it all perfectly. But I know He gave me the grace to go through it and to learn from it.

6/22/2018 13:55 The Book of John says that Jesus is the Word, and the Word created everything with God and was God. Then the Word became man, and God lived on earth for thirty-three years.

6/22/2018 14:04 A lack of forgiveness brings bitterness, bitterness brings hate, hate can do horrible things, so forgive. Outsmarting Satan.

6/22/2018 16:54 The Lord promises to hear the cries of the poor and the suffering and comfort them. Social Justice.

6/25/2018 20:50 Love needs to be the base of all correction. Correction is the demonstration of true love.

6/25/2018 20:52 The Lord is merciful and is willing to forgive us. He only asks us to forsake our sinful ways and follow Him.

6/26/2018 13:59 Anger is the result of self-righteousness. I have been fighting mine for most of my adult life. Having a temper.

6/27/2018 4:53 I thank God that He has lifted my eyes and showed me His vision and carried me on. Never Tire of Doing Good.

6/27/2018 4:56 God rejects a proud spirit.

6/27/2018 4:59   I'm humbled daily. Very Thankful.

6/27/2018 5:00   I am eager to Help.

6/27/2018 5:06   There were times in my life when I did not look to Jesus. I thank the Lord He has given me His heart for the lost; this drives me forward.

6/27/2018 5:10   Satan was full of pride, and that's why He fell from heaven. A humble person's heart is not puffed up. He understands we are all equal in the eyes of our Lord. He becomes a servant of all. As for myself, I am working on that, or should I say God is working on me.

6/27/2018 5:12   We are led by the things we want in our hearts. God places His Word in our hearts so we will want to follow Him with our hearts

6/27/2018 13:48   When things go wrong, my first reaction can be seeking the solution before praying. The Lord Is Our Help. Learning.

6/27/2018 16:38   Everything we do for Jesus is eternal. For most of my 46 years, my vision was to do something for the Lord. There have been a few years in between when I got too busy, and I didn't do as much and wasn't as strong. I fell back quite a lot, but for the last ten years, I've been full time again, always seeking the Lost.

6/28/2018 13:11   I am the peacemaker if I am seeking to allow the Holy Spirit to guide me when things happen.

6/30/2018 13:43	I am so grateful for everything that God has done for me. I don't have too much and not too little, we are pretty much in the middle, but compared to the rest of the world, we in the United States are rich.
6/30/2018 13:44	I found that the Lord is with me when I seek Him in the morning, in the evening, and during the day. He's always with us; it's just at times we get so busy we leave Him behind.
6/30/2018 13:46	Nobody can stand up against God. He is on the side of those who seek Him. He will care for us in ways we don't understand or even realize. Thank you, Jesus. I don't fear anyone except for God. He Will Save.
6/30/2018 13:47	I have had my ups and downs, my hard times, and my not so hard times. Times of glorious freedoms and times with full vision and love.
6/30/2018 13:49	Sin separates us from life, from light. Stopping our sins is both liberating and a trial, but in the end, once we have gotten rid of sin, it's definitely liberating.
6/30/2018 16:19	I love that God watches over me. He has opened many doors and closed some. The open door that I'm truly grateful for is to be able to help others share the Gospel. There is nothing better in this life than seeing someone give their life to God.
7/1/2018 5:29	It's wonderful when we realize that God

watches over everything. I know there are many things we do not understand, but we will when we stand in front of Him. I put my trust in Him and in Him alone.

7/2/2018 17:16   Our Father in heaven's love cannot be measured. To know God is to fear God because He is Almighty. Everything starts and ends with God.

7/3/2018 16:43   Saul had an issue with power, worrying about whether he would lose his kingdom. I have also worried about positions at times in my life. I'm trying to deal with it, I don't really think it's holding me back at all, but yes, it does touch my life at times. There are times I think I want more, but at the same time, I'm thankful for where I am.

7/3/2018 16:46   Being patient, knowing that God is going to handle every situation. He throws different situations our way on purpose so we can deal with our areas of sin. He is a loving Father, nurturing, and training us in the way we should go. May He help us to have the humility to be able to receive all His Corrections and dealings so we can be the people who You want us to be.

7/3/2018 16:48   Our Father in heaven has sent Jesus to show us how to live and guide us so we can live lives that please God. What a blessing.

7/3/2018 16:53   Anyone who believes that they know exactly what God's doing all the time is foolish. God is God; there is no one like Him; no one understands completely What He does. He is the Great I Am. We can grow to know Him better. He gives us wisdom by His grace, but we will never ever catch up to Him because He is God.

7/4/2018 4:05	I am giving and receiving.
7/4/2018 4:11	The fear of the Lord is the beginning of wisdom. The older I get, the more I understand how little I am and how great He is.
7/4/2018 4:13	Mary, Martha's sister, discovered that the best thing we can do stay close to Jesus and learn from Him. We cannot put anything above that.
7/4/2018 4:16	God reminds His people that He delivered them from all their troubles. He does the same with me. He's done many mighty things for me, and when I forget what He's done, I can get fearful; when I remember what He's done, it gives me faith that He will do it again.
7/4/2018 14:05	We need to do as Jesus did. He served the world by dying for every one of us, but even before that as He washed the disciples' feet. He healed people. He shared God's kingdom with us in word and deed.
7/5/2018 4:11	I do give to the Church and to the persecuted Church. I use what I have to assist Churches in training to share the Gospel. I can give more and am waiting on the Lord to show me

where. Compassion.

7/5/2018 12:31	We need to do what we can to reach the world with the Gospel. Do what we can to find ways to relieve others of their hunger, both physically and spiritually.
7/8/2018 5:04	When we truly listen to the Holy Spirit, He leads us and gives us the words that are needed to be said to those He leads us to.
7/8/2018 5:07	Lift someone closer to the Lord.
7/11/2018 14:56	We are God's masterpieces; this truly amazes me.
7/12/2018 1:44	Make Disciples, teaching them to observe God's Laws.
7/12/2018 1:45	Lord help us to pray for the needy.
7/12/2018 3:40	We have been given what we have been given so we can enhance the kingdom of God on Earth in whichever way He leads us. The ministry God has given me has been blessed financially by people who feel led to support the ministry. I truly know it's all by His grace, and I'm very thankful for others who believe in You Lord.
7/12/2018 3:49	We have been blessed in so many ways. Yes, I give my time, money, and effort to reach as many as possible with the Gospel of Jesus Christ. I could still do more. By His grace, He will allow me to do more for His kingdom.

7/12/2018 3:50	We are to lift up Jesus so others will come to Him. That's the one and only way that we can lift people up. Only Jesus can truly lift them up.
7/12/2018 3:51	Jesus is the only true Shepherd.
7/12/2018 3:56	I don't believe there is a stronger love on this Earth than a mother's love for her child. John 3:16 shows God's love is even stronger than that. God's love for all and every person on this Earth is stronger than the love of a mother for her child.
7/12/2018 16:28	In Acts chapter four, we see all that believed lived together, sharing all things. People were attracted to the love and care they saw.
7/16/2018 3:49	When we give as unto our Lord, it is lifting His Kingdom. Time is the hardest part of our lives to give. I am quite busy, but I know I can get rid of some of the fluff and work more for the Lord.
7/16/2018 3:52	True love, sacrificial love is not really seen much in this world. That's why I cry with joy when I see it. Some brothers are showing their love for me by sponsoring God's work that He is allowing me to do.
7/16/2018 3:58	No matter how much good we do, we will always have sins in our lives. God will not allow sin into His Kingdom, not even one sin. I know I need Jesus. He Saved Us.

7/16/2018 4:05	Becoming citizens of Heaven is such a gift. Living as Citizen of Heaven is a gift. We all are still growing in the nature of Christ Jesus, and I believe we will continue to grow to be His creation until the day we enter into his kingdom.
7/16/2018 12:38	When we compare God's Kingdom to the pains and sorrows in this life, which will be left behind, Understanding this truth, we must choose Him above all, we must do all we can to show His light to the world
7/17/2018 12:19	The life of those in the Church today does not compare to those who were in the early Church. The great majority of those going to Church have very little if any guidance of the Holy Spirit. I believe this is why Jesus will say to many that come to Him in His Kingdom. I do not know you. This, truly, truly, truly is horrible and a terrible event; it is heartbreaking. I call out for mercy for my life often. I feel lost when the Holy Spirit isn't guiding me. I feel blessed to be able to train others and help them to memorize God's Word, the Bible, and show them how to share the Gospel. This is a great joy for me.
7/21/2018 15:48	People can influence others to sin. We have to influence them to receive the forgiveness of sin. When sharing with others about their sin, we must take note that we are sinners also. Let's fulfill Jesus's second command to us all, love the neighbor as yourself.

7/21/2018 18:10	Lord, please keep us during hard times.
7/21/2018 18:12	Lord help me to see the people You have directed me to.
7/24/2018 4:31	Our own righteousness means nothing. It's only when we lift up God in Jesus's Name that something is accomplished for God's Kingdom.
7/24/2018 4:35	Only what is done for Jesus will last. Love = Obedience.
7/31/2018 17:02	God is love if what we give is not given in love, God's love, it would be given for self-exhortation
7/31/2018 17:04	We are challenged daily to live in love.
8/1/2018 1:43	Love your neighbor as yourself. I am trying to make sure I reach out to those the Lord has put in my path. My neighbor and others.
8/7/2018 12:27	The rebel, Satan, always starts the disunity.
8/7/2018 12:28	We all are growing in love. Stop Faking.
8/7/2018 12:29	We are representatives of Jesus, something we have to be constantly aware of.
8/7/2018 12:31	Forgiveness is a strength; we feel great when we administer it. Be the first to forgive.
8/9/2018 5:02	I want to live now as if Jesus has returned already. By His Grace, I will be a good representation of His Kingdom here on earth. Jesus is coming and soon.

8/9/2018 5:03	God's is LOVE. We are His children; we too are to live in His love. It's so important to tell others how we became God's children.
8/10/2018 12:57	I believe that Jesus is the only human being who loved our God with all His heart. I am in love with God and His Son and His Holy Spirit. I'm seeking to give all to Him, and by His Grace, I will love God with all my being when I come into His presence and throw my crown to Jesus. Then I will sit at His feet.
8/11/2018 0:53	The best thing in this life and in the eternal life, is the fact that we will be one. We will live in the only real life that exists: life in the Kingdom of God.
8/13/2018 14:35	I believe the devil always tries to divide and conquer. We always have to seek God for His unifying Spirit. I have had leaders that have not learned this yet, and it has held back what could be accomplished for God's Kingdom. They have been so worried about someone usurping their power that they drive away others that could grow with them.
8/13/2018 14:39	There is always somebody that knows more than we do. I try to be humble and listen and be led, but I can't say I always have. I found the best thing to do, even when you're right,' and there's conflict, be quiet and let the Lord take care of it and move on. Most things are smaller than we think.
8/15/2018 12:16	Jesus served humanity and God. We are to

do the same. I believe that most of the Pastors that I have had the joy to meet have been serving humans and God, but many have lost the vision to go into the highways and byways to compel others to come to the wedding feast of the Lamb.

8/15/2018 12:19   I am having a hard time with one of my leaders. I have been humbled by her and continue being humbled by her. I find this hard to take, but I pray for her. I do have sympathy for her and love her in the Lord.

8/16/2018 15:37   We have to have the patience to forgive.

8/17/2018 12:28   Take up our cross daily and give up our life for Him.

8/18/2018 12:14   God is love.

8/19/2018 12:24   Serving our God takes on both physical and spiritual commitment. The world is starving for the Word of God. They don't know why they are unfulfilled, unhappy, and feel incomplete. In the world we live in today, we can reach those around us and abroad.

8/20/2018 13:00   Our Father in heaven is always waiting with arms open. We need to know that He loves us and will never leave us. All He asks is that we seek Him, then we will find Him.

8/22/2018 12:35   When things don't seem to be going your way. When somebody does something wrong to you, what will help is to think about Jesus and what he did and how he reacted to everything. Oh, how I want to be more like Jesus. Dear Friends, Let's Love.

8/23/2018 12:50   Love is the key to everything. Without Love, we can't please God. We can't please others; we can't please ourselves. 1st Corinthians 13. Love Covers All

8/25/2018 14:47   I am so thankful for His gift of salvation.

8/25/2018 14:53   It hurts everyone when love is not real. When love is real, it brings God's blessings of a relationship with Him and others. God's love radiates toward everyone.

8/27/2018 13:01   The most generous gift we can give is a message about the relationship with Jesus that we can have. Giving others the eternal riches of eternal life

8/27/2018 13:03   I need to pray daily to know who to give to. To share what God's given to me. I can't say I have much, but I do have more than many, and less than many others, but my giving does not depend on how much you have. It's in our heart to give.

8/29/2018 13:36   Jesus showed us how to live, how to love, how to reach out to God, through Jesus. This is the only way we can reach out to God since God gave Him total Authority on the Earth and in Heaven. Jesus Loves the Church.

8/31/2018 12:35   Let's give forgiveness, give God's love, give money, food, clothing, and even Godly advice.

9/3/2018 12:53 We are to serve one another just as Jesus served His disciples when He washed the disciple's feet. I'm just so grateful God loves me so much that I can walk with Him, talk with Him, and be with Him daily. Lord, help me to do that in Jesus's Name. A Servant's heart.

9/6/2018 12:36 I can't think of anyone that I have any grudge against.

9/7/2018 17:24 Sharing eternal life with as many as possible.

9/8/2018 12:41 The Gospel of our Lord and King Jesus is truth. Jesus said He was the truth. He said I am the way, the truth, and the life. By his grace, I'm training Fishers of Men to tell this truth to the world.

9/10/2018 13:00 Pray for and uplift one another.

9/10/2018 13:02 For me, my deep desire and prayer is for God to use me, to pour through me. Using His Word, the Bible, I can quote it to others to lift them up to God. When I am, I know that is God smiling on me.

9/11/2018 13:52 Love the Lord with all your heart and your neighbor as yourself.

9/12/2018 12:49 We as Christians need to be willing to be living as we have been commanded to. Which is to love one another. We will be able to live this so much more when we do it together, Harmonious Living.

9/14/2018 15:06	Sin must be pointed out, and Lord willing, when this happens to us, we will repent and change our ways. By putting this in action, we will keep the body of Christ healthy.
9/16/2018 18:09	Are you willing to forgive?
9/21/2018 13:52	Growing in God's Spirit is growing in his mercy and His loving-kindness, understanding that without Him, without His love, mercy, and kindness, I would be lost.
9/21/2018 13:55	Talking to our Father in Heaven is a priority. By Your grace, I'll learn that more and more, day by day, we will take the time to hear from our Father in heaven.
9/22/2018 13:43	God always has our eternal lives in mind.
9/24/2018 13:04	We are all the same. We can learn from everyone. Financial status has nothing to do with it. Harmony is a beautiful word and even Lovelier when we live it.
9/25/2018 12:37	It's always good to give and to do things for other people, but the best thing that we can do is to lead them to Jesus.
9/26/2018 13:22	God's harvest is around me at all times of the day. Lord, open our eyes to see as You see.
9/29/2018 13:40	Lord, please have mercy on me and give my loved ones and me the grace to go through the suffering of our bodies. Help all things be to Your Glory.
9/30/2018 14:13	Most the time, I feel my Lord close and

personal, but there have been times when I felt He was far away. I always remember that He is love and that He loves me. He's God, all-powerful. I know His ways are not my ways. He's so far beyond me.

9/30/2018 14:26 When the light is on, we can see, when it's dark, we can't. When we see the light of God's love, His vision, and His understanding, it opens up our understanding about what the world is all about. Regardless if others are believing in God or not, He still reigns. We will all stand before Him after we die. His plan is that we walk with Him NOW, not only after we die physically, so when we stand before Him, we can say, " I walked with Your Son Jesus, and He showed me the way and paid the price on the Cross for me.

10/2/2018 13:39 Only a loving father takes the time to correct his son or daughter. He's loved us from the foundation of the world. God's design was to walk in love with us. Only by His grace through Jesus can we walk with Him. We can't force it. We can't make it work with our own willpower; we just have to seek Him with all our hearts in Jesus. Trusting God's Word.

10/2/2018 13:44 I love allowing the Holy Spirit to pass through me to others. Many things I've been through and continue to go through, has always driven me to find the favor of my Father in Heaven. There have been times that I've been walking in the dark, and I have no idea why? In these times, I can't sense the Father's Holy Spirit on me, but I know He will never leave me or forsake me.

10/4/2018 4:19   When my parents were alive, I treated them with respect, but they didn't like that I was a Missionary in South America. After returning from Argentina, I took care of my father for about 24 years before he passed away. He was a Catholic, but he said he believed in Jesus's saving Grace. I'm claiming that in Jesus' name.

10/4/2018 13:32   I love bearing fruit for the kingdom of God. Anything we do for God will last forever. The Bible is the Word of God and is what gives us the power to bear fruit unto Him. Our personal lives are testimonies to the Eternal Kingdom of God. Whenever we lead anyone to know Jesus, they will be with Him and us in Eternity. As we grow in Jesus by reading His word, He allows us to bear fruit for his King. All praise to God. John 15.

10/5/2018 12:47   God loves the world. The Bible tells us when somebody loves the world, the love of the Father is not in them. In 1 John 2, John tells us; Do not love the world or the things that belong to the world. If anyone loves the world, love for the Father is not in him. For everything that belongs to the world-the lust of the flesh, the lust of the eyes, and the pride in one's life is not from the Father but is from the world. And the world, with its lust, is passing away, but the one who does God's will remain forever. So, God does what's best for those He loves; therefore, God is patient, even when He takes things from us.

10/9/2018 12:05   I'm being told that I might need a pacemaker to keep my heart going. I'm praying about what to do. I need to hear from You, Lord. I know Your love endures forever. At this time, I sure need You.

10/10/2018 13:38   The Bible says Jesus was angry at times, and He felt deep compassion for the human race. Jesus has given me compassion for those around me, who are crying and feeling lost. The majority of people in this world do not understand that there is life after death.

10/10/2018 13:40   We are called to be light; we're called to show the love of Christ to as many as possible. Holy Spirit, please give us the grace to do so, regardless of anything else that happens. In Jesus' name.

10/11/2018 13:38   I've been asked to pray for others, which I do. I do my best to comfort others in times of need. Have aided friends with needs etc. The best is when the Lord allows me to tell them about what Jesus did for them.

10/12/2018 13:25   John 13:34 says; A new command I give you: **Love one another. As I have loved you**, so you must love one another. By this, everyone will know that you are my disciples. We need this definition of love because it gives us a standard to live up to. The most meaningful for me right now is endurance. God is gracious, and He is helping me through, leaning to Trust in Him regardless.

10/14/2018 13:44   Pray for one another, we are in a spiritual war.

10/14/2018 13:50   Jesus fulfilled the prophecies about the Messiah who would come and take the sins of the world. I need to continue in the work of telling as many as I can.

10/16/2018 12:56   If nobody pays you back after you lent something to them and it's making it extremely hard to have a relationship with them. It's better just to give it to them.

10/16/2018 12:57   Anytime anybody finds out about a lie. It can allow the devil to win. Lies are of the devil. May the Lord help us to be truthful always with mercy and love. Stop Telling Lies.

10/19/2018 21:38   What a great heart King David had. May we have the same.

10/19/2018 21:41   As seen through history, man, can never save himself. May God give us the grace for the moments of need and the power for the moments of need. All glory to God.

10/22/2018 2:59   It is wonderful to see that God, throughout time, has always wanted us to walk with Him on this earth. We are His creation, and we need to give Him Glory for Who He is, the Father of all creation. I am intensely grateful that He is able to keep us and that we will see

His Great Glory with great joy. Thank You, Jesus.

10/22/2018 3:09

I am going through a time of physical weakness and the greatest spiritual battle of my life. The Lord comforted me with two men of God who share their hearts with me without knowing how bad I needed encouragement. Both of which did not direct their message to me personally, but to the whole congregation. I know it was God speaking to me. Thank You, Jesus.

10/22/2018 13:35

The devil wants to do all he can to stop us from doing God's work. God's work is merely believing in His Son Jesus and sharing Him with others. The devil has been around since the beginning, so we can't outsmart him. Our only chance is to yield to God's Holy Spirit and let Him take on the devil. If we do, we can't lose.

10/24/2018 13:17

I cannot think of any enemies at this time in my life. I had enemies in the past. I had an experience of blowing up on a person who would not let us out of a house contract when I had a home Church in Posadas Argentina, even when I showed him the 43 dead scorpions. My home Church home had nine children and eight adults who could have been strung. He was becoming an enemy. The Lord told me to go to him and say I was sorry for blowing upon him. I fought doing it for a few days, but when I did, the hate that was dominating me was lifted off me. Turn the Tables.

10/25/2018 12:40	We are in a battle with not only the devil but also our own flesh. I know for myself; my desire is to live as Jesus did, but it is a daily battle to follow Him. Self-Control.
10/27/2018 14:56	I lived a life away from God until I was 22. Now it seems I am always thanking God for His mercy. Recently my health has been bad, even close to death. I have been calling out to Jesus, and He has heard my prayers and is bringing me back to health.
10/29/2018 12:57	Loyalty is a demonstration of God's love as He will never leave us or forsake us.
11/1/2018 15:42	Jesus called us His friends. I'm so thankful He is, He knows what I'm going through, and He will give me His grace to get through it or take me home. Praying that He Gives me the Grace for that too. In Jesus Name, Amen.
11/2/2018 14:15	Life can be very tough at times. I'm going through a tough time myself right now, but I know all things work towards good for those who love the Lord Jesus. Exhausted.
11/3/2018 14:06	Love is light and life; without love, there is no meaning to life. God is the only Everlasting being. His love is all and all. Jesus showed this when He was on earth. He was God in a physical person.
11/7/2018 18:22	It will be great, outstanding, unbelievable, exhilarating, fabulous, and incredible to see

Jesus when he returns in the heavens. I'm totally excited. We will be pure as He is on the entrance of heaven. In Jesus' name, amen. Eager Expectation.

11/7/2018 18:28   I am going through a life-death situation. I know that God has given me a deeper connection with him because of it. He's given me a deeper faith since going through this episode. Suffering truly does help us grow stronger in faith. God knows exactly what we need. New Strength

11/7/2018 18:31   Taking up the Cross of Christ is nothing more than opening our mouths and telling the world what Jesus has done for us. That's what the first disciples did; that's what we need to do too, Daily. We, as His children, need to tell others about our loving Father and what He has done for us through His Son Jesus. One would think the only way we could be totally like Christ is if we were to sell our homes, give away everything, put on a pair of sandals, and walk the walk he has walked. So, understanding this, I reckon we're all selfish. How to Follow the Leader

11/10/2018 23:53   Jesus was led by the Holy Spirit always. By God's grace, I will reach out to everyone with this truth. Be an Example.

11/11/2018 17:21   The Bible truly is food for our soul. When we take the time to read the Bible daily, our spirit is lifted, strengthen, envisioned, and fed. We eat physical food for the physical body. We must eat spiritual food (The Bible) for our spiritual life. Thank you, Jesus, for showing us the way and making away, the only way to heaven. Sustenance

11/12/2018 16:48   I believe that hate is anything that moves people away from God. Love is anything that brings people closer to God through Jesus.

11/14/2018 14:40   When we have God's peace, we cannot be thankless. In those moments that we stop, look, and listen for the Holy Spirit of God, Who was sent by Jesus, that's when we can experience his peace. For any Christian, anyone that calls themselves a child of God, it is imperative that we stop every day to talk to our Lord. This is the only way that we will walk in His peace and hear the commands of our commander so we can follow what He wills us to do daily.

11/16/2018 16:10   I am unworthy and undeserving to walk with God, but I'm grateful that I am walking with Him now by His mercy alone.

11/16/2018 16:11   I have found it better to encourage rather than be judgmental. To lift up is better than judging.

11/19/2018 0:07   The cross of Jesus was and is the only way God will bring the world back to Himself. So grateful to this to be true. God is for us and not against us.

11/19/2018 0:12   God has promised that He will guide us and direct our path. I am so pleased that He has allowed me to serve Him. God's Guidance.

11/19/2018 14:13   Being 68 years old, I totally understand that my time on this Earth is coming to an end shortly, but then my eternal life will continue forever. Eternity began the moment I received the gift of eternal life by asking Jesus to forgive my sins and guide my life. When I leave this body, I will continue in my heavenly body. Praise be to Jesus and Jesus alone for dying on the cross for me and you.

11/20/2018 13:48   People remember what generous people do for a lifetime or two, but those who use their money to bring others to the knowledge of Jesus Christ will be remembered for eternity—fighting Evil with Money.

11/22/2018 2:51   Jesus "is" the Word of God. The written Words in the Bible show us what God has done and what He is doing.

11/22/2018 15:59   The Holy Spirit gives me peace and guidance and vision for our Fathers Kingdom. The Source of Hope.

11/23/2018 13:36   I know my Father in heaven has a plan for me, and by His Grace, I will walk in the path.

11/24/2018 14:01   To fix our eyes on God means to stay focused daily. When I think about Jesus and the way He loved during His life while He was on Earth, His life inspires me to be like Him. His Words and actions drive my desires. I want to be like Jesus. I fall deeper and deeper in love with Jesus as I read His Word daily. Fix Your Thoughts.

11/26/2018 14:47   The Word says Jesus learned through the things He suffered. It is the same with us. We learn from the things we go through. This way, we can have compassion for others who go through things we have lived through.

11/26/2018 14:49   Jesus is the only person Who was in this world and Who had a pure heart, so when we read and pray about Jesus, we can see God and a pure heart through Him and His Words—seeing God.

11/27/2018 17:17   King David came to the understanding that the only thing that really matters during this life is that we are walking with God. That is the reason we are here and the only way to true reality and eternal life.

11/30/2018 15:36   It says in the Gospel of Luke 6:45, A good man out of the good treasures of his heart brings forth that which is good and an evil man out of the evil treasures of his heart brings forth that which is evil, because out of the abundance of the heart his mouth speaks. So, therefore, it's important for us to study the Word of God daily. All humankind, both male and female, have some evil in their hearts. We are born that way. The ways of the world drive us away from God, and this is very evil. Therefore, the only way to stay close to Him is to stay close to Him through His Word. Please take time today to read and meditate on the word of God.

| 11/30/2018 16:20 | It is imperative that we read the Word of God to see His truth, the only Truth because many lies are being poured through the media. TV, radio, schools, and books. Many are taking these lies as truth. Only the Bible, nothing else's, but the Word of our Creator is truth. He is Alive and Powerful |

11/30/2018 16:22   God lives in each one of His children. Those who have been born again by receiving Jesus as Lord and King. To love others is to love God who lives in us. If we do, we will fulfill the command of Jesus, love one another.

12/1/2018 15:12   God is in control even in the times when we think He's not. So, when the leaders of the country do things that are bad, His Glory will come out of it regardless. Our best position is to seek Him in all situations. When we do, He will see us through our Red Sea and save us for His eternal glory in heaven.

12/3/2018 14:41   I absolutely love serving the Lord.

12/3/2018 14:43   Many times, I have needed to be hidden in the presence of the Lord, driven to seek Him in times of need. I believe that we as humans dislike having hard times, but if we are driven into the presence of the Lord, are these times good or bad? If these hard times drive us to seek God, then they are for our good. Romans 8:28 And we know that for those who love God all things work together for good, for those who are called according to his purpose. May God help us to remember this and seek Him during our times of trouble. If someone does not, then it will drive them towards bitterness, heartache, and farther away from God and others. Matthew 10:28 And fear, not them which kill the body but are not able to kill the soul: but rather fear Him which is able to destroy both soul and body in hell.　Are not two sparrows sold for a farthing? And one of them shall not fall on the ground without your Father. The very hairs of your head are all numbered. Fear ye not, therefore, ye are of more value than many sparrows.　Whosoever, therefore, shall confess Me before men, him will I confess also before my Father which is in heaven. But whosoever shall deny Me before men; he will I also deny before My Father which is in heaven.　Matthew 10:28-33 KJV. Let's remember that God is our Father in heaven, and He always wants what is best for us. Revelation 2:9 I know thy works, and tribulation, and poverty, (but thou art rich) and I know the blasphemy of them which say they are Jews, and are not, but are the synagogue of Satan.　Fear none of those things which thou shalt suffer: behold, the devil shall cast some of you into prison, that ye may be tried; and ye shall have tribulation ten days: be thou faithful unto death, and I will give thee a crown of life.　He that hath an ear let him hear what the Spirit saith unto the churches; He that overcomes shall not be hurt of the second death. Revelation 2:9-11 KJV

12/6/2018 14:18

By the grace of Jesus, we will be ready to daily lay down our pride and take those "Divine Appointments" that God leads us to. We will share the Greatest News that anyone will ever hear that Jesus laid down His life for us. That He has removed sin from the world and all we need to do is give them to Jesus. If someone refuses to surrender to Jesus, they will have to stand before our Creator and confess that they did not want to surrender to the King of Kings, Jesus. The only judgment for this is a continual separation from Jesus for eternity. This is called hell. Let's be bold with this truth. Allow the Holy Spirit of God to give you His boldness combined with His love and mercy so you can share about the gift of God that came through Jesus on the cross. Ephesians 2:8-9.

12/6/2018 14:31

I thank You Lord that You have shown Your love to all human beings.

12/6/2018 17:34

How does remembering God's mercy on you help you to relate to others? Romans 3:23-24 Says; For all have sinned and fall short of the glory of God, and all are justified freely by his grace through the redemption that came by Christ Jesus. When I look over my life, I see both good and bad. As a child, I heard about Jesus. I saw Him hanging on the cross on the few days we went to Church. Did it change my life? No sad to say. As life moved on, I stop going to Church and only talk to God when things did not go my way. After spending time in the Navy off the coast of Vietnam, I returned to the USA and met Jesus when I was twenty-two. My life changed completely. I was blessed to serve Jesus in South America for thirteen years and then four years in Spain. I continue to serve Jesus now. Praise His Name.

12/10/2018 3:36   Ruth had become one with Naomi. What an incredible bond of love. We can stay close to our friends, even when they move far away.

12/16/2018 3:35   There is no better investment than to invest in the Lord's Kingdom. It is really only giving back what God has given us. It's all His in really.

12/16/2018 3:38   There are so many times when God has pulled me through hard times. The last one was when my heartbeat went down to 27. I had lost all my strength and really felt as though I was dying. God saw fit to allow me to get a pacemaker. My energy came back again, so I now can serve Him again for more years.

12/18/2018 16:01   It truly is a mystery to see how God works in our lives. He knows what we need spiritually and what He needs to do to get us to be the men and women that He wants us to be. May the Lord help us to be ready and willing to receive His change at His time, so He can mold us to be who He wants us to be eternally. I've seen in my own life that I need to change in certain areas that I know are not up to His standard. I am seeking the way to correct those areas in my life now.

12/18/2018 16:05   We need to always realize that seeking to hear from the Master is the best and foremost thing we should be doing. There are always pressures in this life, no matter what part of the world you live in. There are pressures on a daily basis; again, our most important job is to seek the Lord and do our best to change the things that need to be changed as soon as we can.

12/18/2018 16:09   Oh, what a comfort to know God is on our side. May He help us to seek Him in all our ways so He can direct our paths.

12/18/2018 16:19   Knowing that Jesus has shown us mercy, kindness, and gentleness. We are to do the same for those around us all the time. We are reflecting God's love towards them. On occasions, I know my strong personality has been overwhelming for some. By Your grace, Lord, You have had them overlook this weakness of mine.

12/18/2018 16:24   Jesus, at great sacrifice, did what He did to bring us back to God. How long will it take for us to become like Jesus? I don't know. I seek to be like Him and have been seeking to be like Him 47 years, and I'm still not there. By his grace, I'm getting closer each day. I know on our entrance into heaven we will be given this gift, but I want to be like Him here too.

12/18/2018 16:25	God is Love, and there is nothing or no one Greater than God. These Three Things, faith, hope, and love. But the greatest of these is love. 1 Cor. 13.
12/18/2018 16:32	Paul shares with us that Jesus Christ is the only way that we, in our sinful nature, can be brought back to God. I agree with Paul fighting our sinful nature is a daily fight and will be till the day we stand before God. We will win, only by the grace of our Lord and Savior Jesus.
12/18/2018 16:33	There is great joy when we serve someone.
12/18/2018 16:37	Oh Lord, help us to learn from the life experience of Jonah. There are so many times we think such and such should happen, instead of knowing that God knows what He's doing and accepting it for what it is, growing by it, and knowing that He is all-knowing. We are to join Him in His labors.
12/22/2018 15:45	I want to submit to the Holy Spirit every day, so He can use me to reach the world with the saving message of Jesus.
12/24/2018 16:12	Thank You, Jesus. You know the hearts of all men and women; therefore, You knew eternal life with You had to be a gift.

12/25/2018 22:18	Give. Love Defined.
12/25/2018 22:19	We are precious in His sight.
12/25/2018 23:56	Jesus came to save the world He created. If we humble ourselves to realize that we are nothing, when we stand in front of a perfect God, then and only then can He begin to use our lives.
12/30/2018 8:45	We can have strength and peace in the midst of storms.
12/30/2018 8:48	Loving God's Word, the Bible, and Jesus give us delight.
12/30/2018 8:51	Being Faithful is actively seeking to be led by the Holy Spirit. This is how Disciples are made.
12/30/2018 8:57	Jesus knew His physical body would suffer. He would be shedding His physical body and taking up His Heavenly body that will never suffer again. In times when I have suffered physical pain, I try to remember this.
12/31/2018 14:07	The Word of God is as sweet as honey. ("God's Word being Jesus") He gives me hope and vision. He guides me and comforts me. He gives me a reason to live and a way to grow. He is the light of life.
1/3/2019 14:07	God is over all things. I must always remind myself of this in the good times and the bad times. I have seen God move in mysterious ways, way above my understanding.

1/3/2019 14:35	God, our Father, and Creator loves us and wants all things to work towards our good and the eternal person He has designed us to become.
1/3/2019 14:38	Jesus washed His disciples' feet to show us what we are to do and how we are to live.
1/4/2019 14:20	Joseph believed God had a plan for him as a young boy, but he went through many trials, sufferings, and pain. I don't think he had any idea the Lord would be using his life to the degree He used it. Suffering is a tough thing for me, but I know God has a reason. I just strive to remain faithful.
1/8/2019 13:15	Jesus has won the battle against the enemy of God, Satan. Only Jesus can give us the victory over any and all that comes before us in this life and for eternity. "We that have come to the end of ourselves seek Him." Then He gives freedom.
1/11/2019 20:24	Jesus forgives our past sins and the sins we are fighting daily. It has to be by grace because I would not have a connection with the Lord if it weren't for Grace. Don't let guilt be a barrier; seek forgiveness.
1/18/2019 14:54	Jesus is more valuable than any other thing or person. Without Jesus, we have nothing.
1/18/2019 14:58	By our Lord's grace, He has allowed me to pray for my persecutors. It takes a few hours sometimes. No Grumbling.

1/18/2019 15:00	God, our Creator, knows all things, guides all things, and if we find His guidance, we have found the best of all.
1/18/2019 15:02	It's so wonderful to know our Father in heaven has our lives in His hands. Be Strong and Courageous.
1/19/2019 4:42	Our God is with us during our ups and downs.
1/19/2019 4:44	God is with us always. It does not seem like it sometimes, but Jesus said He would never leave us or forsake us.
1/19/2019 4:48	All things that happen to God's children will lead them to more usefulness both here and in eternity if we let them.
1/24/2019 2:54	By His Grace, I lift His Name up to those He leads me to daily.
1/24/2019 2:57	Pleasing God is when we seek to hear from His Holy Spirit and obey Him.
1/24/2019 2:59	Humbly serve. Imitate Jesus.
1/24/2019 3:02	Humility is a great gift. Learning it is not easy.
1/24/2019 13:44	Lord, You know my heart. Thank You for Your continued Love and care for me. Thank You for not letting me go. Please help me to be the son You want me to be. Throw Off the Old.
1/26/2019 15:33	I hear God is saying, don't be afraid I know your health and life span. Trust Me, Your

Father.

1/26/2019 15:36   Jesus says, Trust Me. He Is Our Salvation.

1/28/2019 13:56   The death of my father was hard to go through. I know he believed in Jesus, so I will see him again. Still was awfully hard to see him suffer. Sorrow.

1/30/2019 14:18   Practice mercy, sometimes if we don't, the child of God may become so discouraged that the devil would have an easier job of making them fall away from the faith. I have felt like this at times, so I know we are always to seek to lift up and not put down. Forgive Others.

2/7/2019 14:09   Lord help us to live what we preach.

2/7/2019 14:11   It is a fearful thing to fall in the hands of the Lord, and it is a fearful thing not to fall into the hands of the Lord. Incredibly grateful for Jesus. Heart Examinations.

2/7/2019 14:12   Praise the Lord for Godly women.

2/8/2019 13:56   Lord, I ask You to help me yield to You when speaking and praying with others. Please let me know how to let You shine through me.

2/9/2019 17:15   We all have a blessed life when we allow love to control us. We spent so much time of our lives with our parents; our lives are set in motion with them, so strive to love them in their passing years. It also reflects our Father in heaven and is a commandment.

2/10/2019 13:18	It is a joy for me to get people excited about reaching others for Jesus. It breaks my heart, knowing that many are almost blind to the reality that without the saving grace of Jesus, everyone will be going to Hell.
2/11/2019 14:51	I try to pay debt off as soon as possible. Don't let debt be your Master.
2/13/2019 21:12	Our Lord has reasons for everything that happens in our lives. Yes, we are fragile beings. We are on an eternal path, either towards the Kingdom of Jesus or Hell.
2/14/2019 19:48	This, by far, is the most important thing we have to do as children of God. Listen for the small still voice of His Holy Spirit. Be led by the Spirit, for those are the children of God.
2/20/2019 13:20	I want to be like Jesus 1. Because He told us to follow or be like Him, 2. He came to Earth to show us how to live.
2/20/2019 13:21	Getting better by receiving constructive criticism.
2/20/2019 13:24	God is light, and there is no darkness in Him. We are human, and we are not perfect like God, so we have darkness. Seek to walk in Jesus daily. He is my only hope.
2/23/2019 14:17	So grateful for those who see how the Lord is using my life to reach the lost and teach others how to share the Gospel.
2/23/2019 21:51	God has commanded us first and for most to tell people about His Saving Grace given by

Jesus.

2/23/2019 21:56 Moses was in the presents of God. His life was controlled and kept by God to do His will. He was used to set forth the Commandments of God for the world. Jesus said they were fulfilled with two Commands. Love God and Love your neighbor.

2/24/2019 13:56 I try to and live as a temple of God, showing Him in my life. I love it when I see Jesus shine through me. The closer I get to God, the more I see myself and the sinner I am. The light, love, and mercy of God shown through Jesus is amazing. My goal is to be like Him.

2/26/2019 13:37 God is the Creator of us and all things. He does what He will because no one can judge Him except Himself. He has told us that His Word is forever and that it is to be trusted. We as His children can hold Him to His Word, but with fear and trembling. He is Almighty.

2/28/2019 14:06 Every day is a new day with Battles and victories. Only holding on to Jesus can we get through with Joy.

2/28/2019 14:09 When I look over my life, I see the hand of God. He has had grace on me even when I didn't deserve it. His mercies are new every morning. I love being with Him.

3/1/2019 14:58 To obey is to go and share with others about His gift of eternal life.

3/2/2019 14:20 Christ was the visible image of God because

He is God.

3/4/2019 16:13	I pray for mercy. Mercy for my loved ones. For Susie, please Jesus rebuke the devil and any demon who is trying to keep her away from knowing You better by studying Your Word. Please protect and guide her and allow her to have an even closer relationship with You, Jesus. In Jesus Name.
3/4/2019 16:14	Thank You, Jesus, for Your victory. We can have no victory without You. You are the Vine, and we are the branches.
3/6/2019 14:23	Our physical bodies are weak, but Jesus in us is our strength. Thank You, Jesus, for coming to Earth and dying for us. Thank You for sending Your Holy Spirit to guide and care for us. I need You. We are fragile clay jars.
3/8/2019 1:05	Our Lord is so gracious to me and to all those who come to know Him. No one will ever be good enough to walk with God. We all sin. Many in this world think their good deeds will get them into heaven, but good works do not get us into heaven. Only being perfect in God's eyes gets into heaven, so we have to be cleansed by the blood of Christ Jesus in order to have our souls cleaned.
3/8/2019 14:09	Sad to say the higher percentage of so-called Christians never study the Bible, so how can they keep God's Word? I know Salvation is a gift, but once we receive the gift, I mean truly receive the gift, how can we

not seek to study to be good followers of Jesus. And how can we not desire to share His gift with as many as possible?

3/10/2019 12:42   By telling people about our King Jesus, we become His Ambassadors.

3/11/2019 13:00   The goal is to be like Jesus. The closer I get to Him, the more Holy I'll be. This is my desire. Now the battle is getting out of my old ways. The victory is Romans 12:2. Holy Is as Holy Does.

3/13/2019 13:53   We have many trials in life. We can allow them to harden our hearts or break our hearts. Jesus wept for the hardest of hearts. Lord, allow me to do the same.

3/13/2019 13:54   Godly discipline = Love

3/16/2019 18:01   God created the world for His purpose. We know He loves the world. John 3:16.

3/16/2019 18:02   Jesus is the Shepard of His sheep, me, and you.

3/16/2019 18:06   Our Father in heaven has our eternal best in mind, always.

3/18/2019 2:28   I only need enough money to keep going to Churches and training leaders in Evangelism. Each leader that starts training others in Evangelism is worth everything I can give to assist it to get set up.

3/18/2019 17:03   Considering that I will be with God for eternity, I definitely want to dedicate my time and loyalty to Him while here on Earth.

3/20/2019 16:05 , God is our Creator. He can do as He wills. Fear not them who kill the body but can't kill the soul. Fear God who can kill both body and soul. This also leads to loving Him 🖤.

3/20/2019 16:59 Our roots are our foundation in The Word. I pray daily, read, and study the Word most every day, and claim Titus 3:5.

3/22/2019 15:36 John's baptism was one of repentance. We need both baptisms. Repentance of the heart and baptism of the Spirit. All those who are led by the Holy Spirit are children of God— wearing Christ, Like Clothes.

3/22/2019 15:37 By His grace and mercy, I'm growing day by day. By His Grace, I will continue for eternity.

3/23/2019 13:28 I want God in my life. Jonah had a very difficult thing to do. Nineveh was a very bad place, and Jonah was putting his life on the line. May the Lord help us to be willing to put our life on the line when he calls us.

3/24/2019 12:31 We are teaching people who don't even realize they are rebelling against God. When sharing God's Words with others, do it with wisdom and mercy.

3/26/2019 13:07 One of the most important things to learn is that we are to love others as ourselves. This means do not do things to others that you don't want them to do to you. So, when they say, "let do something, and they leave you waiting or don't even show up," how does that make you feel? Well, don't do it to them. This will lead to a blessed life. Unreliable Friends

3/29/2019 12:56   My goal in life is to be a man of God, showing His love in the world. I do my best to serve both God and man.

3/29/2019 13:01   In jail 13 times in South America. I was rejected by family and friends. I am pleased to say I have been able to win some of them back, even seeing some come to Jesus.

3/29/2019 13:07   God created humans and gave them a job. Without a vision, the people perish. When people have nothing to do, they lose a reason for living. It's a blessing having the vision to win the world for Christ.

3/29/2019 13:09   These things make it harder to serve God and man. 1. A lack of financial backing and 2. being persecuted from both the society and so-called brethren.

4/3/2019 3:17   Paul said to be winsome. Wise and Gracious.

4/7/2019 12:51   It's true when God's Holy Spirit moves through me, I feel full of Joy.

4/7/2019 12:52   Jesus will never leave you or forsakes you.

4/10/2019 1:24   , God wants to give us the desires of our hearts. I'm asking You, my Lord, to allow me to be used by your Holy Spirit. Give me the gift of hearing You and Your Holy Spirit and help me yield to You.

4/11/2019 15:22   I clearly remember when I didn't wait on the Lord and went to Argentina instead of Brazil. I was 24, and after eight months of trials and times in jail, I obeyed and left for Brazil. I found peace and protection there.

4/11/2019 15:24   Prayer and living the life of a Christian allows us to walk humbly in His ways and in His Words.

4/13/2019 14:43   Traffic Patience.

4/14/2019 13:21   We become faithful and used by God by studying His Word, Living His Word, Sharing His Word, and listening to the small still voice of the Lord's Holy Spirit.

4/14/2019 14:25   Righteous anger is against the devil and anything fighting to stop God's will. God hates sin, which is rebellion. Lord, please forgive my hidden sins.

4/18/2019 13:18   Beating evil by taking flowers to my wife.

4/18/2019 13:21   Jesus told us; In my father's house or many mansions and if it was not so I tell you I go and prepare a place for you that where I am you may be also.

4/18/2019 13:24   I usually claim my own weakness as my problem, but as time goes on, God's giving me wisdom to overcome some of my weaknesses. So thankful that we will be like him when we stand in this kingdom

4/20/2019 19:19	Our ordinary deed of the day reflects our faith. Whereby by their fruits they will know us. Whatever You Do.
4/23/2019 13:33	I have a long road ahead of me to become like Jesus. I praise God for His mercy every day. His love overwhelms me.
4/24/2019 13:10	Prayer, Reading the Word, and accountability with weekly communications with brethren is what helps us grow.
4/26/2019 12:49	Discipline is close to the word disciple. A disciple follows Jesus as He has directed them.
4/26/2019 12:53	People who are not reading His Word don't have His direction, therefore erred from His way.
4/27/2019 13:38	I need to seek God with deeper conviction and take more time with Him daily. I need to look to Him for the power to win the battle of my sins.
4/29/2019 17:18	There were times I could have been described as an inpatient, even angry man, but by his grace, this did not stop me from seeking to live close to Jesus daily. I will get closer to Jesus by reading his word and letting it become part of me, by praying and sharing His Gospel, remembering all have sinned and fall short of the glory of God. I know it's not by works of righteousness which I have done. Still, according to his mercies, Jesus saved me by the washing of

regeneration and renewing of His Holy Spirit, so stay faithful, and Jesus will help you grow out of your sinful ways so you can become a child of God.

4/29/2019 17:20 After hearing David Platt's event on the secret Church, it has driven me to be more desperate with the Lord. I know it's only by His grace that He allows me to understand His wisdom when I asked Him. Oh, I desire His wisdom.

4/30/2019 15:07 Jesus told us the world would know we are His disciples if we have love for one another. So, let's shine His light of love to each other and the world.

5/2/2019 12:58 I am so thankful that God has allowed me to shine His light by sharing His amazing Grace and the Gift of eternal life with thousands. All Glory to God. The treasure in heaven Jesus told us about are partially those who we assist getting into heaven.

5/2/2019 13:06 When Jesus was on earth, He lived a life full of love and grace. I want to live as He did.

5/2/2019 13:09 I know my weaknesses are many, I know only in lifting Jesus is my strength.

5/3/2019 12:25 To give begrudgingly is not giving.

5/5/2019 12:45 I tell my wife, "did I tell you I love you today"? daily.

5/6/2019 14:09 Our Lord is allowing me to overcome many sins. Sins of submission to Him and others, sins of loving the world and the things of the world, sins of the flesh. God's mercy and Grace are so full and overwhelming.

5/7/2019 12:58   I love seeing the Spirit of God move.

5/9/2019 2:30   There are so many differences between the world's ways and God's ways. It would take many books to share them. I am so thankful for submitting to God's Word and His ways.

5/9/2019 12:10   I try to be loving. I love it when He leads me, as I see incredible things happen. God is Love.

5/11/2019 12:34   , Losing my dad last year was is still hard. Mainly because I became accustomed to calling him daily, and I miss this. Knowing that I will see him again in heaven helps comfort my heart.

5/12/2019 13:47   God has told us not to put anything above Him. In today's society, the pressures of the cares of this life and luxury have driven personal desires into first place; this is a sin.

5/13/2019 12:35   I love, trusting God. With Him, all things are possible.

5/15/2019 12:07   We are in a spiritual war, and it starts from our births and goes until our deaths. Therefore, we need correction and guidance. If it isn't given, the enemy of God will guide instead.

5/17/2019 13:06   Pray and listen to His small, still voice.

5/17/2019 13:11	Oh Lord, You know I seek to lift You up to others during my daily life. Only by Your Grace, truly all Glory to You.
5/19/2019 13:06	I feel insecure in many of the things God asks me to do. I do them anyway.
5/19/2019 13:08	God has given me a desire to seek a deeper understanding of His Word. Every time I read through the Bible, I learn something new. I just can't read it enough.
5/20/2019 12:57	When a Mocker tells a joke at another's person's expense, it is wrong.
5/21/2019 13:46	, I seek to see how God sees me.
5/22/2019 12:39	We have a choice, self-glorification in the things we do or to give Glory to God.
5/23/2019 13:46	We know that God has shown anger, and even Jesus overturned tables, but His anger was righteous, and ours are for stupid things, like when someone cuts us off in traffic or says something we don't agree with. Lord, help me to have the self-control I'm asking You to give it to me. I want to be meek, but Bold in sharing Your Gospel. IN JESUS NAME.
5/24/2019 19:35	We all fall short of the Glory of God. I do my best to live the love of Jesus daily. I know even with my shortcomings, the best I can do is lift up Jesus and what He has done for us.
5/26/2019 13:10	When we learn that His way is the best way, we gain the peace that passes all

understanding. Then we will be children that desire to follow and obey Jesus.

5/27/2019 17:32   Lord, You know that every day is a new day, and Your mercy is new every morning. It needs to be as we are in a war, and this war will be continuing until the day You return to subdue the enemy, the devil. Thank You, Jesus, for allowing us to be on the winning side, Your side.

5/28/2019 17:02   Knowing God's Word is knowing God. I want to be faithful to read and study the Bible daily.

5/29/2019 20:08   Only God is Good.

5/30/2019 13:32   A Godly nation lifts up God by recognizing the one He sent, Jesus.

5/31/2019 14:18   God loves us, and He knows every thought we have. Through His love and mercy, He will lead us in the way of His light.

6/1/2019 13:18   Our Lord knew from the beginning of the creation of the world that He would show us, and all the heavenly beings, His love and mercy through Jesus the Christ. He knew we would go the wrong way; then He showed us the way back through Jesus our Lord and Savior

11/13/19   My Degenerative Spondylolisthesis is causing me sleepless nights and a lot of pain. While praying about it, I saw that if we allow pain to push us closer to God in prayer, it is great. It's like when we have a boil on our skin when we push on it; the bad stuff comes out. God allows pain and even suffering, so we His people will grow closer to Him in prayer. Today I had one of those experiences. I felt God in a wonderfully comforting way. All things work towards good for those who love the Lord Jesus, His Holy Spirit, and our Father in heaven. Let's keep sharing the Gospel no matter what, until we stand before Him in heaven.

Contents

Chapter 13

My great nephew's Dominick Memorial service

Hello Everyone, my name is Vincent, and I am Dominick's great uncle. I have been here in Akron for about a week, and I have seen and heard so many people speak and show such love and compassion towards Dominick and all his family; this has shown me Dom's heart and your hearts. Thank you.

I live in Maryland, so I have not been able to get to know Dominick as well as I would have liked. Through your comments, I have been able to understand how great a person he was. I am so deeply sorry we have lost Dominick. He will be missed. I am going to share a few of the things I've read in your comments.

I read that he had some amazing adventures at camp, also meeting some of his best friends there. He made you laugh with some of his goofball antics, and that you could not help but smile when he smiled. Everyone genuinely enjoyed themselves whenever they were with him. He was the life of the party. He had a heart as big as the moon. He left a memorable impression on many lives that he touched. He loved spending time with his family, especially his little sister Angelina. He loved watching and playing basketball, and he dressed to impress.

I had to smile when I read about Dominick's pinkly promises, I don't really know if that truly locks in a promise, but it's fun to think about him doing it. Another person shared about his kindness, which all of us remember. When I read this comment, it brought a proper vision to my eyes; it said, God bless you, Dominick may you rest in the arms of the Angels.

The reason Dominic has been taken from us is because people yielded to evil and the darkness that Satan leads people into. We live in a fallen world, and there are people that live with evil thoughts and hate in their hearts daily. A very large portion of this world has fallen away from God, and many have fallen away from the wisdom, compassion, and love that He wants us to live.

To help you understand how it all started, Lucifer, also known as the Satan or the Devil, rebelled against God in the Kingdom of God. He led 1/3 of the angels in the rebellion against God. God knowing all things, knew what to do about this rebellion. He created the world and cast Lucifer and the angels who followed him to earth. Then God created Adam and Eve and told them to have children and to multiply and fill the earth with people. God told them not to eat of the tree of knowledge of good and evil. They did eat from it, and every human being since has eaten from it. Most people try to do good and not evil, but it is a choice we make daily. God has allowed this earth to bring children to Himself. Children who choose to follow Him and now His Son Jesus and His children refuse to do evil. Every one of us and everyone who has ever been born has been given this choice, Love God or do evil. God has used the rebellion of the devil to create full-hearted children who love Him. This was the reason He created the earth in the first place, as I said. The people who killed Dominick were led by evil and the devil.

About 2000 years ago, God placed Himself in the womb of a virgin and walked on our earth as a person. We know His name, it is Jesus the Christ. This is why Jesus could give sight to the blind, heal the sick, and He even came out of the grave Himself. After rising from the grave, He walked with His disciples for 40 days, and hundreds of people saw Him. His new resurrected body could walk through walls, eat, and He even cooked a fish dinner for His disciples and ate it with them. When Jesus walked this earth, He told us and showed us, through His life, how we should be living. Jesus told us He was with God when the world was created. When it was the right time in the history of the world, He came from Heaven to earth in the form of a man to share with the world about Heaven, how to get there, and many incredible things about Heaven.

Jesus said, if we, the human race, would live just the two commandments that He gave us to live, the world would be an incredible place to live, and it would fulfill everything that They wanted the world to be. The first commandment is that we are to love God with all our heart, all our mind, and all our soul. The second is a continuation of that commandment; we are to love our neighbor as our self.

God must give every human being the right to choose, as He did not want a bunch of robots running around on earth. He wants children: children that want to follow Him and love Him and each other by choice. You cannot mandate or force anyone to love.

The majority of the people in the world today are not living the two commandments Jesus gave the world, love God, and love each other. It is up to each one of us to remember and live those two commandments every moment we live.

If anyone here thinks they want to retaliate against the ones that did this, it is not what Jesus would do or want us to do. They are not allowing God to punish the guilty as He will. We cannot take the law in our hands. If someone takes the law in their own hands, it will just make things harder for all of us, as we may lose someone else that we love, and that will make things even worst. I know God will punish all the guilty, Trust in that.

The Word of God, The Bible, tells us that there is life after death, that we are spiritual beings, living in a physical body. Please know that Dominick is in the hands of the Angels.

I am so glad I have read through the Bible many times. I have seen in it that the prophet's that came hundreds even thousands of years before the arrival of Jesus told us in their writings of things that Jesus would do. The Prophetic prophets wrote many Prophecies about Jesus, thousands of years before Jesus was born, and Jesus fulfilled all 333 of these Prophecies. You see, the Prophets were writing what God told them to write. They were men and women who lived to hear from God, and they lived, allowing God to speak through them. These Prophets told us that God would send Jesus, and He would show us things to come and would give us a new life and visions of His Kingdom. Then He would suffer many beatings and would be nailed on a cross. Jesus the Christ died exactly as the Prophet David said He would (in Psalms 22). Please understand nailing people to a cross did not even exist during the time this Prophet wrote about it. This and many other fulfilled Prophecies show us that God told them what to write because God is the only one who knew what Jesus would have to do and go through. God showed it to the Prophets, and they wrote it down so we could read it and understand that He is real and to show us His ways.

Many prophets told us in many ways that Jesus would take the sins of the world. Jesus, Himself, gave us many promises that we can depend on. In one of those promises, He told us, "Let not your heart be troubled; you believe in God, also believe in Me. He said, In My Father's house are many mansions; if it were not so, I would have told you. Jesus said I go to prepare a place for you in Heaven.

Heaven has many dwelling places. If we choose to believe Jesus, now, in this world and we accept that He can live with us and in us. He will give us a full life now in this world, and we will live for eternity in the heavenly Kingdom of God with Him. This is not saying we will not have problems and heartaches here on earth. He's promising He will help us through our problems and heartaches. Jesus will give anyone this comfort and eternal security if they ask for it. There is a place for us in Heaven. In Heaven, everyone is free from stress, relational drama, and endless 'to-do' lists. Jesus will give those who seek Him rest and of peace; He has promised this and will give it to those who seek and trust Him. Most importantly, Heaven is about knowing and learning from our heavenly Father. Jesus even gave us a prayer to say; whoever knows it say it with me silently.

Our Father which art in heaven,

Hallowed be Thy name.

Thy kingdom come.

Thy will be done

On earth, as *it is* in heaven.

Give us this day our daily bread.

And forgive our Trespasses,

As we forgive those, who Trespasses against us.

And do not lead us into temptation,

But deliver us from the evil one.

For Yours is the kingdom and the power and the glory forever and ever. Amen.

Our Father in Heaven offers us His security. He is a Father we can count on, even in times like this. Many people haven't had a good relationship with their biological father. Some may have never even known their father on earth or their Father in Heaven. Some may have greatly feared their earthly father, while others may have been loved by their father.

The type of Father Jesus is describing might be difficult for some to imagine, but heaven is going to be a perfect home with the perfect Father. In heaven, we will finally experience the world the way that God intended, free from brokenness, pain, and disappointment with a Father who is strong, loving, fair, dependable, and kind.

We have all been hurt or let down by life's circumstances, but if we look to Jesus, we will be comforted knowing we too will be with Him someday. If your earthly father has failed or disappointed, you look to Jesus; He will give you guidance, vision for life here and in eternity. Those who trust in Jesus, the best is yet to come!

Let's pray.

Father, we are hurting because of this horrible deed that was led by the devil. We need Your peace; we need the comfort of Your Holy Spirit. Thank you for allowing us to be together today to remember Dominick. Give us the strength we need to fight evil with Your love as Jesus did. Thank You for coming to earth in the person of Jesus. Please remove all our sins, past sins, present sins, and future sins. Help us to see what we are doing that is not pleasing to You and give us the strength to repent of it, to turn away from it, and make our lives to be as children of God. Thank You that by Your grace and mercy, we will be with You in Heaven for eternity. In Jesus Name. Amen.

Contents

Chapter 14

Final thoughts

I would like to finish my story with you by clarifying who I am. I have made many mistakes during my lifetime. I have not become a perfect person since following Jesus, but I have become a student of God's Word and a son of the living God because of what Jesus did. I have the desire and vision to become more like Jesus, always wanting to be as loving and kind as He. No one has completely become as Jesus is in this world. We are all on the journey seeking to live His perfection. I know I am in a war, the spiritual war that is talked about in Ephesians 6:12. We wrestle not against flesh and blood, but against principalities, against powers, against the rulers of the darkness of this world, against spiritual wickedness in high places.

The Lord has helped me through battles of hate, lust, lying, stealing, cheating, deceit, and drugs. His love has never failed me. He stands with me, no matter what. I can joyfully say that He has given me the Grace to overcome many sins. Somehow, He has seen fit to use me to share the Gospel with many. Some days I shared the Gospel with six or more people; other days, I did not share Him. If I took a rough estimate, even if it averaged to 2 a day for the 48 years I have been serving Him, it would come to 35,040 people and multiplied by an average of 6 brothers and sisters sharing with me while on mission in South America. At times in the USA, this number could be multiplied by 6. These are people who we share the Gospel face to face. The reason I am sharing this is not to boast but to bring to your attention that if we are faithful to share the Gospel daily, our influence for the Kingdom of God adds up. If we train others to share the Gospel, our influence in this world multiplies. He is faithful to use our lives, even if we are not perfect. He's perfect, and that's what counts.

I acknowledge that Jesus Created the world with His Father. He came to be the Savior and is the King of Kings. He has all authority in heaven and on earth. I need Him. I have submitted to His Lordship over my life. I understand that eternal life, "the entrance into Heaven" is a free gift. When Jesus died on the cross, He removed all sin. Every human being has a choice to believe in what He has done and allow Him to take away their sins or not believe and stand before God at judgment without the cleansing blood of Jesus the Christ. It's a choice. It's your choice.

When someone becomes a believer, they need constant cleansing from defilement contracted in this pilgrim walk through this fallen world. Titus 3:5 tells us; not by works of righteousness which we have done, but according to his mercy he saved us, by the washing of regeneration, and renewing of the Holy Spirit. We all need this washing of our souls and renewing of the Holy Spirit daily to keep an open connection with God through His Holy Spirit. Heaven is a non-returnable gift. The Holy Spirit's cleansing allows us to live in a pleasing way in our Father's eyes while we walk in this world. It also allows us to be used on earth to lift His Glory so others can see Him in us. His Holy Spirit is able to shine through us.

When we understand that Jesus created the world with His Father, See John 1:1-14 and that He wants us to walk with Him and to love Him, our outlook on life changes.

From the beginning of the world, humankind was unable to understand what God wanted with His creation, so Jesus came to earth in a human form. Jesus was totally God and totally man when he walked this earth. He showed us how God wants humans to live then made a way for us to walk with God on earth by taking all sins on the cross, fulfilling the prophecy of Psalms 22, which had been written about 1000 years prior to His death. He offers to take anyone's sins, but He has given every human being the choice to humble ourselves and ask Jesus to take our sins. You see, we all choose to sin. Sin is anything that keeps us from living our daily lives with God.

To help, guide, and bring all things to our remembrance, Jesus sent His Holy Spirit to us. Anyone can receive the Holy Spirit by asking Jesus for Him. Luke 11:13 If ye then, being evil, know how to give good gifts unto your children: how much more shall *your* heavenly Father give the Holy Spirit to them that ask him? (KJV) After we receive the Holy Spirit, our obedience comes into play. To be able to keep the connection with the Holy Spirit. If we continue in known sin, it shuts down our communication through the Holy Spirit. Our open communication with God will be blocked by sin, and the cares of this life.

In the Book of Romans, it says the wages of sin is death, but the gift of God is eternal life. Death means living without God because, in God, there is eternal life. Without eternal life, we are spiritually dead, walking without God, now and for eternity. The Bible calls Hell.

Something for you to think about: if someone is not happily loving Jesus here on earth, they will not be happy living with Him for eternity. If you are not happily loving Jesus here, you will not be happy in heaven. God doesn't send anyone to Hell. Going to Hell is a choice. This is chosen by receiving or rejecting God's gift given through Jesus.

God wants to pour His light and love on us, but He has given us a choice. If that choice is to seek to walk with Him, then He will walk with us. If we choose not to walk with God, then He will not walk with us. It is that simple. According to the Bible, Satan, also known as Lucifer, took a choice to rebel against God. One-third of the angels followed him in his rebellion. We have the same decision, follow Jesus, or follow Satan. These are the only two choices.

The majority of the human race considered evil to be satanic and loving acts heavenly. Truth be told, the Bible teaches us that evil is when someone rejects Jesus Whom God sent. There are people who are good in the eyes of the world, but if they have rejected God's gift of eternal life through Jesus, they will still be going to Hell. As Jesus said in John 14:6, **Jesus saith** unto him, I am the way, the truth, and the life: **no man cometh unto the Father, but by me**.

Jesus lived a perfect life while He was here on earth. He showed the human race how we should strive to be living. If we could live as loving as He did, the world would be a different place.

We are all guilty of falling short in this life because none of us have lived a perfect life. Most people look for worldly things to bring happiness. If we seek the world and the things of the world and not God, we are looking in the wrong direction. David, in Psalms 14, said the fool has said in his heart, "*There is* no God." They are corrupt; they have done abominable works; there is none who does good, no not one. The Lord looks down from heaven upon the children of men, to see if there are any who understand, who seek God. They have all turned aside; they have become corrupt; *There is* none who does good, No, not one.

God loved us so much He gave His human physical body up to get us to look at Him. At the same time, He has fixed the problem of all sin.

Let us say you have two glasses; one is full of deadly poison, and the other glass only has a drop of very deadly poison in it. It does not matter which glass you drink from; if you drink either one, you will die. You may be a great person. You may know of some very corrupt persons, but even one sin will keep you out of God's heaven. God will not allow even one sin into His heaven because sin, in truth, is a rebellion against Jesus. God will not let any rebellion into His heaven. This is why, without receiving the forgiveness of God through Jesus, no one will get into heaven. If someone refuses to believe in what God said through Jesus, then God cannot forgive his or her sins. John 3:36 says He that believeth on the Son hath everlasting life: and he that believeth not the Son shall not see life, but the wrath of God abideth on him. (KJV)

If someone believes their good deeds done in this life outweigh their bad deeds, therefore they will get into the Kingdom of God. That being good enough is good enough; if so, they are missing the point of what Jesus said in John 1:12, but as many as received him, to them gave He the power to become the sons of God, even to them that believe on his name. And verse 13, which were born, not of blood, nor the will of the flesh, nor of the will of man, but of God. Also, what the Bible tells us in Titus 3:5 not by works of righteousness which we have done, but according to His mercy He saved us, through the washing of regeneration and renewing of the Holy Spirit.

Stop and ask Jesus to forgive you of all your sins, past, present, and future. Start praying, daily wherever you are. Start reading the New Testament so you can know for yourself what Jesus said. Find a good Bible-teaching church, one where the Pastor reads and explains the Bible from the pulpit. Start finding Christian friends who read the Bible, talk about the Bible, and share the Bible with others. Know that Jesus is God, as Thomas said in John 20:28. When he saw Jesus appear in the upper room three days after He was buried in the tomb, Jesus being risen from the grave in His new body, told Thomas, "Put your finger in His nail holes of My hands and your hand into My side," Thomas said to Jesus "my Lord and my God. Stop and pray now. Ask Jesus to take your sins. Repent of the things you know are not pleasing in His sight. Do it today. We truly do not know the day we will be standing in front of the great white throne of God. You could die today. Get right with God through Jesus. He loves you, and nothing will stop His love for you. Give in, humble yourself before Him, and He will give you peace even in the storm.

Resources

https://afreegift.blog/